The People Make the Peace: Lessons From the Vi presents an insightful examination of the Việt Nam antiwar movement, with fascinating stories by nine activists who made wartime trips to Việt Nam to establish people-to-people contacts. The book shatters stereotypes of protesters and shows the activists as thoughtful, courageous, and compassionate strategists whose dedication to peaceful diplomacy helped end the war earlier that it would have otherwise. Anyone interested in putting a halt to our current state of perpetual war—and stopping future ones—will get inspiration and direction from the lessons so brilliantly conveyed in this book.

MEDEA BENJAMIN
Co-founder of the peace group CODEPINK and
the human rights organization Global Exchange

A marvelous collection that comes full circle in understanding America's past and present relationship with Vietnam, and that reminds us of the power and impact of the antiwar movement through the voices of peace advocates from that era who recently returned to Vietnam.

DAVID CORTRIGHT
Director of Policy Studies at Notre Dame's
Kroc Institute for International Peace Studies

This is a wonderfully moving, inspiring, and instructive collection of autobiographical essays by prominent Vietnam War activists who kept the faith over the decades since they joined in signing an extraordinary treaty of peace between the American and Vietnamese people in 1973. The authors succeed, above all, in making us realize how profoundly wrong it was ever to wage war against this proud people who so often returned our violence with their love. Everyone who cares about this country needs to read this book in a hurry.

RICHARD FALK
Professor Emeritus of International Law and Practice,
Princeton University

The American movement against the Vietnam War was the largest, most complex, and most effective antiwar movement in history, but neither its scope nor its complexity have gotten their due in the historical record. The essays in this collection help fill in many blanks, adding essential color to the story of this astounding citizens' movement, especially the remarkable saga of the 1970–71 People's Peace Treaty. They inspire reflection that America still sorely needs.

TODD GITLIN
Professor of journalism and sociology at Columbia University

The People Make the Peace is an invaluable document describing the varied experiences of one significant segment of the movement against the war in Vietnam. Activists who engaged in what Hanoi and the NLF called "people's diplomacy," recall their experiences and place them in the context of a more recent visit to the country as well as current U.S. foreign policy. In addition, five veterans now living and working in Vietnam to alleviate the damage done by the war they fought talk of their past and present experiences. The volume will be of interest to all who cherish peace and work towards achieving it.

MARILYN YOUNG
Professor in the Department of History,
New York University

THE PEOPLE
MAKE
THE PEACE

THE PEOPLE MAKE THE PEACE

Lessons from the Vietnam Antiwar Movement

Karín Aguilar-San Juan & Frank Joyce, Editors

Just World Books
Charlottesville, Virginia

Just World Books

Timely Books for Changing Times

Just World Books is an imprint of Just World Publishing, LLC.

Front cover image is from a vintage antiwar poster by an unknown artist. Courtesy of Lincoln Cushing / Docs Populi.
Cover design and typesetting by Diana Ghazzawi for Just World Publishing, LLC.

Publisher's Cataloging in Publication
(Provided by Quality Books, Inc.)

The people make the peace : lessons from the Vietnam
   antiwar movement / Karín Aguilar-San Juan & Frank Joyce, eds.
      pages cm
      LCCN 2015947153
      ISBN 978-1-935982-59-3
      ISBN 978-1-935982-58-6 (ebook)

      1. Vietnam War, 1961-1975--Protest movements--United
States. 2. Vietnam War, 1961-1975--Personal narratives,
American. I. Aguilar-San Juan, Karin, 1962- editor.
II. Joyce, Frank H., editor.

DS559.62.U6P46 2015   959.704'30922
          QBI15-600171

To the future peacemakers of the world....

And to Frank's grandchildren, Nathan, Luca, and Sofia, in the hope that they will be among the future peacemakers of the world.

Finally, to Fred Branfman, for his lifetime of dedication to the people of Laos and the cause of peace.

CONTENTS

EDITORS' INTRODUCTION: THE PEOPLE MADE THE PEACE

KARIN AGUILAR-SAN JUAN AND FRANK JOYCE

Students were shot dead.[1] Hundreds of thousands of citizens from all walks of life marched in the streets—repeatedly. Civil disobedience took place on a scale never seen before in U.S. history. Draft cards were burned, and draft board offices were non-violently attacked. Entertainers who opposed the War had TV shows and performances canceled in retaliation. Soldiers rebelled against their commanders. At least eight U.S. Americans immolated themselves in public places. Fed up with their own government, ordinary people became diplomats and reporters, meeting face-to-face with the Vietnamese enemy in Viet Nam and other locations around the world.[2] Former secretary of state Henry Kissinger later said that the antiwar movement rubbed President Nixon's rawest nerve.

The fact that a movement against the Vietnam War came into being in the first place is something of a miracle. Majority support for war has been the rule throughout U.S. history; mass opposition to war has been the exception.

To be clear, virtually every U.S. war has faced opposition. But the Vietnam War stands out. What made it different? What forces called an antiwar movement into existence? Did the antiwar movement help to end the War? If so, how? How do the activists who opposed the Vietnam War understand "Vietnam" today, as an era, a war, a country, and a people?

This book addresses these questions and more. *The People Make the Peace* features the reflections and analyses of nine activists who made wartime trips to Viet Nam. The authors of this book tell many stories that are previously untold. They address issues of how the War affected them and how it affected our society that every generation needs to consider.

While each person's journey differs in its specific details, circumstances, and lasting impact, all share a high degree of moral conviction and political courage. During the War they went to Viet Nam to learn about the Vietnamese people and to observe first-hand the terrible impact of the War. Looking back now, each of them sees their encounters with the Vietnamese land and people, devastated by war yet determined to set their own future, as a defining and instructive moment in their lives.

In 2013, the group that playfully came to refer to itself as the "Hanoi 9" returned to Viet Nam to participate in observances of the 40th anniversary of the signing of the Paris Peace Accords. That trip was a major force behind this book.

The Vietnam War

How far back do we need to go to trace the origins of the Vietnam War? We share the view that the Vietnam War came at the end of an arc of U.S. imperialism in Asia and the Pacific.[3] From the settler colonial conquest of the West on to Hawaii, the Philippines and beyond, the U.S. military has a long history of brutality. All of which comes wrapped in an alibi of Western benevolence and tutelage.[4]

As World War II ended, a new set of "Cold War" animosities emerged, led on the capitalist side by the United States and Europe; and on the communist side by the USSR and China. Viet Nam was among the many Third World nations that, having recently fought off their colonial masters, sought to remain neutral with regard to the Cold War superpowers. But instead of achieving freedom from French rule and garnering U.S. support for their independent status, the Vietnamese found the United States inserting itself into the role of substitute colonizer. In convincing ways, Jeffrey Kimball establishes that it was Nixon's war, because of all the U.S. presidents, he had the longest tie to it. Nixon, as a young vice president in the Eisenhower administration, got invested in his own personal Vietnam War as early as 1953.[5] John F. Kennedy observed the seeds of U.S. war in Viet Nam in the 1950s. Fredrik Logevall traces the path of Kennedy, then a congressman from Massachusetts, on a trip with his siblings to Saigon in 1951. Even then, the Kennedys saw the United States taking on the mantle of colonialism, and they knew that the picture did not have a bright future.[6] Historians debate whether Kennedy would have ended the War earlier had he not been killed in 1963.

Everyone knows how this story ends. The United States ultimately failed in its war objectives and was forced to withdraw in April 1975. North and South Viet Nam were reunified as the Socialist Republic of Viet Nam; 29 years later, Viet Nam became a significant participant in the global economy. But debates still rage about the origins, meaning, purpose, impact, legacies, and implications of the Vietnam War. Nearly all of those debates focus on the consequences for U.S. history and policy. For some, the devastating results for Viet Nam may be too much to consider. Jimmy Carter declared the damage from the Vietnam War to be "mutual," a message that simultaneously points to U.S. vulnerability and to the War's devastating impact on the Vietnamese people.

The War produced at least one legislative consequence: The War Powers Resolution of 1973—also referred to as the War Powers Act—which sought to limit the power of the president to commit U.S. forces to combat without the authorization of Congress. Nixon tried unsuccessfully to veto it. This resolution came as a response to Nixon's escalation of ground and air troops in the Vietnam War and could be interpreted as an achievement of the grassroots antiwar movement. Most U.S. presidents abide by the spirit of this resolution while also claiming they are not required to do so.[7] Yet the War Powers Resolution did not prevent the U.S. government from: ousting Chile's democratically elected socialist president, Salvador Allende, in 1973; backing up a dictator in the Philippines from the early 1970s to 1986; or cozying up to F. W. de Klerk's regime of apartheid in South Africa, just to name a few interventions from that era. As this book was being written, President Barack Obama was trying to get Congress to authorize U.S. attacks on Islamic State of Iraq and Syria (ISIS) while continuing U.S. engagement in several other conflicts in the Middle East.

Since the Vietnam War ended, successive U.S. leaders have had to contend with the "Vietnam syndrome," a hesitation to commit troops to combat and thus repeat the mistakes of that War. In fact, successive presidents from Jimmy Carter to Bill Clinton have twisted the meaning and public memory of the Vietnam War in order to develop a new justification for military intervention abroad. Ronald Reagan called the Vietnam War a "noble" and "just cause." Subsequently, the U.S. government engaged in low-intensity warfare in El Salvador and throughout Central America, prompting a new antiwar slogan "El Salvador is Spanish for Vietnam." Upon sending troops to the Gulf War in 1991, George H.W. Bush exclaimed, "It's a proud day for America. And, by God, we've kicked the Vietnam syndrome once and for all."[8]

President Obama sings in that choir too. On May 28, 2012, in a speech aimed at Vietnam War veterans, he said, "You were often blamed for a war you didn't start, when you should have been commended for serving your country with valor. You were sometimes blamed for misdeeds of a few, when the honorable service of the many should have been praised. You came home and sometimes were denigrated, when you should have been celebrated." The president went on to endorse the mythical widespread mistreatment of returning Vietnam veterans as "a national shame and a disgrace that should never have happened" and to accuse the Vietnamese of brutality. He also issued a proclamation calling for "a 13-year program to honor and give thanks to a generation of proud Americans who saw our country through one of the most challenging missions we have ever faced."[9]

The Vietnam Antiwar Movement

If you have seen the movie *Forrest Gump* (1994), you probably remember the quote "life is like a box of chocolates." Actually, the film is a box of propaganda, especially when it comes to how it portrays the antiwar movement. The movie is populated by caricatures: flag-wearing hippies; militant and sexist Black Panthers; and air-headed, would-be feminists. Forrest, a charming simpleton, never has a meaningful or specific discussion of the Vietnam War. But his sideways encounters with antiwar activists leave the distinct impression that the movement was wasteful, annoying, insignificant, and possibly unethical. For viewers who will go no further to investigate any other perspective, *Forrest Gump* serves as a main cultural and political lesson on the 1960s, creating disdain and hostility toward the antiwar movement. It is but one example of a sustained and multipronged effort to do so.

The truth is that the antiwar movement fomented and channeled opposition to the War, both from ordinary people and elites. Over time, the War became the anchor issue for activists, journalists, and politicians. Vietnam was the first televised war, but television alone did not create opposition to the War. As Susan Sontag pointed out, the TV showed the War, but TV viewers saw those images through the interpretive lens that the antiwar movement created through their struggles and protests.[10]

Between 1965 and 1968, Lyndon Johnson relied on the draft to build the number of U.S. troops in battle from 100,000 to 500,000.[11] Draft resistance and conscientious objection became a key strategy of antiwar activists. The draft resulted in disproportionate numbers of working class, black, and Latino men fighting and dying in Vietnam. These inequities further enraged antiwar activists, who then targeted the race and class bias of draft

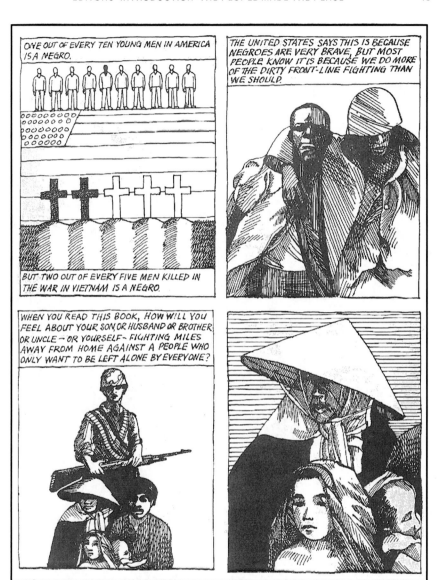

Julian Bond made an antiwar comic book after he was expelled from the Georgia House of Representative for his antiwar views. Reproduced with permission of Julian Bond.

This poster connects Chicano struggles to the antiwar movement.
Artwork by Malaquias Montoya.

*Filipino labor leader Philip Vera Cruz spoke at a
Vietnam Moratorium in San Francisco, 1972.
Photo by Leon Sun.*

deferments. Richard Nixon lowered overall troop numbers in part to defuse opposition to the draft. In 1973, the draft ended and was replaced by an all-volunteer service.

Working alongside blacks in the civil-rights movement in the South provided a crucial learning experience for the young, mostly white university students who would later join the antiwar movement. Hundreds were recruited to join the Mississippi Freedom Summer Project; in their poignant letters home, they describe transformative, eye-opening moments confronting institutionalized white racism and state-sponsored violence.[12] The connections between Jim Crow in the South and the U.S. war in Viet Nam were not lost on them. One white project volunteer asked a Justice Department official: "How is it that the government can protect the Vietnamese from the Vietcong, and the same government will not accept the moral responsibility of protecting the people of Mississippi?"[13]

The antiwar movement is generally treated as white turf, yet people of color—black, Latino/Chicano, Native/indigenous, and Asian—also actively opposed the War.[14] In the late 1950s, leaders including Ella Baker and Bayard Rustin connected U.S. racial justice issues to anticolonial struggles in Africa, Asia, and Latin America. Later, the Student Non-Violent

Vietnamese foreign students on U.S. campuses organized against the War, 1972.
Image courtesy of Steve Louie.

Coordinating Committee (SNCC) clarified the links between "the suppression of Blacks' political rights and the continued violence in the South as part of the larger U.S. war against nonwhites, including Vietnam."[15] In April 1967, the Rev. Dr. Martin Luther King delivered his powerful speech against the War, denouncing the United States as "the greatest purveyor of violence in the world." An editorial in the *New York Times* headlined "Dr. King's Error," denounced the speech. As explained in *Death of a King* by Tavis Smiley, other establishment figures and institutions piled on.[16] Even some of King's allies thought he was putting the civil rights movement in jeopardy. One year later to the day, he was assassinated. And today the United States is still "the greatest purveyor of violence in the world."

By looking at the Vietnam War as part of an extended arc of U.S. imperialism in Asia, we surface the historic and material connection between U.S. wars and Asian-American populations. Yet many people continue to ignore Asian-American participation in the antiwar movement. Actually, the Vietnam War provided a catalyst for a pan-ethnic Asian-American social consciousness. For example, Philip Vera Cruz was a leader of the Filipino farmworkers, and a key organizer in the Delano grape boycott of

1965. By speaking up at an antiwar rally organized by Asian-American activists, Vera Cruz helped to solidify a feeling of a shared racial bond.

Chinese, Japanese, and Filipino Americans who served as soldiers in the War saw themselves in the faces of the so-called "enemy." They personally experienced the contradiction between their status as U.S. citizens, and the way their battalions treated them—sometimes as target practice.[17] Indeed, the racism directed against Vietnamese people during the War served as a wakeup call that propelled many Asian Americans—students, intellectuals, laborers, and cultural workers—to embrace Viet Nam as a symbol of "third world" peoples and struggles all over the world.[18]

Toward the end of the War, at least 2,000 Vietnamese foreign students based on various U.S. campuses organized themselves into the Union of Vietnamese. Their antiwar position crystalized after the 1972 murder of Nguyen Thai Binh, a student of fishery at the University of Washington. On graduation day, Binh walked across the stage, shed his black gown, and revealed a demand to stop the War, written in his own blood. He was then deported to South Vietnam. At the airport in Sai Gon, he was shot dead. His death spurred his peers to hold a memorial for him and to form alliances with other U.S. liberation struggles.[19]

The first large-scale protests organized against the War by Students for a Democratic Society (SDS) and National Committee for a Sane Nuclear Policy (SANE) were triggered by President Lyndon B. Johnson's 1965 air bombing campaign called Operation Rolling Thunder. Like all social movements, this one grew in phases. The phases involved: selecting and framing the issues, establishing decision-making processes, developing expertise, finding a common denominator among many conflicting viewpoints, attacking dominant values and assumptions, and sustaining participation. Sometimes, the goal was to mobilize public opinion about a specific aspect of the War or the draft; at other times, it was to provoke a response from policy makers at the highest levels of the government. Always, the ultimate aim was to stop the bombing, negotiate for peace, and end the War.

Framing and isolating the War with a "single issue" point of focus is one way that the antiwar movement became a primarily white movement rather than a multiracial coalition. That is why black antiwar activists in Committee Organized for Racial Equality (CORE), the Southern Nonviolent Coordinating Committee (SNCC), and the Black Panthers criticized white activists for being unable to include the broader concerns and experience of black communities.[20] The single-issue focus clarified the goals and objectives of the movement, but it also narrowed the agenda. Precisely how did U.S. military aggression abroad connect to domestic urban growth and social control? Once the bombing ended and the U.S. troops were withdrawn, in whose hands would the responsibility for the long-lasting damage and destruction fall? Racism and patriarchy shaped antiwar activism back then, and continues to shape how we look at the movement and the Vietnam War today.

The Vietnam antiwar movement was most visible on streets and campuses, but antiwar sentiment also influenced the political atmosphere in the upper echelons of society, in newsrooms, inside the halls of Congress, and even within the military itself. Some elite families were directly affected by the War, and the children of presidential staff showed up at antiwar rallies and protests. Mainstream journalists revealed civilian casualties and bombings that the Pentagon denied. As the War seemed to be less "winnable," Congress proposed at least 10 resolutions to cut military funding. In March 1968, President Johnson's unofficial group of senior advisors, called the "Wise Men," told him that he should "take steps to disengage" from Vietnam. Days later, Johnson announced that the United States would enter into negotiations with North Vietnam, and that he would not run for re-election. In March 1971, Daniel Ellsberg leaked the "Pentagon Papers" to the *New York Times*, a secret study commissioned by Robert McNamara about the poor decision-making behind the War. Nixon tried to suppress Ellsberg and the *New York Times*, which triggered events leading to the Watergate scandal and Nixon's impeachment.

At the grassroots level, the antiwar movement was subjected to repression through various means, including Operation CHAOS and COINTELPRO. The CIA, the FBI, and local police departments infiltrated, harassed, threatened, and provoked activists for expressing their opposition to the War and for encouraging others to do so. Although the act of gathering in public places is theoretically protected by the Constitution, the government prepared itself for large antiwar protests at the Capitol by amassing tens of thousands of fully armed city police, National Guardsmen, and even federal troops.[21]

One way to examine the antiwar movement would be to present a chronology listing all of its major public events—rallies, marches, sit-ins, teach-ins, moratoria, and more. Besides the huge gatherings in Washington D.C. organized by SDS and Mobe (Mobilization to End the War in Vietnam), this list would include: the Chicago Conspiracy Trial after the 1968 Democratic National Convention; the Yippies humorously running a pig named "Pigasus" for president and attempting to levitate the Pentagon in 1967; and the first coordinated act of non-violence against the draft by the "Catonsville 9," a group of Catholic priests and nuns who broke into a Selective Service agency, poured blood on the files, burned them with homemade napalm, and then waited calmly for the police to arrest them and take them to jail. A complete list would also mention the GI "coffee houses" where feelings of anger and betrayal among the ranks of the military fed the antiwar movement.[22] In 1971, more than a thousand veterans staged "Operation Dewey Canyon III," an action sarcastically described as "a limited incursion into the country of Congress." The five-day event organized by the Vietnam Veterans Against the War dramatically closed as decorated soldiers took their medals and hurled them onto the steps of the Capitol. The symbolism of this act was effective and long-lasting.

Like a fast-moving trailer for a feature film, this chronology presents fascinating snapshots of the movement. But it does not reveal or emphasize the subtle details behind the scenes, or tell what it really meant to be involved in creating the movement and keeping it going. Wholeheartedly investing themselves in the movement against the War, many activists were themselves transformed, and the impact of the historical moment was forever imprinted on their lives.

While the movement is generally portrayed by its protests, there was far more to it than that. This book offers an extensive discussion of the People's Peace Treaty, a remarkable story of people's diplomacy that even Melvin Small—a skeptic when it comes to the achievements of the antiwar movement—describes as "the most innovative approach to ending the war."[23] Fed up with the glacial pace of negotiations led by the older generation, the student organizers of the People's Peace Treaty took matters into their own hands. The simple and direct language they crafted for ending the War came about as they met face-to-face and discussed together across the United States, South Viet Nam, and North Viet Nam. The authors of this section speak from direct experience, a perspective on the People's Peace Treaty that has never been published as far as we know.

As the nation learned more and more about the scope and brutality of military operations—not only in Viet Nam but Laos and Cambodia as well—skepticism, mistrust of the U.S. government's reports on the War, and outright opposition grew larger still.

Increasingly, that opposition penetrated the military itself. An accomplished journalist for the *Washington Post* and author of *Long Time Passing: Vietnam and the Haunted Generation* (2002), Myra MacPherson toured Viet Nam in 2013 with five U.S. veterans, ex-soldiers who now live in Viet Nam. In Chapter 9, she tells the stories of this "band of brothers in peace"—a poet, an ex-cop, a former gang member, a psychiatric social worker, and a former aid to a U.S. senator. Today, each is dedicated in his own way to dealing with the most painful legacies of the War, including widespread contamination from Agent Orange. Their examples shine a new light on the ideals of military service, and on the patriotism and brotherly love that is often touted as a sustaining force among troops in combat in Vietnam.

As the War dragged on, the Vietnamese were so effective on the battlefield and the opposition became so intense within the United States that the U.S. government was compelled to open the formal peace talks that ultimately resulted in the Paris Peace Accords, which was signed in 1973. To some, then and now, it might seem that escalating opposition to the War was some accidental mood shift. This book shows otherwise. Relating their own personal experiences as leaders of the antiwar movement, the authors in this book offer first-hand and concrete examples of innovative strategies and tactics they devised to express public opposition to the War and to challenge the war-makers' version of what the War was about and how well it was going.

As it turned out, some of the worst consequences of U.S. military and foreign policy intervention happened in Laos and Cambodia. In the 1970s, Fred Branfman, an antiwar activist based in Laos, made crucial revelations about military operations that were being concealed by the U.S. government. Those returning from trips to Laos and Viet Nam brought home information about the effects of the War not being reported by either the government or the mainstream media.

The "Hanoi 9" represent thousands of others who eagerly interacted with the Vietnamese, not just for information unfiltered by media or the government, but for important human bonds across the boundaries of nation-states and ideologies. Even as antiwar activity in the United States has waned since the end of the Vietnam War, citizens still work to counteract the U.S. military juggernaut. From Latin America to the Middle East and beyond, "people's diplomats" take trips, arrange conferences, make media, and bear witness in a multitude of efforts to change perceptions and policies.

Traveling to Viet Nam

Presidents Johnson and Nixon tried to discredit antiwar activists by claiming that they were "dupes," spies in the service of international communism. But precisely because antiwar activists did not want to be mindless pawns for anyone, they purposefully searched beyond the conventional sources of news for the truth about the War. After Tom Hayden's trip to Ha Noi in 1965, approximately 200 U.S. citizens followed his path, bypassing the Cold War travel ban implemented by the State Department so that they could meet face-to-face with Vietnamese people and see with their own eyes what the U.S. military was actually doing in Viet Nam. Neither journalists nor combatants, these travelers became known as "people's" or "citizen" diplomats because they established an unofficial line of communication between the two countries.

The people's diplomats represented a variety of peace or antiwar perspectives, social groups, and professional backgrounds. Many of them were prominent and influential cultural figures, such as writers, doctors, or entertainers. By going to Viet Nam and returning home with first-hand observations and anecdotes about the War, they became credible witnesses for the antiwar movement. They delivered speeches, made documentary films, and wrote books and essays that exposed the realities of U.S. military and political intervention in Viet Nam. Some also criticized the underlying attitudes and assumptions about what "winning" the War would mean. The travelers made practical connections, carrying mail between POWs and their families. In a few remarkable instances, the travelers took on even more serious responsibility, escorting POWs back to the United States. These communications with POWs were made possible by the Committee of Liaison with Servicemen Detained in North Vietnam, a group formed by Women Strike for Peace (WSP) in 1969.[24] Over time, the people's diplomats developed trustworthy international relationships that continue to shape the dialogue about the War even today.

Predictably, rather than take advantage of the unofficial diplomatic channel opened to Ha Noi by these travelers, the State Department either ignored or punished their efforts. Passports were revoked, then returned—but only after courts ruled in favor of the right to travel. Some became subjects of government investigation and surveillance because of their trip. Many people who might have considered the trip were deterred because of the potential backlash or harassment they expected to receive upon their return.[25]

Going to Viet Nam as a war witness presented other obstacles as well. In one direction, the trip required ten or more days of travel through three or more nations, boarding several different planes. To enter Ha Noi, travelers had to be flown in on tiny aircraft operated by the International Control Commission (ICC), a neutral agency composed of troops and officers from Poland, India, and Canada. Entering contested space, the ICC planes created a safe corridor meant to pause fighting on the ground and in the air. Once in Ha Noi, many travelers experienced war-time bombing by U.S. aircraft. For their protection, Vietnamese children and elders were evacuated to the countryside and remained there during the War. But the remaining residents of Ha Noi were on constant alert, driving at night time with their lights off, and ready to hide in bomb shelters at any moment during the day.

Traveling to Viet Nam as sympathetic observers was possible in large part because the Vietnamese in Ha Noi actively cultivated people's diplomacy as a solution to their lack of access to international media. They arranged face-to-face encounters not only in Ha Noi, but also in Paris, Bratislava, and Canada.[26] They established organizational structures to handle "delegations" of foreigners; for example, the Viet Nam Committee for Solidarity with American People met U.S. travelers at the airport and provided drivers, guides, and translators for the duration of their stay. Essentially, the Solidarity Committee created an antiwar travel-and-study circuit that kept travelers safe and yet allowed for an exchange of views and information that would have otherwise been forbidden. The international networks and friendships that were created by the dual efforts of the Vietnamese and sympathetic individuals around the world were a unique and distinctive aspect of the antiwar effort.

The "Hanoi 9": Students, Rebels, Diplomats

With the exception of the five U.S. soldiers featured in Chapter 9, "Voices of Veterans: The Endless Tragedy of Vietnam," all of the authors featured in this book visited Viet Nam during the War as representatives of the antiwar movement in the United States. In January 2013, this group returned to Viet Nam on a special trip that coincided with the 40th anniversary of the signing of the Paris Peace Accords in January 1973.

The "Hanoi 9" were treated as special guests of the Vietnamese government because of their visible role in the U.S. antiwar movement. Among the invitation-only activities they joined: a government sponsored and nationally televised event commemorating the Paris Peace Accords that involved a police escort, a red carpet entrance, and a marching band; a brunch attended by President Truong Tan Sang and high-ranking members of the Communist Party; a tree-planting ceremony with the President; and a home-style dinner with Nguyen Thi Binh, known throughout the world as "Madame Binh."[27] The royal treatment that the U.S. travelers received in Viet Nam is diametrically opposite to the way they were treated in the United States during the years of the War. And certainly today, no branch of the current U.S. government has any intention of inviting them to anything.

After five days in Ha Noi, the group then headed south via train through Quang Tri and Da Nang before ending in Sai Gon/Ho Chi Minh City. Along the way, the group stopped to speak with local and provincial government leaders, veterans, and other community representatives. An

President Truong Tan Sang receives a framed photograph of the
May Day March on Washington DC, 1971. Appearing from left to right:
Nancy Kurshan, Frank Joyce, Rennie Davis, and John McAuliff.
Photo courtesy of Frank Joyce.

important segment of the trip involved encounters with victims of Agent
Orange and unexploded ordnance. Decades after the War, these effects still
manifest in death, injury, illnesses, and physical defects in subsequent generations of the Vietnamese population. Being exposed to this most enduring consequence of the War enabled the group to see one way that they
could extend the commitments they made in their youth into their current
political agendas.

How the Trip Happened

The "Hanoi 9" project started in an ad hoc way. In 2006, the co-editors of
this book met on a trip to Viet Nam led by the late Erwin Marquit, editor
of the journal *Nature, Society and Thought*. We quickly discovered we had
many things in common. Perhaps most important: we share an irreverent
and active sense of humor that has served us well throughout the process of
creating this book. Furthermore, despite quite different paths in life, we felt
a love for Viet Nam and a hatred of the long, ugly history of U.S. imperialist
and racist interventions. On top of that, from Frank's lifetime of political
activism in Detroit and Karin's repeated visits to the city, they found much

to discuss about Detroit's role as an emerging multicultural, multiracial icon in the effort to create viable economic solutions to Detroit's problems.

One conversation after another led to the idea of the timeliness and importance of looking back at the Vietnam antiwar movement and forward into the contemporary relationship between Americans and Vietnamese, including Americans of Vietnamese heritage. From that came the idea of focusing on those who had taken the considerable risks of traveling to Viet Nam during the War. Countless phone calls and emails later, eight other people came forward and the 2013 trip finally happened. The group was joined by six others who included scholars, a filmmaker, and spouses.

And yet, the "Hanoi 9" might not have made it to Viet Nam but for Frank's encounter with John McAuliff at the 50th anniversary conference of SNCC in Raleigh, North Carolina, in April 2010. John and Frank were among those whites who shared experience in both the civil-rights and the antiwar movements. As McAuliff explains later in this book, he had developed and maintained relationships with many Vietnamese in the years since the War ended. Those ties were invaluable in planning the itinerary and the logistical details of bringing the visit together.

Last but by no mean least, the Viet Nam USA Friendship Society provided invaluable support for the trip. Bui Van Nghi, Secretary General of the Viet Nam Union of Friendship Organizations (VUFO), along with his colleagues who served as our hosts, guides, translators, and cultural interlocutors were all essential to the trip's success.

As editors, we share important values and attitudes in common although our life stories and professional experiences differ greatly. For example, we are both interested and invested in the grassroots, multiracial struggles to rebuild Detroit. Frank, a lifelong Detroiter and trade union leader, actively participates as an elder white male in multiracial, intergenerational dialogues about community activism and urban development based in the Boggs Center and elsewhere. As a writer-activist and college professor, Karin developed an interest in Detroit and took her students there many times to experience Detroit Summer, a youth-oriented initiative to rebuild the city.

Being committed to Detroit means that when it comes to the Vietnam War and the antiwar movement, we both prioritize the multiracial/anti-racist aspects of struggle. We both understand place-based struggles as a valuable paradigm for coalitions and solidarity work. It also means we each position ourselves in certain ways vis-à-vis the histories of people of color and other subjugated groups in the United States and around the globe. For Frank, it is important to identify and acknowledge the continuing dynamics of white supremacy in U.S. society. For Karin, it is important to connect as an Asian American, woman of color, and lesbian feminist.

In addition, we do not want to set off stereotypes about Vietnamese or for that matter other people of color as helpless populations in need of rescue by heroic white savior nations. We want to fill the void left by *Forrest Gump* but we do not want to perpetuate an idealized Western projection of revolution in place of a realistic assessment of a place, people, or struggle. The "Vietnam" of our memories needs to be in constant dialogue with the contemporary nation, culture, and diaspora of Viet Nam. We greatly appreciate the work of Ngô Vĩnh Long and other Vietnamese-American scholars and peace veterans who continue to explain and analyze contemporary developments in Viet Nam and in the U.S.–Viet Nam relationship.[28]

The Editors' Perspective on the War and the Movement

As we tell the story of the antiwar movement, we are often torn between explanation and advocacy. In what circumstances do we need to explain what happened in literal terms, and when is it necessary to advocate for a particular angle on the story? In this introduction, we strive to balance a view that emphasizes on one side the long historical cycles of war, domination, exploitation, and repression, and on the other side, the continuing and overlapping struggles for peace and democracy. In other words, our interpretation of U.S. history leads us to expect the negative cycles to repeat over and over again. But we also recognize the traditions of rebellion and resistance especially among indigenous and enslaved peoples, migrant laborers, and poor and urban minorities. To borrow from Antonio Gramsci, we hope this project achieves a tricky combination of pessimism of the mind and optimism of the will.

The examples we provide show people who stood up against a colossal global power structure to fight for what they believed was right. They were not just "clicktivists" posting antiwar messages and collecting "friends" on Facebook. Yes, social media is a powerful tool for bringing people together as we saw during Occupy Wall Street and the 2011 Egyptian Revolution. But during the Vietnam War, activists had to explain the consequences of the War without the Internet. They had to be able to present their ideas to people they did not know or necessarily like, and argue convincingly for a new way to look at the world. The antiwar movement gained traction because activists were able to shift people's thoughts and feelings about the War. In return, the lives of antiwar activists were transformed.

We celebrate the accomplishments of the Vietnam antiwar movement knowing full well that it was also rife with conflict, factionalism, and everyday human flaws. Every struggle for justice in the course of U.S. history also bears the traces of the problems it is trying to solve; the antiwar movement was not alone in this shortcoming. But what propels this book forward is the hope that we do not mindlessly re-invent racism, sexism, homophobia, or other "isms" as we draw out the lessons of the Vietnam era.

We understand as well that climate change and many other problems demand our attention today. Consequently, neither the Vietnam War nor the antiwar movement ranks high on anyone's agenda. One might even ask: Why look backward at all? The fact is that Vietnam antiwar movement was one of the most significant collective mobilizations of the twentieth century. Spanning from 1965 through 1971, the movement fomented so much dissent that observers refer to an "internal war" within the United States involving students, grassroots activists, liberal Establishment figures, business people, clergy, and the media.

Admittedly, current U.S. wars, especially those in the Middle East, differ from the Vietnam War in important ways. Viet Nam never attacked the United States; Al Qaeda did.

Furthermore, the U.S. military is not drafting soldiers to go to Iraq or Afghanistan, or other theaters of conflict. This alone merits further scrutiny, particularly because it is often argued that opposition to the War was primarily driven by a reluctance to serve. Draft resistance (called "dodging" by supporters of the War) and conscientious objection to the draft were huge components of the Vietnam antiwar movement.

In pointing this out, however, we do not intend to give in to the arguments made by supporters of the Vietnam War that the protests were merely an attempt to avoid the draft on the part of cowardly activists. Many draft resistors exhibited courage by their deeds. Thousands risked arrest and a significant number were imprisoned or otherwise punished. Widespread protests on college campuses invariably involved women who were not subject to the draft at all. For that matter, males on college campuses were among those best positioned to avoid the draft because of student deferments and other opportunities available to the more affluent. Yet in massive numbers, they opposed the War anyway. Furthermore, the Korean War was sold to the public in "WE MUST STOP COMMUNISM IN ITS TRACKS" terms virtually identical to the Vietnam War. The Korean War, too, had a massive draft. What it did not have was significant draft resistance.[29]

The contrast between the absence of opposition to the Korean War compared to the Vietnam War is indeed striking. Clearly the times were very different. If there was some sort of thermal imaging technology allowing satellites to register political dissent and upheaval, on any given day in the 1960s the planet would have been glowing bright red. Within the

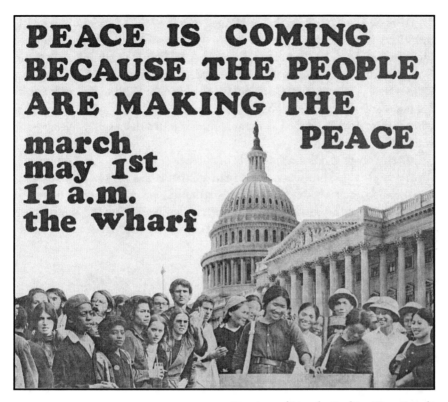

Courtesy of Lincoln Cushing/Docs Populi.

United States alone there was conflict over racism and civil rights; the place of women in relation to men; and the pay, benefits, and status of workers. Students in the United States and Europe took to the streets. In Africa, Asia, and Latin America, people were throwing off the yoke of their colonial rulers. Across the globe, more and more people were sympathizing with the Vietnamese "David" taking on the U.S. "Goliath."

Big social movements do not happen all the time—especially on the scale of the 1960s. They are the exception, not the rule, occurring every few decades, not every few years. Mass movements against war in the United States are especially unusual. To be clear, antiwar and pacifist sentiment in the United States has a long and proud tradition. A strain of what is often called isolationism has always been strong. Many U.S. Americans opposed involvement in World War II because they supported Hitler or Mussolini or both. Becoming a mass antiwar undertaking, however, is exceptional and, in that regard, the Vietnam opposition stands out.

This book recognizes and celebrates making face-to-face contact with the Vietnamese on the other side of the War as an essential component of the spirit of defiance that characterized what Tom Hayden has called the "long 1960s." Herbert Aptheker, Tom Hayden, Staughton Lynd, Cora Weiss, Diane Nash, Joan Baez, Eldridge Cleaver, Noam Chomsky, and Susan Sontag were among the highly visible writers, activists, and intellectuals who went to Viet Nam not as combatants or journalists but as citizen-advocates for peace.

Their travels did not necessarily make them experts in Vietnamese culture or politics; in some cases, they realized that it was very hard to relate as Americans and as Westerners to the Vietnamese people they had hoped to befriend. But in the context of the War that was destroying the Vietnamese land and people, not to mention costing U.S. soldiers a great deal, it was important to look for a greater truth.

The Movement Did Not Endure

In January 2013, the 40th anniversary of the Paris Peace Accords was commemorated in events throughout Viet Nam that received considerable media attention around the world. This was not so in U.S. media.

The failure of any U.S. media, including alternative media, to carry a single story about the 40th anniversary of the signing of the Paris Peace Accords is a glaring example of the role played by media in encouraging a process of forgetting what, for many, are unpleasant events and outcomes. Yet this example also highlights an important reality of the antiwar movement: it left no institutionalized organizational legacy. Thus, there was no group to lobby the U.S. media to pay attention to the anniversary of the Paris Peace Accords.

With a few small exceptions, none of the organizations and coalitions that emerged to oppose the Vietnam War exists today. This is not unique to the antiwar movement. Most 1960s movement organizations including the Student Non-Violent Coordinating Committee (SNCC) and Students for a Democratic Society (SDS) did not endure.

Groups such as the American Friends Service Committee, the Mennonites, the War Resisters League, and the Fellowship of Reconciliation constitute an ongoing voice for peace. They continue to be involved in Viet Nam, Laos, and Cambodia in various ways, but each of these organizations existed long before the War.

Since the War ended, several organizations have been formed in Europe, the United States, and within Viet Nam itself to deal with ongoing consequences of the War such as Agent Orange and unexploded ordnance.

They have also facilitated travel by U.S. military veterans back to Viet Nam. The "Hanoi 9" met with leaders of several of such organizations and visited a number of their projects during their trip. These groups are listed in the Resources section of this book.

Once we returned from the 2013 trip, the idea of a book featuring the "Hanoi 9" became even more compelling. One reason was the richness of their diverse backgrounds and perspectives. Some came from leftist families and grew up critical of U.S. foreign policy. Some came from the civil-rights movement and through that movement, came to identify with anti-colonial struggles around the world. Others are pacifists, committed to non-violence even in the midst of war. Some came from the cultural rebellion wing of the movement of the 1960s. Others joined the movement as students against the War. Several resisted the draft.

The sad truth is that while opposition to the War was strong throughout the U.S. population, antiwar organizing largely reproduced the lines of racial separation within society. Furthermore, the demonstrations and protests against the War that were mostly white, on campus and off, received the greatest media attention. And while the draft put the War very much in the face of all young men, whites had access to a far greater range of strategies for avoiding service. To be fair, as noted previously, the extent to which black and brown men were disproportionately represented, especially in combat, was part of what motivated many whites to oppose the War.

Many antiwar whites saw the War as a deviation from what they thought were the nation's core values. For them, the War was a "mistake," evidence that the country had gone off track. Secretary of State John Kerry's famous question, "How do you ask a man to be the last man to die for a mistake?"[30] captured this viewpoint perfectly.

In any case, the scale of opposition took the nation's leaders by surprise. In retrospect, it is clear that the architects of the War made at least two miscalculations. First, and most importantly, their colossal arrogance led them to think they could succeed in subduing the Vietnamese, even though the French and others before them had failed. Second, they did not anticipate the domestic resistance to the War. Why would they? Arguably the previous intervention in Korea was an expensive failure. The ill-fated attempt to invade Cuba during the Bay of Pigs certainly was. Nevertheless, neither action aroused all that much opposition. Why would generals, senators, or presidents think that Viet Nam might somehow be different?

Ironically, the current times make it easier to understand their mindset. We think this book is important in no small measure precisely because opposition to war has again become muted and marginal.

Opposing War Today

While there was initially intense ad hoc opposition to the 2003 invasion of Iraq, once that war began in earnest, the U.S. military has operated with a mostly free hand. It has gone wherever it wants, using any and all weapons (except nuclear) that it sees fit.

Tom Hayden in particular has been outspoken and relentless in working to mobilize opposition to the Iraq War. CODEPINK has also been creative and steadfast in keeping the serial military interventions in the Middle East before the public. The reality, however, is that there has been no sustained mass movement against these wars.

A meme of failure to "support the troops" retains deep and strong roots in U.S. culture. Furthermore, the widely held belief that the United States "lost" the Vietnam War energized a backlash against the antiwar movement—the effects of which linger to this day. The election of Ronald Reagan in 1980 was both effect and cause of a national rededication to war, violence, and racism.

Part of rededicating the nation to war involves revising any memories of the movement against it. Professor David Steigerwald, a historian at Ohio State University, observes that when he teaches the history of the Vietnam antiwar movement, his students imagine "pot-smoking, tie-dyed, anti-American hippies who heaped public scorn on soldiers." Steigerwald argues that instead of having *no* ideas about the War, the U.S. public *mis*-remembers it just as the lead character played by Tom Hanks did in *Forrest Gump*.[31]

An even more sharply distorted perspective on the War and the antiwar movement was institutionalized in 2008 when Congress passed legislation authorizing and funding the Pentagon-sponsored Vietnam War commemoration, which is scheduled to run until 2025. President Obama enthusiastically endorsed the commemoration in his 2012 Memorial Day proclamation.

Since then, the commission has developed a robust website at www.vietnamwar50th.com. It has already organized hundreds of events to commemorate the Vietnam War—including plans for half-time celebrations at university football games around the country—and has thousands more in the works. As far as we know, there is no meaningful reference to the antiwar movement. Veterans of the antiwar movement, including some of the authors in this book, are waging their own campaign to counteract the Pentagon's perspective.

The key to what made the Vietnam War different than previous wars was that U.S. military and technological prowess could not secure or maintain U.S. domination. Millions of tons of bombs were dumped on the Vietnamese people, causing more than three million deaths. Nevertheless, a unified Vietnamese nation emerged that was determined to control its own cultural, historical, and political agenda, despite severe losses and deep trauma that would continue for generations.

During their 2013 trip, members of the Hanoi 9 repeatedly inquired about how the Vietnamese *won* the War against the United States. People of all ages and walks of life invariably had a similar response: "We didn't," they said. "All we did was defend our country. Besides, the losses we suffered make the notion of winning nonsensical."

Indeed, as U.S. citizens we can hardly stop ourselves from thinking in terms of "winning" or "losing" any competition or sports event, never mind a major war. In Chapter 3, Alex Hing comments that our Western "either/or" patterns of thought can make it more difficult to understand our contemporary realities. For example, most of us see the casualties of the Vietnam War only in terms of "Americans" or "Vietnamese." But at least one million Vietnamese Americans, including refugees, immigrants, and people of Vietnamese heritage born in the United States are also deeply divided over the origins, meaning, and consequences of the War.

Far too often, those who opposed the War stereotype Vietnamese Americans as simply anti-communist, or worse, stooges of U.S. imperialism. On the other hand, for good reasons, Vietnamese Americans frequently assert that they are tired of being seen only through the lens of the Vietnam War. They might think that U.S. antiwar activists are pathologically nostalgic about "Vietnam," constantly referring to a place and culture they hardly know.

Today, scholars of Critical Refugee Studies are exposing a particular motif of the Vietnamese refugee: tragic, docile, helpless, and in need of rescue by the United States. In order to justify future wars in Iraq and elsewhere, Vietnamese, Hmong, and other war refugees are woven into a "good refugee means good war" story.

When a Vietnamese-American poet like Bao Phi seethes with anger about racism and poverty in his hometown of Minneapolis, Minnesota, this story breaks apart and new divisions appear.[32] This much more complicated view of the intersections of U.S. racism and imperialism emerges from struggles and lived experiences within Vietnamese American communities. No longer strapped to one single narrative, people of Vietnamese ancestry in the United States are more openly reconsidering their relationships to the history of the United States and Viet Nam. Many Vietnamese Americans feel they have lost all meaningful connection to their homeland; others have resolved those conflicts and returned to Viet Nam.

The very idea of the United States "losing" the War reflects a certain point of view. The United States "lost" because it failed to overthrow the government of another country—not because *the U.S. government or way of life* was attacked by another nation. When the War ended, the sovereignty of the United States was intact. For the failure of the United States to change the government and economic system of Viet Nam or any other country to be described as a loss presumes the legitimacy of the United States' determining how other countries should be governed in the first place. To put it another way, to argue that the United States "lost" Viet Nam is to believe that its fate was up to the United States to begin with.

Even beyond that, if the goal was to either gain or maintain world hegemony—remembering that beyond regime-change in Viet Nam, "containing communism," was the stated objective of the War—then the outcome did not prevent the United States from becoming "the sole superpower."

In fact, Viet Nam is now a valued U.S. economic partner and strategic ally in the game of geopolitics. Recent documents signed by the governments of Viet Nam and the United States give some reason to think that ever so slowly the United States will take a little bit more responsibility for the ongoing death and pain caused by the massive use of chemical Agent Orange and unexploded ordnance at least in Viet Nam if not in Laos and Cambodia. Or, for that matter, in the Philippines, because the U.S. military bases in the Philippines were a staging area for Vietnam, and Agent Orange has left its traces there, too.

Which brings us to a pressing question: *What exactly did the antiwar movement achieve?*

Achievements of the Antiwar Movement

In the 40 years since the War ended, there have been few, if any, conferences or symposia bringing Vietnam antiwar leaders together to "debrief" the movement. Scholarly attention to the civil rights, feminist and student movements of the 1960s significantly exceeds that given to the antiwar movement as well.[33]

The Resources section of this book lists some of the studies that have been done, as well as biographies and autobiographies of those who were leaders or participants in the antiwar movement. We are proud that this book will add to that literature. We do not submit that this book is the definitive history, let alone analysis, of what the antiwar movement did or what it meant.

That said, from our vantage point, several things seem clear. First, the antiwar movement made a tangible and significant difference in how people thought about the War. From beauty shop conversations to presidential politics, it put the legality, morality, and efficacy of the War into question in ways that would not have happened otherwise.

Transcripts of White House tapes reveal that the highest level of government paid close attention to the antiwar movement's actions and its leaders. Without the visibility and controversy generated by many, many courageous and creative protestors in the United States and around the world, the War would have been longer, and the death and destruction would have been worse.

It is harder to prove, but still possible, that the antiwar movement prevented the use of nuclear weapons against Viet Nam. The United States offered its nuclear weapons to the French during their nine-year war with the Vietnamese (1945–54). To their credit, the French declined. As Nick Turse notes in his book, *Kill Anything that Moves: The Real American War in Vietnam* (2013), the U.S. military deployed chemical weapons, bombing on an unprecedented scale, torture, mass assassination, and every other weapon of war as never before in history. But perhaps because of the pressure of the antiwar movement, the United States did not cross the nuclear line.

These are remarkable achievements. But there is even more to the story. As we have said earlier, neither before nor since has the machinery of perpetual war been as seriously challenged as it was over this War.

People in the United States think that every other country is absorbed in one or more wars 365 days of the year, year after year after year, just like we are. They are wrong. The sole superpower stands alone in its dedication to all war all the time.

Obviously, the antiwar movement did not reverse that pattern. To be fair, however, that was not its objective. The forces that dominated the movement were never about ending all war—they were about one war at one time in one place. It was the *pro-war* movement that propagated the notion that the antiwar movement would bring the whole edifice of the government and everything else crashing to the ground. They still do.

Were there those within the movement who wanted a more fundamental and radical shift in U.S. foreign and military policy? To be sure. And some of them played an important role in the creative strategy of the movement. But they were always a minority. Noam Chomsky, Chris Hedges, Juan Cole, Kathy Kelly, David Swanson, Christian Appy, Medea Benjamin,

Father Roy Bourgeois, Bishop Thomas Gumbleton, Richard Falk, and others continue to voice strong condemnation of U.S. foreign and military policy. A range of critiques of current U.S. policies occasionally enters mainstream political discussion, but these criticisms do not begin to approach the impact of the movement against the Vietnam War.

Could the Vietnam antiwar movement have been more effective in generating more pressure sooner and thus ending the War earlier? Probably. Could it have had a more lasting impact on future wars? Perhaps. Does the fragmentation of today's social movements continue to impair the impact of war opponents as it did decades ago? Sadly, the answer is yes.

Nevertheless, we are convinced that understanding the experiences of the Vietnam antiwar movement, including its strengths and weaknesses, can contribute to ending U.S. wars and preventing future ones. If there is one message that we hope comes through loud and clear from this book it is this: If the people could rein in the war-making mania of the United States government once, they can do it again.

SEEING VIETNAM WITH MY OWN EYES

RENNIE DAVIS

Editors' Note: The stories of this chapter are more fully presented in a forthcoming book, Generation Arise, by Rennie Davis.

It seemed hard to imagine I was going back to Vietnam with an American antiwar delegation 40 years after the signing of the Paris Peace Accords. It was harder still to explain what I experienced when I came back to the United States. This book was organized to share the experiences of our delegation to Vietnam's 40th anniversary of the Paris Peace Accords. We attended official meetings and ceremonies from Hanoi to Ho Chi Minh City. We met the president of Vietnam, the U.S. ambassador to Vietnam, the head of Vietnam's national assembly and Madame Nguyen Thi Binh, a living icon in today's Vietnam. What happened on our trip is set out in this book. It was the continuing love and appreciation that the Vietnamese have for the millions of Americans who joined massive mobilizations against the war that most stood out for me during this trip back to Vietnam. To share my own experience, I want to paint a picture of who the Vietnamese actually are and what really happened during those years of war between the United States and Vietnam.

In January 2013, nine Americans with their spouses and significant others returned to Vietnam. We had all previously traveled to Hanoi during the war. On our first night back in Hanoi, Madame Nguyen Thi Binh unexpectedly invited Frank Joyce, his wife, Mary Anne Barnett, John McAuliff,

Kirsten Liegmann, and me to a private dinner with her son and grandson. She held hands with me most of the night and presented me a gift of her autobiography, recently translated into English and just off the press. [2]

When I read her book, I saw again her incredible love and appreciation for the U.S. antiwar movement. She described her relation to me like "a mother to a son" and since first meeting her in 1967, I have always felt the same. Before the negotiations in Paris began, the American public had a blurry image of Vietnam's resistance leaders. No one imagined the official representative of the South Vietnamese National Liberation Front would be a woman, much less the enchanting and elegant Madame Nguyen Thi Binh. When she first stepped onto the world stage on November 4, 1968—a wise, sensitive, and articulate spokeswoman—she stunned and inspired the public. As hundreds of delegations made the trip to Paris to meet her, she won their hearts with her sincerity and kindness as she patiently explained the deeply flawed and brutal American war policy.

Madame Binh's grandfather had been a beloved national scholar and early advocate of democracy for Vietnam. Her father had been a surveyor with the French administration who moved to the Mekong Delta when she was a child. Growing up, she lived with her family and later attended a French school in Cambodia where she excelled in math and sports and competed in cross-country races and basketball. In April 1951, her education was halted when she was imprisoned by the French. She spent three years in the most notorious French prison of the time after someone who had been brutally tortured gave up her name. In her autobiography she wrote, "I was cruelly beaten without stopping because an earlier arrestee had broken down under torture and given my name. First, they tortured us by savage beatings. Then they submerged us in water, then with electricity, then—I wanted to die so they would finish—I was most worried about breaking under torture and giving names, leading the enemy to arrest others.... Fortunately, the torturers saw they couldn't wrest any information from me." In recalling those brutal years, she said it gave her strength—the strength "to survive the most intense conditions imaginable."

U.S. reporters who covered the events in Paris had little if any awareness of this personal history. Instead, many wondered why a woman was selected for Paris at all. Ho Chi Minh, the president of Vietnam, had traveled abroad and even lived in the United States. The time he spent in New York City and Boston was during the woman's suffrage movement before World War I when he came to deeply believe that a woman should represent Vietnam to the world. He also knew that Madame Nguyen Thi Binh possessed the intelligence, openness, and kindness to win over the skeptics.

When the Vietnamese launched their final nationwide mobilization that overran Saigon, ending the Vietnam War in 1975, Madame Binh became Vietnam's minister of education and integrated two very different systems of education. During 1992 to 2002, she was subsequently elected twice by the National Assembly to serve as Vietnam's vice president with oversight of state diplomacy, health, education, and judicial reform. When she "retired" in 2002 at age 75, her close friends watched her become busier than ever. About her retirement she said, "I can't be still. I must continue to take a full part in life" until Vietnam is "truly democratic, equal and cultured."

I visited her frequently during her years in Paris. Now it was the 40th anniversary of the Paris Peace Accords and she was in front of me again, still expressing her appreciation for the Americans who opposed the horrific U.S. war. In her book, she acknowledged many of the specific U.S. groups that came to Paris during the war, from Congressional delegates to families of American prisoners of war to antiwar activists. She wanted the people of Vietnam to remember the names of the Americans who had fought to end the war, especially those who sacrificed their own lives, some setting themselves on fire to protest the war. She specifically mentioned the work of Dave Dellinger, Tom Hayden, Jane Fonda, Cora Weiss, Benjamin Spock, and myself.

For the 40th anniversary of the Paris Peace Accords, Vietnam decided to host a national event in Hanoi with past and present political and military leaders, ranking members of the national assembly, chief justices, members of the secretariat and politburo, the minister of foreign affairs and other ministers, along with diverse representatives of foreign governments, NGOs, and organizations that had supported Vietnam during the war from around the world. The national ceremony included the past and present political and military leadership of the country. Our delegation joined the gathering along with hundreds of representatives of foreign governments, NGOs, and antiwar organizations around the world that had supported Vietnam during the U.S. war.

Following stunning performances from dancers, singers, and leading artists of Vietnam, President Truong Tan Sang spoke of the January 1973 Paris negotiations as the ultimate achievement in Vietnam's "history of diplomacy." Acknowledging the pivotal work of Madame Binh, she was awarded Vietnam's highest recognition that evening, the military's hero award.

Today, Madame Nguyen Thi Binh is Chairperson of Vietnam's Children's Fund, Honorary President of the Association of Victims of Agent Orange, and President of the Peace and Development Foundation where she

Dave Dellinger, David Ifshin, and Rennie Davis confer
near the White House, February 8, 1971.
Photo courtesy of The Baltimore Sun.

is devoted to supporting Vietnamese victims of chemical Agent Orange. To paint a picture of who the Vietnamese people really are, I should begin with my first visit to Hanoi during the fall of 1967.

My first contact with a Vietnamese person was at a Vietnamese-American conference held in Bratislava (now the capital of Slovakia). Forty-two Americans came. Martin Luther King was invited but declined at the last minute due to a scheduling conflict. The U.S. delegation was a cross-section of antiwar, civil rights, and women activists with a handful of journalists. We flew to Paris, then to Prague before taking a bus to Bratislava where we met 23 Vietnamese delegates, including members of the North Vietnamese national assembly and ranking leaders of South Vietnam's Provisional Revolutionary Government.

I slowly came to realize during the conference that the Vietnamese delegation was the highest-level gathering of officials outside of Vietnam since the Geneva Convention in 1954—the historic conference that had ended the Indochina War between France and the Viet Minh. That's when I first met Madame Nguyen Thi Binh. I had no idea at the time that she had traveled six months from South Vietnam to attend this conference herself. She greeted us warmly, wearing a simple but elegant full-length, high-collared Vietnamese dress. In a few short years, she would become a world sensation, appearing in Paris as the articulate individual to head the South Vietnamese "Viet Cong" delegation—one of the four parties to the U.S.–Vietnam peace accord.

I could have left this Bratislava conference with a richer perspective on Vietnam if I had simply returned to the United States as planned. I would have come home more educated. But something unexpected happened—shifting my Vietnam awareness from educated and informed to up close and personal. At that conference, I was invited with six others to visit Vietnam and see for myself. I had no idea what that meant but knew I wanted to go. In Bratislava, I sensed correctly that I might be seizing the moment of a lifetime by saying yes to this invitation and seeing Vietnam with my own eyes.

Every American invited felt the same. We wanted to go. As risky as travelling to Czechoslovakia may have been, there was no comparison with the possible consequences of an unsanctioned trip into "enemy" territory. While I never considered declining the invitation, I found it hard to evaluate the risks. I could be bombed by U.S. Navy war planes stationed on carriers near Vietnam. I could be vilified by the press upon returning home. Believing the United States had strayed from its greatness—and longing for its return to democratic ideals—I felt motivated to be among the first Americans to evaluate the Vietnamese claim that American air raids routinely targeted civilian infrastructures resulting in large-scale casualties.

And so I joined one of the first delegations of antiwar activists to see what our Defense Department did not want any American to witness—the effects of the U.S. air war raining down its anti-personnel and 2,000-pound bombs on North Vietnam. Our delegation to Hanoi that year was Tom Hayden, Carol McEldowney, Vivian Rothstein, Norman Fruchter, Robert Allen, Jock Brown, and myself. We boarded an International Control Commission (ICC) aircraft heading for North Vietnam. ICC was an off-shoot of the Geneva Convention established to monitor the implementation of the international agreement that followed the French war in 1954. When its purpose to unify the country with nationwide elections was blocked by the United States, ICC continued to provide an airline connection to the divided country with flights from Saigon to Hanoi through Laos.

Our nighttime flight into Hanoi from Laos was the final leg of a journey that had begun in Prague and taken us through Beirut, Dubai, Bombay

Traveling by train from Hanoi to Ho Chi Minh City (Saigon) in 2013, with stops in Quang Tri and Da Nang. From left to right: Alex Hing, Rennie Davis, and Judy Gumbo. Photo courtesy of Judy Gumbo.

Rangoon, Phnom Penh, and Vientiane, Laos. We faced stormy weather that night that hurled our tiny prop plane sharply upwards before dropping it hard, over and over, making the passengers tightly bound to their throw-up bags. I was relieved not to feel sick as we descended into the pitch darkness of this mysterious Asian city. At the last moment, just before touching down, a row of bright lights went on to illuminate the runway and then turned off quickly as the wheels made contact with the ground. Walking down the plane's stairs, a group of excited Vietnamese welcomed us like U.S. tourists from the mainland are often greeted by natives in Hawaii. As I got my travel bag and walked to a caravan of jeep-style military vehicles,

I felt overwhelmed with questions. Given the need to turn off the lights of Hanoi's airport, were we in danger from bombs being dropped by our own country tonight? How would we get into a blacked-out city if the bridges into Hanoi had all been bombed?

Returning to Vietnam in 2013 and returning again in January 2015 just after Hanoi's new terminal had opened, it is clear that Vietnam on one level has dramatically changed. These days, international flights to Hanoi don't use ICC prop planes anymore. Instead, 500 passengers crowd onto one Airbus. The old airport is gone. Terminal two of the Nội Bài International Airport was inaugurated January 4, 2015, boosting the total capacity of the new Vietnam airport to 19 million passengers a year. Traveling the 17 miles from the airport to downtown Hanoi uses a brand new world-class highway that crosses the spectacular Nhật Tân Bridge, where many circles of gardens are in development but not yet finished.

When I came to Hanoi the first time, getting into the city was not that easy. The Red River—a major waterway flowing from Yunnan in Southwestern China to the Gulf of Tonkin—had to be crossed and the main bridge into the city had been repeatedly bombed. While it was never destroyed, it was deemed safer for us to board a ferry and cross the Red River discreetly. The United States was at war with Vietnam but on my first humid Vietnam night with its bright tropical moon casting a liquid silver light onto the faces of every Vietnamese passenger, they looked friendly and open to me. Except for the sound of the boat's motor and one radio tuned to the music of a bamboo flute, all was quiet on the Red River. The music was elegant too. As I took in the idyllic scents and the serene scenery, I felt like a person who had stepped out of a modern world and time traveled into some ancient century.

Looking directly into the faces of the people around me, no one seemed stressed or worried at all. Not one person looked guarded or hateful like I typically experienced taking a commuter train from the O'Hare airport into downtown Chicago. If I had to pick one word to describe the demeanor of these war-time passengers, I would say innocence. Strange to say; nevertheless, that was my first impression of the Vietnamese people and it took me by surprise. Vietnam was being bombed every day by the United States of America, yet ordinary Vietnamese seemed entirely comfortable with our group of Americans and strangely free of any body armor, defenses, or cunning. Suddenly the radio music was interrupted by the voice of an announcer. Everyone hushed to listen. Unable to understand the language, I could only watch in amazement at everyone's rapt attention to every word. Then the boat erupted in celebration with cheering and clapping. I turned to our guide to hear his translation as he said, "it was just reported a U.S. F-16 flew over the country and was shot down by an 18-year-old woman with a rifle."

Now I was truly stunned—and conflicted too. My immediate thoughts went to the pilot. A U.S. serviceman had been shot down by a woman's rifle and I was surrounded by a heart-felt flood of excitement and passion. Frankly, it is only possible now decades later to share this story publicly. That night on that ferry, I wanted the war to end but wasn't prepared for this. I did not think it was possible that an American advanced fighter plane could be shot down by a Vietnamese teenager with only a rifle. As my emotions slowly settled down, I let myself see how the Vietnamese actually felt about this war. There was a genuineness in them I would witness again and again in the coming days. From my very first hours in Hanoi, I realized the United States might not be fighting an ideology after all or the narrow agenda of a rigid political elite. None of these people appeared like they were forced to celebrate the cause of their military. They seemed more like the perfect nation for "containing China" as our State Department mission had stated the United States was determined to accomplish.

Throughout my first trip to Vietnam, I watched everyday Vietnamese demonstrate over and over this was their country and their duty to fight for their freedom and independence. I felt like someone who had slipped into an American colony from Great Britain to witness a small band of freedom fighters during our own country's war of independence. I was like that invisible Brit that got to overhear the news of a victory won by a ragtag American army fighting for its freedom and independence. In Vietnam, I was witnessing something similar.

It never previously occurred to me that the Vietnamese might actually succeed in defeating the world's most powerful and advanced military on the battlefield. The Vietnamese, however, seemed completely convinced that, in the end, they would prevail, just as they had many times in the past—against the French at Dien Bien Phu, against the Japanese during World War II, and against the Chinese and Mongols to the north repeatedly over many centuries. The Vietnamese I met clearly lacked the sense of desperation one might expect from hopelessly outgunned underdogs. Instead, they displayed a confidence that caused me to consider, for the first time, the possibility that the war in Vietnam could be more than just a misguided foreign policy about containing China. Anyone visiting Hanoi in those early days of the U.S. air war had to wonder if this was a completely foolish military strategy as well. It was difficult to believe the American argument that Vietnamese guerrillas were Russian or Chinese pawns in a global cold war game of chess. The people I met seemed like genuine patriots, fighting to preserve a nation they deeply loved and respected.

Where I lived in Chicago, most people had only a vague idea of what the Vietnam War was about. Unless a person was part of a military family fighting in Vietnam, there was little stake in the outcome beyond the safe return of loved ones in combat. Everyone on this river ferry, however, appeared to have a passionate stake in the outcome.

During my first visit to Vietnam, I realized what most Americans never fully got to appreciate: The Vietnamese people loved America's founding principles and cheered us on as millions of Americans figured it out and turned against this misguided war. In Vietnam, we were the heroes as we still are today.

One evening in 1967, I strolled through the streets of Hanoi with one of my hosts. We came to a large truck caravan parked and waiting. Its destination was clearly South Vietnam. I noticed many of the waiting trucks had pictures on their windshields. A picture of Ho Chi Minh, the President of North Vietnam, was proudly displayed as I would expect, but a Western face was also common. I asked several drivers through my translator who that was—the Westerner next to Ho Chi Minh? Norman Morrison was the response. I had heard the Morrison story. He was an American Quaker who had committed suicide in an act of self-immolation at age 31, protesting U.S. involvement in the Vietnam War. The date was November 2, 1965 when he doused himself in kerosene and set himself on fire just below Defense Secretary Robert McNamara's Pentagon office. He followed the emulation of Buddhist monk Thich Quang Duc, who had also burned himself to death in downtown Saigon to protest the repression of the South Vietnam government.

Morrison's story was known to me but not widely known to the public in the United States. In Vietnam, he was a national hero. He had influenced Robert McNamara too. Filmmaker Errol Morris, who interviewed McNamara for his documentary *The Fog of War* (2003), captured the U.S. secretary of defense saying, "[Morrison] came to the Pentagon, doused himself with gasoline. Burned himself to death below my office...his wife issued a very moving statement—'human beings must stop killing other human beings'—and that's a belief that I shared, I shared it then, I believe it even more strongly today."

Americans who knew Morrison remembered him as devoutly and sincerely sacrificing himself for the Vietnam cause. While he was not a folk hero in the United States, when he died, Vietnamese poet Tố Hữu wrote a poem titled "Emily, My Child," as if Morrison was speaking *to* his daughter

Emily and telling her the reasons for his sacrifice. North Vietnam later named a Hanoi street after Morrison and issued a postage stamp in his honor. Years later, during a visit to the United States, Vietnam's President Nguyễn Minh Triết went to the Potomac near the place where Morrison immolated himself and read the poem by Tố Hữu to commemorate the act of Morrison sacrificing himself.

Vietnam had a different culture than our own. They truly enjoyed listening to bamboo music on loud speakers throughout the city. Broadcasting air raid alerts was the reason for the public sound system and when the flute music stopped and the alarms went off, our 1967 delegation was hustled into the nearest bomb shelter. During these intensive bombing raids, I couldn't see anything in the shelter but I could feel the bombs exploding in the city. The ground would shake under my feet in our shelter. When we left Hanoi to visit a rural village, our hosts became more nervous about our safety. On one occasion, our jeep caravan was flagged to an abrupt stop by local residents shouting the words "danger, danger" that even I could understand. I was pulled out of my jeep and carried by one of my Vietnamese hosts to the nearest "bomb shelter," which was a ditch on the side of the road. I was put in the ditch and covered with the body of my Vietnamese guide. Then in what seemed like seconds a U.S. fighter jet buzzed our position at very low altitude trying to stay under the radar on its way to its bombing target.

Hanoi today has certainly changed. It is bustling now with people and commerce. There must be ten million motorbikes. Crossing a street is a decision to make a life commitment to a great dance of trust in the Vietnamese motorist. With the end of the war, the countryside has been booming and developing too. Like every major city in the world, the growth and consumption in Hanoi and Ho Chi Minh City are not sustainable and the endless accumulation of cement is unhealthy, but one thing has not changed at all: The people of Vietnam are still stunning and beautiful. Their love for family and country has continued into a new generation. When I went back to Vietnam, everywhere I looked, people seemed bright-eyed and shining like few other places I know. Vietnam's greatest resource without a doubt continues to be its amazing people.

What is not seen by tourists today visiting this new century of Vietnam are the third and fourth generation Vietnamese victims suffering from chemical Agent Orange toxins or unexploded U.S. bombs that still go off. In 1967, when I first visited, the United States defoliated 1.7 million acres in South Vietnam in the pursuit of a U.S. policy to clear the jungles. It was a war crime that left devastating birth defects and other unthinkable health effects that continue today. Four decades after signing the Paris Peace

Accords, clean-up of the U.S. contamination had been limited to three U.S. military bases where the chemicals were physically stored. The toxic U.S. poison is still in ponds and lakes where fish and animals swim. As the people drink the water or consume the fish, new birth defects result in the present time from the chemical Agent Orange sprayed decades ago. It was the U.S. military policy to clear trees, shrubs, jungles, and food crops in Vietnam. The toxic chemical employed for that job was a mixture of two deadly herbicides, 2,4-D and 2,4,5-T. While Agent Orange does degrade over time, its human and environmental effects persist. Vietnam's pre-war lush forests and jungles took hundreds of years to achieve their balanced mixture of flora and fauna, and natural regeneration may take centuries to re-create these extraordinary landscapes again. In some areas, land erosion and landslides have significantly decreased the nutrient levels of the soil with invasive grasses taking over.

Dioxin is a pollutant resulting from the accelerated production of one of the two Agent Orange components (2,4,5-T.) This dioxin is toxic over a far longer period and does not degrade easily. It attaches itself to soil particles, which are carried by water into ponds and lakes. People today, especially in the southern part of Vietnam, eat dioxin-contaminated fish or fowl and get sick. Genetic deformities are occurring in third-generation Vietnamese now. A vast remediation of Vietnam's contaminated soils and water is urgently needed on a scale far greater than the three U.S. designated "hot spots" where the U.S. is cleaning up some of its worst contamination.

What I came to realize on my 2013 return to Vietnam was that the 1967 dioxins previously used in Vietnam had changed people's internal cellular and chemical balance, creating severe health challenges or death today.

With the signing of the Paris Peace Accords on January 27, 1973, the four parties to this conflict agreed to the unconditional withdrawal of U.S. troops from Vietnam. They also agreed to "support the healing of the wounds of war." Despite that agreement, the war continued until April 1975. Normalization of U.S.-Vietnam relations took even longer through many difficult years and only with the considerable leadership of President Bill Clinton. I had to go back to Vietnam to fully realize myself that "healing the wounds of war" would need far more than a modest U.S. government clean-up of three toxic chemical hot spots. Virtually no U.S. public awareness even exists that 40 years after the Paris Peace Accord, new wounds of war continue to be inflicted today. Our own American Vietnam veterans continue to suffer under the radar as well.

Third-generation Vietnamese are born with deformities because their grandparents were exposed to the chemical Agent Orange or because they live in a village where a buried unexploded ordnance is unearthed during an ordinary play day. When a buried bomb explodes, a lifetime of new suffering is created. For these victims, the war in Vietnam continues. Normalization of relations between the United States and Vietnam has certainly taken giant strides forward in recent years, but the U.S. desire to avoid its legal liability for unexploded ordnance or the genetic effects of chemical Agent Orange has kept the U.S. government immobilized regarding its 1973 pledge to heal the wounds of war.

It is not just the general public who is unaware of this reality. The historic U.S. antiwar movement has also failed to keep up with this development. In addition, a younger American generation has little knowledge of what the U.S. even did in Vietnam. That's why I want to briefly explain again what actually happened.

American troops stationed in Vietnam escalated from 3,500 Marines—initially deployed for "defense"—to 450,000 servicemen and women. When I first visited Vietnam in 1967, the U.S. was raining down 2,000 bombing sorties weekly on North and South Vietnam. The total ordnance dropped that year was 1.5 million tons of explosives—a nearly inconceivable carnage that grew to nearly 8 million tons by the war's end, making an area the size of New Mexico the most bombed nation on Earth.

After the Vietnamese decisively defeated the French at Dien Bein Phu, an international conference split French Indochina into three countries—Vietnam, Laos, and Cambodia. Vietnam was provisionally partitioned along the 17th parallel pending a countrywide election in 1956 to unify the country and democratically elect a new national leadership. With direction from the U.S. State Department, the American-backed South Vietnamese President Ngo Dinh Diem rejected the elections, knowing his country's overwhelming public support for the popular Vietnamese resistance leader, Ho Chi Minh.

In other words, the United States completely lost its way in Vietnam. Fortunately, tens of millions of Americans did not. We figured it out. In one of America's greatest historical moments, millions of people, many in their twenties, broke free of the entrenched mindset that always insisted that protesting an unjust American war was somehow unpatriotic. We challenged the traditional American view of patriotism. When our antiwar movement pushed and demanded that the United States become a better nation, it wasn't treasonous at all. A massive citizen effort opposing an ill-conceived war in Vietnam emerged in America like a breath of fresh air. I felt proud to oppose a ruinous war in which our own country supported one of the most brutal dictators in history and rejected the legally required elections to unify this ancient country. Looking back, everyone can see today that it was our own U.S. policies that were the only real threat to the American homeland. Eventually, the vast majority of American public opinion came to agree with us—even Robert McNamara, the U.S. secretary of defense, joined in after the War's conclusion to denounce the Vietnam War policies he had once managed.

Nevertheless, throughout this entire antiwar history, the U.S. government mostly struggled to figure it out. Our officials could not comprehend how a peasant country such as Vietnam could endure thousands of planeloads of bombs and chemicals along with our vast U.S. troop build-up. The odds of a Vietnamese victory was considered "impossible" by the U.S. military, but the fact remained that Vietnam was able to successfully mobilize the most advanced guerrilla force in modern history. No media network fully explained to the American public why millions of ordinary Vietnamese were willing to pay any price to defend their freedom and independence. While the U.S. government publicly insisted the "Vietnamese communists" were an "enemy" that had to be "contained" to secure the "free world," I belonged to an amazing generation that came to appreciate the people of Vietnam as inspiring and not that different than our own rag-tag patriots that defeated the British at the beginning of our country.

When the Vietnam War ended on April 30, 1975, the last U.S. helicopter was barely able to lift off in time. For every person who escaped the final Vietnamese offensive that overran Saigon, there were a thousand more that could not. The world's superpower had been militarily humiliated. It was curious to me why our U.S. commanders were unable to understand the reasons why. Visiting Vietnam during the war and coming back again in 2013, the reasons could be plainly seen.

I made a second visit to Vietnam in 1969 to bring American prisoners of war back to their families. I knew no Westerner had traveled to the area between the 19th and the 17th parallel since the U.S. air war concentrated on this tiny region. Facing challenging logistics to make a trip into this area, I wanted to go but did not think it could happen. I was, of course, delighted when our hosts said yes.

And so seven Americans traveled from Hanoi to the Panhandle. I was especially curious to see the "gateway to the south"—the city of Vinh—that had once been an important center of revolutionary activity in earlier centuries. Ho Chi Minh's birthplace was near Vinh. During the French occupation of Vietnam, the city was developed into an industrial center. During the U.S. invasion of Vietnam, Vinh was returned to the "stone age," to hear U.S. pilots tell it. I had a picture of Hamburg or Dresden, where urban areas were carpet-bombed during World War II. In those horrific devastations, a bombed out structure might have one wall standing. A person could speculate that a bombed out building had once been a house or factory. In Vinh, however, the landscape more closely resembled the moon. There was crater upon crater with no evidence that any building ever previously existed. Vinh looked like an atom bomb explosion without the radiation.

What I never anticipated were the people of the Panhandle. They looked like a community that had missed the largest aerial assault in human history. A parade of smiling, energetic people had dug deep into the ground to set up living quarters inside the Earth. During my visit to the Panhandle, I squeezed through one of the narrow passageways to see for myself one of the underground corridors that led to a large open space under the ground. Our delegation sat in an underground theatre watching a play with local actors singing and dancing about a free and independent Vietnam. In "basement" theaters like this, Vietnam's culture seemed alive and buoyant despite the unimaginable bombardment from the sky.

Vietnam knew from the start the horror that was coming from the United States. By 1965, the country had made the decision to survive the complete destruction of their nation. With the passage of decades and 20 years of "normalization," there has been a steady public recognition in our country that Vietnam is not an American enemy after all. Perhaps now that we have gotten over our "mistakes" in Vietnam, we can shed our historic blinders and finally figure it out. We could let ourselves see what really happened during the war in Vietnam and why the Vietnamese deserve our respect and admiration.

Vietnam was a people's war where every citizen became a soldier and every village, street, and plant were made into a battlefront fortress. In North Vietnam, cities were moved to the countryside. By the time I visited in 1967, Hanoi's population had been reduced by half. The entire economy was decentralized. Large factories were relocated in caves or small rural villages. In the Panhandle region, people built tunnels and then moved into their underground complexes. While food shortages were widespread, people shared and supported each other. When a bridge was destroyed, it was quickly replaced by dirt fords or ferries that were durable, easily repaired, and nearly impossible to stop with bombs.

Inside the Panhandle in 1969, I saw for myself what I still see today in Vietnam. The nation's greatest resource is not its military equipment, but the spirit and enduring strength of its people and culture. Even earlier, as the U.S. war started to escalate, nearly 500,000 Vietnamese organized in the North just to repair the coming bomb damage. Supply trains and truck convoys were formed into small units that traveled only at night. There were trucks and equipment to carry and haul supplies but the largest logistical capacity consisted of carts, wheelbarrows, and two baskets on a pole carried on a woman's shoulder.

There was no possibility that a national political party in the United States was going to go down in history for losing a war. Consequently, neither the Democratic nor the Republican Party was able to withdraw from an undeveloped nation half the size of Texas because they were wrong. "Losing a war" did not compute in the Oval Office of the White House. Both Lyndon Johnson and Richard Nixon constantly reminded their advisors that the United States was the military leader of the "free world" and its foreign policy in Asia had to "contain communist China." Losing a war was not going to happen on their watch. The Vietnam War was the only way to prevent every Southeast Asian country from falling like dominos into Communist hands. The fact that this bedrock assumption was proved altogether inaccurate by subsequent events—that no dominos went falling after the U.S. military left Vietnam and a divided Vietnam was successfully reunited to become an American trading ally—did not mean the architects of America's war strategy could grasp what actually happened.

History will remember the Vietnam War as one of America's saddest, darkest chapters. This year is the 50th anniversary of the Vietnam War. The Department of Defense is organizing 10,000 events across the United States as part of the anniversary. I personally believe the antiwar movement should insert itself into these events. It is time for our country to remember that the American public came to its senses about the Vietnam War. We should remember at this anniversary that out of a small 1965 antiwar march of 25,000 young people in Washington, D.C., organized by Students for a Democratic Society, the U.S. antiwar movement grew to a thunderous chorus to withdraw U.S. troops from Vietnam. Following demonstrations at the Chicago Democratic National Convention where a police riot assaulted demonstrators to the horror of the whole world, public opinion polls shifted and our demand to end the war was supported by a majority of the American people. Even many of the officials who managed the war eventually joined in. Civil rights, women's rights, and human rights also took flight during this unique historical moment, creating one of our great American legacies. For the 50th anniversary, let us never forget the history of what actually happened.

The participation of Vietnam veterans against the Vietnam War became the great turning of U.S. patriotism that had always previously proclaimed, "my country, right or wrong." With thousands of GIs choosing to leave that point of view to become new patriots for America, many of them gathered in front of the U.S. Capitol Building in 1971 to return their medals and awards won for valor in Vietnam back to the government. No previous American generation ever witnessed such a phenomenon. The bedrock of American patriotism was challenged from every quarter of society, including the GIs themselves. Let's not forget that, either.

I once walked onto the base at Fort Bragg with Jane Fonda. It was just the two of us with no security. Thousands of GIs surrounded us as word spread like wildfire that she was there. It was a moment when I experienced her courage. What I saw in her was impressive and beyond words even today. She stood before the crowd and spoke her convictions that nearly every American would agree that the war was brutal and a mistake for our country. While the audience included many antiwar GI friends, not every soldier was ready to embrace her new patriotism that day. Her message of patriotism at Fort Bragg that day was to support GIs by bringing them home, but it made for a tense moment. When Jane Fonda traveled to Hanoi, a picture was taken of her with Vietnamese women defending their homeland. That photo went around the world, and the American patriots who still proclaim "my country, right or wrong" have mocked and ridiculed her for years because she did not support our GIs; however, I remember her supporting our GIs with her call to bring them home. Perhaps one day, the people who "hate" Jane Fonda for traveling to North Vietnam during a time when U.S. war crimes in Southeast Asia went utterly and completely out of control will consider taking a page from our own revolution. During that time, there were many Americans like Jane Fonda who had the wisdom to leave the British tradition of "my country, right or wrong" to support the dream of a better world. Because she believes in the ideals of this country, I understand why she might wish that picture had never happened and prefer somehow to take it back if she could. Should you ever have the opportunity to speak with her, may I encourage you to remember that Jane Fonda pioneered, along with millions of Americans, a new patriotism that must never fade away. Use your good fortune of being with her to thank her yourself for what she did to support and advance the dream of a wiser United States.

Changing the bedrock of a nation's patriotism takes decades or centuries. During the time when the United States lost its way in Vietnam, Gold Star Mothers and veterans against the Vietnam War became the shining light of our movement with its new American patriotism. Vietnam veterans marched to Arlington National Cemetery in support of the Gold Star Mothers who had lost their sons in Vietnam. When the mothers were refused entry to lay their wreaths in the national cemetery, the veterans refused to back down until those antiwar mothers were eventually let in to the national monument.

In 1932, World War I veterans camped out at the nation's Capitol demanding to be paid their promised service bonuses. President Hoover sent in troops and used tear gas, bullets, bayonets, and torches to destroy the veterans' camp and drive them out of the city. In 1971, Vietnam Veterans against the War came to Washington to return their medals for bravery back to the government. In doing so, they touched the heart of America. Recognizing the public mood had changed, Nixon announced, "I see no reason to go in and arrest the veterans and put them into jail at this time."

Standing on the steps of the nation's Capitol, American veterans from every service stated their names, units, and citations before throwing their awards and mementos back to Congress. One by one for three hours, they tossed their decorations earned with bravery back to the government. One veteran said, "I hope someday I can return to Vietnam and help rebuild the country we tore apart." Another announced, "here are my merit badges for murder." Veteran Paul Winter took the microphone to pray for forgiveness as he threw back his Silver Star, Bronze Star, and Distinguished Service Cross before limping away.

Fifty years after the Vietnam War, that spirit is urgently needed again. The U.S. Department of Defense with its 10,000 ceremonies that will remember the 50th anniversary of the Vietnam War has no plans to remember what actually happened. A majority of the American public opposed this war, including many GIs. That's what happened. The overwhelming majority of the Vietnamese nation mobilized every man and woman to drive the United States out of its country. That also happened. Will the Defense Department during the 50th anniversary be pointing out that the wounds of war continue today? That is what is happening now. Since we have shown in the past that we can rise to the occasion and shift an "inevitable" outcome in a new direction, we could reconnect and do what is needed ourselves. Because there are new technologies that could dramatically assist victims of chemical Agent Orange with safe, non-toxic therapies and breakthrough water and soil clean-up discoveries that could be made available to Vietnam today, the tens of millions of Americans who once opposed the Vietnam War are needed again to come back and support Vietnam once more with their donations, volunteer services, health therapies, and soil and water clean-up technologies. If the government won't heal the wounds of war, why not do it ourselves? A citizen-to-citizen America–Vietnam Initiative would be welcomed in Vietnam. We could develop our own victim income-generation programs. We could build victim home construction projects ourselves that support rehabilitation and vocational education schools for disabled children as well. We could bring our own breakthrough energy medicines to Vietnamese and American victims for our own 50th anniversary. We have among us thousands of health professionals and humanitarian activists who could significantly support the war-affected communities of Laos and Cambodia as well as Vietnam. The Vietnamese would love our volunteers to plant trees and help them build victim rehabilitation centers or provide large-scale financial support for the professional organizations working tirelessly in Vietnam to remove unexploded ordnance.

For our 50th anniversary, a new generation could take bold steps to heal the wounds of war ourselves. In fact, we may be the only ones who can.

VIET NAM TIME TRAVEL, 1970–2013

JUDY GUMBO

Editors' Note: Portions of this chapter are adapted from Yippie Girl, a memoir in progress. You can find a slideshow of the Viet Nam trip on the website www.yippiegirl.com.

> *Here's to the land that you tore out the heart of*
> *Richard Nixon, find yourself another country to be part of....*
>
> —"Here's to the State of Richard Nixon," Phil Ochs

I am one among millions of people around the globe who protested the war in Viet Nam. I am also one of perhaps 200 people from the United States who visited Viet Nam while the war still raged. I was born Judy Clavir in Toronto, Canada, on June 25, 1943, and raised a "red diaper baby," or child of Communist Party parents. I am perhaps best known as an original member of the Yippies, or Youth International Party, a late 1960s political and countercultural group dedicated to performance activism. In late 1967, I emigrated from Canada to Berkeley, where I met Stew Albert, who became my lover and partner of 40 years. Luckily for me, Stew also happened to be a close friend of both Yippie founder Jerry Rubin and Black Panther Party leader Eldridge Cleaver, who gave me the name Gumbo since, in his mind, Gumbo went with Stew. I, along with Stew, Nancy Kurshan, Jerry Rubin, Abbie and Anita Hoffman, Paul Krassner, and folksinger Phil Ochs were

Nancy Kurshan, Genie Plamondon, and Judy Gumbo protest
outside the U.S. embassy in Moscow, 1970.
Photo courtesy of Judy Gumbo.

among the 10,000 people tear-gassed in Chicago in August 1968 when the Yippies ran a pig named Pigasus for president to protest the war.

By the end of 1968, public opposition to the war had become a fact of American life. More than 14,500 young American soldiers had been killed. More than 485,000 U.S. military personnel had served in combat. Even though President Lyndon Baines Johnson had by then been replaced by President Richard Nixon, a claim by Johnson's top general Curtis LeMay that the United States would bomb Viet Nam back into the Stone Age still resonated. Pro-war America labeled Vietnamese people as gooks; demonizing combatant and civilian as a slant-eyed, black-pyjama'd enemy who fought relentlessly by day and insinuated themselves at night into tunnels, encampments, and nightmares of foot soldiers and presidents alike. At the same time, hundreds of thousands of antiwar activists like me looked on North Vietnamese freedom fighters and their compatriots, the NLF (the National Liberation Front of South Vietnam, or Viet Cong, as the media liked to called them) as Davids battling the high-tech killing machine of the American Goliath. By the time I visited what was called North Viet Nam in 1970, U.S. troops had been waging war in that country for six years.

I remember myself from those days: curly brown hair to my shoulders; a red, blue and gold NLF flag painted on one cheek; orange woman's symbol on the other; green marijuana leaf on my chin, speaking into a microphone in my best take-no-prisoners' voice: "Richard Nixon and his arrogant pig generals are traitors to America. They betray the American people by invading and bombing Vietnam. Vietnam has a 1,000-year history of defeating foreign aggressors. The Vietnamese will win. All the American war machine does is condemn young people like us—and millions of Vietnamese—to death. I belong to a New Nation. We believe in peace, justice, sex, drugs, and rock and roll. Youth will make the revolution! Yippie!"

The American War in Viet Nam would come to an end in 1975, making it, for its day, the longest war in U.S. history. By then, an estimated two million Vietnamese civilians had died, plus another one million combatants—10 percent of their entire population. Fifty-eight thousand Americans, primarily young men, many drafted against their will, also perished—.00027 percent of the population of the United States in 1975. As our guide to Viet Nam's Cu Chi tunnels told us in 2013, "We didn't win the war. You can't say anyone won the war. We lost three million people."

I arrived in Hanoi in May 1970, along with Nancy Kurshan and Genie Plamondon of the White Panther Party. We were a Yippie women's delegation. Our goal was to bring back to our respective cohorts what we discovered about the consequences of war. Three weeks before our departure, on April 30, 1970, the world had learned that U.S. and South Vietnamese Army troops invaded Cambodia, a neutral nation and Vietnam's next-door neighbor. It did not cross my mind to cancel our trip. The antiwar chant "Ho, Ho, Ho Chi Minh, the NLF is gonna win" was not, to my way of thinking, propagandistic wish fulfillment—Vietnamese victory was, I felt, inevitable.

On our way home from Viet Nam in 1970, Genie, Nancy, and I, dressed NLF-style in black "pyjamas" and conical straw hats, held an antiwar demonstration outside the U.S. embassy in Moscow. I also carried with me 143 letters from American pilots who had been shot down and captured. This unorthodox route was, at the time, the only reliable way for uncensored mail from servicemen detained in Viet Nam to reach their families. It would take three more years of intense carpet bombing of North Viet Nam, Cambodia, and Laos, plus continued Vietnamese resistance combined with increasingly large and militant demonstrations in the United States, for President Nixon's secretary of state Henry Kissinger and Special Advisor Le Duc Tho to sign the Paris Peace Accords. They did so on January 27, 2003. Two years later, on April 30, 1975, Saigon became a liberated Ho Chi Minh City.

In 2013, I returned to Viet Nam as part of a delegation of nine former antiwar activists, plus spouses, partners, and supporters, invited to help celebrate the 40th anniversary of the Paris Peace Accords. I had been ridiculously nervous before the trip. I put it down to fear of losing my illusions.

I could not help but ask a selfish question: Would this country for which I once held the most romantic of ideals still maintain their moral hegemony in a brave new world of Starbucks and a Ho Chi Minh City stock exchange?

1970: The Munitions Factory

A dilapidated dark green school bus with the number 4709 stenciled on its windshield waited for Nancy, Genie, and me on Ngo Quyen Street outside the Reunification Hotel, the former colonial French Hotel Metropole. As did Do Xuan Oanh, the man who had invited the three of us to visit Viet Nam. Oanh, pronounced "Wine" with a nasal intonation and "nnnng" at the end, was more than just the go-to person for visiting anti–Viet Nam War activists. Oanh was a composer, a poet in the romantic Vietnamese/French style, a watercolor artist, and a translator of Mark Twain's *Huck Finn* into Vietnamese. Everyone from the inner core of the U.S. peace movement knew him. The literary icon Susan Sontag put it this way: Oanh had a "personal authority, (he) walks and sits with that charming 'American' slouch, and sometimes seems moody or distracted."[1] I would come to recognize that moodiness. If I had to guess, I'd say Oanh's brooding stemmed from the fact that his wife, the granddaughter of the chief of staff of the French government in Indochina, had been arrested in the early 1950s and held at the Maison Central, a concrete building in downtown Hanoi that would become known as the infamous Hanoi Hilton. Oanh told me in 1970 that his wife suffered chronic headaches and would pass out every time she saw a snake. It would take me to 2013 to grasp the implication of Oanh's story when I saw on the wall of the War Remnants Museum in Ho Chi Minh City a depiction of a woman being held down by two burly, bare-chested men who raped her with a snake.

In 1970, our bus drove Nancy, Genie, me, Oanh, and three Vietnamese guides, two men and a woman, three hours south until we crossed the Ham Rong Bridge in Thanh Hoa province. To me, the bridge did not resemble a bridge at all, instead it looked as if a deranged spider had spun a web out of steel girders, gouged and pitted. A hole in the bus's rusted floor allowed a view of brown muddy river water rushing by mere yards under my feet. Oanh told us the North Vietnamese army moved war materiel by train, ox-cart, bicycle, and foot across this bridge to the South. American planes had made at least 400 sorties, laying down a carpet of bombs. "Every day this bridge is demolished." I recall Oanh saying. "Every night it is rebuilt. The courage of the peasants is a local legend."

I could not fathom living such a life. Before I could find words to respond, I saw a mountain loom on my right. At its base, railway cars lay in a graveyard of rusting brown. One-half of the mountain's top had been sheared away; as if some industrial-sized backhoe had strip-mined giant bites from it. I made out the words "QUYET THANG" carved into the mountaintop in letters of white chalk. I asked Oanh what the words meant. Oanh replied.

"Determined to win. So American pilots will see this as they fly over."

Thoroughly cowed, I did not think to question why the Vietnamese believed American pilots could translate this slogan. Then I realized mine was an Americo-centric point of view. The slogan was much more to inspire resistance among peasants undergoing bombing than a deterrent to pilots. By the time the bus stopped, I was feeling no small measure of guilt and remorse, as if I was in some way responsible for the destruction I had witnessed.

A woman in a stained lightweight patterned shirt, visibly pregnant, led us through a narrow passage into a dark low-ceiling cave hollowed into the mountain's core. Bare bulbs attached to wires flickered orange; tons of black mountain earth above us tamed Vietnam's humidity and heat. Seven or eight women and men bent over lathes that resembled oversized sewing machines. Oanh said that despite daily bombings, this munitions factory had remained in continuous production. I shivered, not from fear or from my cooling skin but because the air around me felt infused with such resolve I could not help but sop it up like a sponge. Suddenly the machines stopped. The cave fell silent. I heard water dripping with a faint *ping ping*. The pregnant woman began to chant, bird-like and trilling. Oanh translated line by line:

> If you love me come back to this beautiful province with me
> I stand on guard at this bridge, for seven years strong here
> Through cold and rain
> I stand looking at the yellow star flying in the flashing light
> And each call that I hear from the South tears into my heart.

Behavior change is hard, yet events, as Oanh once said, can remold your spirit. That song combined inside me with what Vietnam's president Ho Chi Minh had called the spirit of resistance. I told myself if Oanh and his compatriots could make a life amid such devastation, I could re-make myself. I would act more like my heroes: Madame Binh, Che Guevara, the Trung sisters, and Emma Goldman. I would become less self-centered. I would sacrifice my happiness for the good of others. I'd learn empathy, compassion, determination, and resistance. The promises I made to myself in that factory cave in 1970 feel pretentious to me now but at the time they felt genuine. I would change my understanding of myself, and thus my life.

2013: The Garco 10 Factory

It's Thursday, January 24, 2013, our second day in Hanoi. Having over-dressed the day before, I had underdressed this day. I'm freezing. I ask our guide Minh, a smiley rotund man who I've just met, if our group could stop at the hotel so I can grab an extra layer, but there's no time. Minh offers me his jacket with that same warmness of heart and desire to help that I remember as characteristic of the Vietnamese I met 40 years previously. I decline. It would be too great a sacrifice for Minh and too oversized (and grungy) a garment for me. I remind myself that since Vietnamese guerillas fought under conditions incomparably worse than mine, the least I can do is get through a chilly day.

Our bus has no holes in its floor; rather, it is equipped with upholstered dark blue seats, wide windows and an up-to-date microphone and speaker system. The traffic has also updated itself; the waves of bicycles that I encountered in 1970, carrying women in black trousers, white blouses, and conical straw hats, and men in white short-sleeved shirts, have morphed into honking, seemingly unstoppable motor scooters.

During the war, this factory had produced uniforms for the North Vietnamese Army. Today's Garco 10 Corporation manufactures shirts, tailored suits, trousers, and jackets for men, women, and children. For companies such as Pierre Cardin, J.C. Penney, Perry Ellis, Liz Claiborne, Tommy Hilfiger, DKNY, and Target. Inside a low-slung building, women and men in sanitary white uniforms, cloth masks over their mouths, sit under florescent lights behind rows of high-tech white sewing machines. Bolts of cloth in dark violet and brilliant blue dominate the room like flowers in a field. Garco 10's 11,000 workers can make wages of $200 a month; well above those made by most factory workers in modern Viet Nam.

Our delegation climbs three flights of stairs past a sign that promotes recycling.

Than Duc Viet, the director, has been delayed. We wait at a conference table in a large, windowed room furnished with a bust of Ho Chi Minh and chairs covered in pink slipcovers with the Garco 10 logo. Its three swooshes rising to a stylized peak remind me of the mountain under which the munitions factory lay. The COO tells us that his factory is designed with ecological principles to take advantage of the daylight and stay cool, and that employees can own shares of stock in Garco 10, which their children can inherit. He promises to show us the preschool the factory provides for workers' children and workers' on-site dental care.

Director Viet arrives; her eyes twinkle under black bangs. Introductions and an official program begin. Suddenly there's a tap on my shoulder. I tiptoe to a room across a hall. It's occupied by two women and a man. And a short pile of coats. A stream of Vietnamese consonants and diphthongs runs past me but I am mute, unable to comprehend the language. The older woman looks me up and down then, with no hesitation, selects one coat from among her stack of three. It's deep Army green and made of soft polyester. The coat has black leather piping on collar and sleeves plus silver buttons with a heraldic crest. I do not question the woman's choice. The coat is warm. And Judy Gumbo–style gorgeous; a revisionist version of what I imagine was once North Vietnamese army design. What better fashion to appeal to my revolutionary sensibilities? The man, clearly an accountant, hands me a slip of paper. I hand him $35 in U.S. currency. I walk back inside the meeting, no more a former antiwar activist with silver hair, but a 69-year-old model for the latest Garco 10 design. Director Viet embraces me, laughing with pride. I notice she has pinned on her yellow jacket a white and black button, the universal symbol for peace.

Director Viet tells us that she's learning from her American partners how to take advantage of Viet Nam's position as a player in the new, competitive marketplace. Americans, she says, know how to adapt to risk and come up with quick solutions. At the same time she expresses what, to me, is an un-American point of view. Her workers "are our parents to respect and our children to take care of." In two years' time she has met each worker personally. Whether or not they feel free to take advantage of it, all workers have her phone number. Three days after our tour of Garco 10, I stand beside antiwar activist and trip organizer John McAuliff as he introduces a delighted Viet and her COO to U.S. Ambassador David Shear.

Ho Chi Minh famously said, "nothing is more precious than independence and freedom." To me, the Garco 10 factory feels like a twenty-first century Vietnamese version of Pete Seeger's "Talking Union": "shorter hours, better working conditions, vacations with pay, take your kids to the seashore." At the same time, I realize that to navigate the worldwide capitalist free market, companies such as Garco 10 must make a profit or go under. Before my 2013 trip I'd read that, in today's post-war world dominated by the triumph of free market capitalism, the Vietnamese government is promulgating what they call a "socialist-oriented market economy." The day after the factory visit, I have an opportunity to ask an official, a charming man with an ironic sense of humor who is the Deputy Director of the government's Americas Department, what the phrase actually means. He responds in what diplomats label an "open and frank" manner. I pick up that the Vietnamese want to transition to a new economy that will combine socialist values with capital markets while avoiding the systemic economic collapse of the former Soviet Union. The Minister emphasizes process. "We have to go slow," he says, "because we must make sure not to fall down."

Creating a socialist-oriented market economy in Viet Nam in 2013 may not be the outcome I anticipated in 1970, but I fought against the war so Viet Nam could gain its independence. The future is up to them.

1970: Remnants of War

All the photos I took in Viet Nam in 1970 are black and white, yet the vivid greens and earth tones of my memory are closer to my actual experience. In Thanh Hoa province, I took one photo of eight women lined up in formation, four abreast. Each wore a pith helmet and those ubiquitous black silk pants. They were a platoon of artillery gunners. They appeared as short as I was and, like me, looked in their mid-20s. One woman was barefoot; the others wore black sandals recycled from used rubber tires. Behind them, a six-foot-tall anti-aircraft gun stood erect, mounted on what looked like a tractor spattered with mud.

I can picture myself now in my pink-and-blue tie-dye tank top, hair braided to ward off the heat, climbing into the metal swivel seat of that Russian anti-aircraft gun and staring out through its elongated sights into a blue Vietnamese sky. Jane Fonda had her picture taken in this same model gun when she visited North Vietnam two years after I did, an act Jane says she now regrets. Jane's enemies used the photo to brand her a traitor. Her friends tell me that photo made the task of winning mainstream Americans to the antiwar cause more difficult. I have never regretted my choice to sit in such a weapon, but I do remember feeling like a fraud. My life was one of privilege. How could I compare myself to women for whom making it through one day meant aiming a gun mounted on a tractor at airplanes out of whose bellies fell canisters filled with shrapnel, white phosphorous, or napalm jelly engineered to stick to clothes and skin? Chi, our female guide, introduced Nancy, Genie, and me to the brigade of women soldiers saying, "These are American friends, come to observe what we do to liberate our country."

"You are an inspiration to me." I replied. Chi translated.

"No, no," a barefoot soldier said. "You, dear friends, inspire us. You help us end war in your country."

The barefoot soldier handed me a grey-green metal ball as if it were detritus of little value. It was round and hollow; two and a quarter inches wide, three-quarters of an inch deep with a jagged hole in its side as if a single tear had burned acid-like through its metal casing. It looked like a baby pomegranate cut in half; except instead of seeds its skin contained ball bearings; testament to the lethal promise of a weapon designed to shred the flesh of any human being or animal unfortunate enough to be in range. In a mathematical progression of expanding death, each of these bombs, known as pellet bombs or "pineapples," contained 250 steel pellets. From 1964 to 1971 the U.S. military ordered at least 37 million such pineapples. Pineapples like mine would be housed inside "mother" bombs dropped by B-52 Stratofortress bombers. A single B-52 could drop 1,000 pineapples over a 400-square-yard area. Between 1965 and 1973, the U.S. Strategic Air Command launched at least 126,600 sorties of B-52 bombers.

In addition to the POW letters I brought with me when I left Viet Nam in 1970, I also brought my bomblet. I use it to this day to illustrate the in-humanity of war.

2013: Remnants of War

I did not understand before my 2013 visit the unprecedented level to which the war had polluted Viet Nam's countryside with toxic waste. A sign at the Mine Action Center in Quang Tri Province reads: "Welcome to Quang Tri, American Peace Activists on 40th Anniversary of Paris Agreement." It's there I encounter displays of unexploded pellet bombs. Not just a single one like mine, but hundreds. The tools available for clean-up are handheld hoes and metal detectors. Supplemented by bright red signs warning *Danger!* with a graphic of a skull mounted on two crossed bones. Quang Tri's capital district was carpeted by 3,000 bombs per square kilometer. Pellet bombs remain buried in the soil out of which they rise, unbidden and undead, to maim and kill children who mistake the orbs for playthings.

At Quang Tri's Cemetery of Fallen Combatants I wander past tomb-stones, steles, red pagodas, engraved with names or lists of names; row on row of white stone each bearing a gold star emblazoned on a red circle. The words of a World War I Canadian poem I had memorized in grade school intrudes: *We are the Dead. Short days ago we lived, felt dawn, saw sunset glow, loved and were loved but now we lie in Flander's fields.*[2] On the bus I notice we pass the occasional one-room three-sided box, a painted doll-house perched on a concrete pole in squares of green rice paddy. These turn out to be traditional Vietnamese grave markers, scattered like multicolored psychedelic mushrooms in the fields. I'm a widow now. I've been best friends with inconsolable grief; still I am surprised by the intensity of remembered sorrow and pain that rises in me from the uncountable numbers of graves I see in Quang Tri province.

We arrive at the former U.S. airbase at Da Nang. Here is where American GIs offloaded barrels of the toxic herbicide Agent Orange. We're told the Da Nang airbase is the most contaminated area in the world. Today a creek flows between green grasses, next to what look, from a distance, like abandoned, brown apartments. At first the creek looks innocent enough, but then I start to feel my mouth burn. *Could this be real?* I ask myself, or merely psychological, an empathetic reaction? A guide gives us a simple formula: dioxin is a byproduct of Agent Orange. Dioxin adheres to soil. Contaminated soil in ponds and streams gets incorporated into ducks and grass. The consequences to human health are not so simple: lung cancer, diabetes, lymphoma, leukemia, kidney disease, and mental disorders. I am shown a photo of a recent visit by a delegation of Americans and Vietnamese. They hold a banner that reads, "Even today, U.S. Veterans and Vietnamese People are Dying from Agent Orange."

Da Nang is just one "hot spot," and I'm told of others: Bien Hua and Phu Cat. The United States Agency for International Development (USAID) has committed funds to clean up just this one. The plan: 100,000 cubic meters of earth at the former U. S. airbase will be dug down 10 feet, then put inside a mountain of concrete boxes that look like a stack of gigantic evil Legos. The contaminated earth will be heated to 300 then 700 degrees. Such thermal heating is supposed to change the chemical nature of Agent Orange to render it nontoxic and usable for building roads. Walt, a stocky former Marine now a clean-up USAID technician with a beard, orange hard hat and wire-rimmed glasses, warns me that I would not want to grow anything in such soil. Or breathe its fumes. Even after de-contamination. I look Walt in the eye, confess to being a former antiwar activist and ask what he thinks now about the war. "I'm a patriot. I used to despise you guys," he tells me. "But what happened here is wrong."

Our final stop in Da Nang is Friendship Village, a complex of white stucco classrooms. Warm sun shines through high windows, a blue banner hangs across the room's front. Emblazoned on it in capital letters are these words:

WELCOME
AMERICAN FRIENDS/PEACE ACTIVISTS
TO DA NANG CENTER SUPPORTING FOR AGENT ORANGE
VICTIMS AND UNFORTUNATED CHILDREN.
Da Nang 31/01/2013

This trip has been fast paced, but now time slows. I hate the word *victim*, but in this case it feels apt. The center director, a man half my size, his legs bent and body contorted, tells our group that 1,400 intellectually disabled children live in the Da Nang area. I sit among them; girls and boys, faces and backs of heads flat, eyes slanted in that recognizable way, some with feet deformed and four toes, and one little girl, her body perfectly formed but at best only three feet tall. This girl appears ageless, with an expression under her straight brown hair and pixie face of such unbearable sadness it breaks my heart. The other children laugh and clap, but she will not join in or smile, as if she understands she has been cheated of a normal life by toxic chemicals leeched into and poisoning the soil of her community two generations before her birth. I believe, although I have no evidence of this, that this young girl knows whatever chance at normality her soul might have possessed had it been born into another body, has been cruelly taken from her by military decisions made in the United States and implemented at the Da Nang Air Base 40 years ago. I am unable to join in the raucous Gangnam-style imitation dance that the other children and my compatriots on the trip enjoy. The girl disappears, as if unable to tolerate the noise and celebration with its fun-loving intensity that disabled children can muster. I am responsible for the tragedy of this life, I tell myself as I leave. Yet I feel powerless to help.

1970: Celebration

I recall a story Oanh told our final night in Hanoi. It was June 6, 1970. Like his male colleagues, Oanh had dressed in grey pants, a white shirt and combed his black hair back 1950s style; Chi and the women from the Committee for Solidarity with the American People wore *ao dai*'s of faded reds and blues carefully preserved for special occasions. I knew the Vietnamese population suffered war-related food shortages, yet this banquet in our honor felt sumptuous; a traditional gesture of farewell and gratitude. Spring rolls fried a delicate brown, a green salad piled with bright red prawns, steaming bowls of Pho served concurrently with fish braised in brown sauce plus a beige vegetable unfamiliar to me, cut in fantastical shapes, gave off an alien scent. After a dessert of ripe yellow pineapple came slices of fruit with white flesh specked with tiny black seeds. The fruit was unfamiliar to me, as if an ironic Mother Nature had created a cluster bomb of peace and friendship just for us.

I'd learned by then that Oanh's way was to teach through aphorism. His story on our last night was personal, unusual for him. It came from his own childhood, something his father had said to him when Oanh was a child, "You must not wait until the score is achieved to know who is the real hero." Oanh said he did not have to wait until revolution would be achieved in America to know that Nancy, Genie, and I represented the future. He ended with this advice: "Be good to friends who are good to you; also be good to friends who are bad to you, for only friends will go with you on the long road to revolution."

In 1970, I could not have asked for a more inspirational farewell.

2013: Celebration

It's Friday, January 21, 2013, the 40th anniversary of the Paris Peace Agreement. With a police escort to stop traffic and get us to the celebration on time, our bus whizzes past lines of cars and motorbikes driven by women in parkas, white masks over their faces to keep out pollution. We arrive. The bus door opens. To the rhythm of a military band, we walk up a red carpet past honor guards in white uniforms standing at attention. I wonder if our presence as American antiwar activists could be more significant than I thought. What looks like 800 guests are gathered inside a vast auditorium. Ten older men, grey haired, balding, dressed in white uniforms, plus one woman in green military garb sit near me in a row of red plush seats. All display on their chests a cornucopia of medals, ribbons, and red stars. I seize the opportunity and make my way down the row, an impromptu ambassador from Woodstock Nation, shaking each of their hands as I say, in English, "Thank you." They beam with delight.

Madame Nguyen Thi Binh and diplomat Luu Van Loi are escorted up to an oversized stage. The two stand in front of red curtains on which a gold star and hammer and sickle hang, behind a gold bust of Ho Chi Minh at least three times their size. As a red diaper baby, I understand such symbols must accompany any official occasion celebrated by a communist government. Madame Binh and Luu Van Loi are given the Heroic Award of Armed Forces—the equivalent of a "lifetime achievement award." At 86, Madame Binh is now the only living signer of the Paris Peace Accords. She had been my ideal romantic hero since the late 1960s; a foreign minister of the Provisional Revolutionary Government of South Viet Nam, and a leader of the Viet Nam Women's Union. She had headed the PRG delegation at the Paris Peace Accords.

Onscreen, an arc of Vietnamese resistance unfolds as Vietnamese orchestral music swells: young Ho Chi Minh with wispy beard fighting French colonizers; bombed-out buildings and pagodas with metal remnants of U.S. B-52s; bicycles and oxcarts guided by peasants in rubber tire sandals

Judy Gumbo (with drum) at the women's antiwar march,
Republican National Convention, Miami 1972.
Photo by Jeanne Raisler, courtesy of Judy Gumbo.

transporting goods down the Ho Chi Minh trail; Madame Binh signing her name to the Paris Peace Accords; destruction caused by two more years of carpet bombing; and finally tears of those who realize that what remains of their families, once torn apart by war, will soon be reunited. At the same time, women with fans and multi-colored *ao dai*'s of brilliant reds and yellows, and men in blue silk fill the stage in front of the screen in a pageant of traditional dances, accompanied by an ever-changing chorus of singers. The music slows. A line of young people enters, students, clearly non-Vietnamese. They're dressed as hippies in jeans and multicolored shirts, and include a young man who plays an air guitar as if he is Bob Dylan. They burst into song: "Ho Ho Ho Chi Minh," written by our movement's very own Red Star Singers. It's a sublime public recognition of U.S. antiwar efforts.

Madame Binh enters the banquet hall. Her walk is steady, her hair still black and not yet grey, and her eyes shine behind her glasses. Even at age 69 my heart pounds in the presence of my hero. I approach her table, introduce myself, and hand her a black-and-white photograph I've brought with me from the United States. It's of a 1972 women's antiwar demonstration at the Republican National Convention in Miami Beach. "Women In Revolt, Sisters Unite!" our banner reads. The Judy Gumbo I remember marches in cutoff jean shorts at the center of the front line of demonstrators, pounding out a militant beat on a wooden drum I've slung over my shoulder. On my left in the photograph is a woman later identified as a police agent. On my right is Patty Oldenberg, who wears a "Mme. Binh Livelikker" t-shirt. I call it the "Livelikker" t-shirt because above a graphic of Madame Binh's head, the word "Livelikker" appears; an unfortunate outcome of a volunteer designer squishing our women's slogan "Live Like Her" into a single silkscreened word. Past meets present: I say to Madame Binh that I and my antiwar compatriots did our best to live like her. I tell her, "Thank you for what you have done." As if in recognition of a common history and shared future, she replies, "And we will continue to do it," then squeezes my hand.

When I left Viet Nam in 1970, I had fallen in love with the country and its people. Those were my exact words. When I left Viet Nam in 2013, I felt like I was saying farewell to a friend with whom I had not had enough time to share our intervening 40 years of pain and triumph. My trip in 1970 had been life-changing; my return in 2013 was life-affirming.

JOURNEY TO THE EAST

ALEX HING

In 1970, when I first visited Viet Nam, I was a 24-year-old revolutionary nationalist. Viet Nam, along with China, helped to shape my identity. As a Chinese American, I was a part of a very small nationality in the United States—barely 1 percent and often times listed as "others" along with Asians from other countries, Pacific Islanders, and American Indians. Life in San Francisco's Chinatown was similar to that of African Americans. I lived in a ghetto. We had the highest suicide and tuberculosis rates in the nation; jobs for youth were very hard to come by. There were very few public places to hang out since Chinatown had the second highest population density in the nation and my generation was the Baby Boomers. Racist tourists would trample through our community looking at us as something exotic—women as sex objects, men as boys, meek and passive. Chinatown was politically and economically controlled by the reactionary KMT (Kuomintang) from Taiwan, and America's stifling culture on its coming-of-age generation was exacerbated in Chinatown by Confucianism. The police did the bidding of the KMT and targeted youth who strayed from the stereotypical norm, mainly those of us who hung out in the pool halls of Manilatown on the edge of Chinatown. My buddies and I kept track of the Civil Rights Movement. In high school, we felt more akin to Blacks than to Whites. The war in Viet Nam looked very much like genocide waged by a racist government against a people who looked just like us.

Becoming a Revolutionary

I was opposed to war after seeing the U.S. military footage of the immediate aftermath of the nuclear attack on Hiroshima in high school. Not much later, when I was in reform school reading a textbook on world history, I wondered why the march of humanity was a never-ceasing series of war—a stupid way to organize society. In juvenile hall, I made a decision to dedicate my life to ending war. I was a pacifist for a hot minute. As an atheist, the religious pacifists, though they were doing good work, did not appeal to me. I thought they had the same agenda as the Christian missionaries in Chinatown who condemned me to hell because I did not believe in God. I was a godless outlaw. What I did believe was that humans had to create a society on Earth without war and to do that was man's work, not God's. I also could not relate to the flower power pacifists who were flaky and not just a little racist. I wanted to work with people in the real world to build a society that would end racism and war; one that would end all oppression.

I searched for answers. In college, I fell in with a group of students who wanted to discuss the war in Viet Nam and the civil rights movement in public forums. The administration of the City College of San Francisco would not allow this, so we organized a Free Speech Movement. I ran for student body president and, although we lost in a very close race, the administration met nearly all of our major demands, but not before calling in the police to stop our mass rallies. Through the process of participating in antiwar and Civil Rights support activities, I became increasingly aware of socialism as a vision of the society I wanted. Capitalism, and the resulting imperialism, was a brutal system of theft that created poverty, racism, and war, as well as other forms of oppression that enabled an elite, obscenely rich class of men to own the means of control over society through its police, courts, schools, and armies. Democracy, so-called majority rule, was a sham under capitalism where Black people were being murdered for registering to vote and the selection of leaders was a fix between two parties who both perpetuated poverty, racism, and war at the bidding of the capitalist elite. Capitalism had to be overthrown by the oppressed people of the world led by the working class. It would be replaced by socialism, a system by which the working class would ensure capitalism's destruction by building a new society based on the vast majority of humanity that produced real wealth for a living. The system would evolve into communism, a global society where the full potential of every human being would be realized to the benefit of humanity and the world. I became a revolutionary.

If there was one thing that made this an easy choice, it was the draft. The possibility of being forced overseas to kill Vietnamese while Black schoolgirls were being murdered in a church in the United States raised the question: Where do I fight? If I were going to die fighting, for what cause would I be giving up my life? When the Civil Rights Movement advanced to the Black liberation movement, the direction was clear. The Black Panther Party for Self Defense (BPP) emerged not only as a fighting force for Black liberation but was advancing socialism and a critique of U.S. imperialism as the alternative to our condition. In the summer of 1968, following the assassination of Martin Luther King, Jr., I participated in the Poor People's Campaign, billed as the "last chance for non-violence." Led by Dr. King's Southern Christian Leadership Conference and supported by the Black Panther Party, I travelled with a group from Northern California in a bus caravan through the South rallying in Black churches from Oakland to Washington, D.C., where 6,000 of us built plywood huts and camped out on the National Mall. We demonstrated daily for economic justice and civil rights. The campaign ended after six weeks when thousands of police backed by the National Guard and army bulldozed our "Resurrection City" flat. During that whole experience, I met only two other Asian-American activists, even though many poor constituencies participated: Blacks, Latinos, American Indians, even poor Whites.

I was determined to return home and organize for socialist revolution in Chinatown. During the bus caravan to Washington, D.C., I read Edgar Snow's *Red Star over China* (1937), an inspiring account of the Chinese revolution. It made me proud of my ancestry to know that the Chinese people—a quarter of humanity—were opposing U.S. imperialism and building socialism, led by Mao Zedong and the Chinese Communist Party. In 1968, the National Liberation Front of South Viet Nam (NLF) launched the Tet Offensive that rocked U.S. imperialism and gave momentum to the antiwar movement. Students and workers in France and Mexico City were striking, crippling their governments. At home and abroad, and particularly in Asia, revolutionary socialists were on the offensive.

San Francisco Chinatown's Red Guard

The Red Guard Party was formed under the direct leadership of the Black Panthers, drawing members from the lumpen proletariat—the street youth I grew up with—and students. Some of us had personal contacts in the Panthers from jail, in high school, or as lovers. We studied with them and developed our program based on the Black Panther Party 10-point program with the addition of the United States recognizing the legitimacy of the

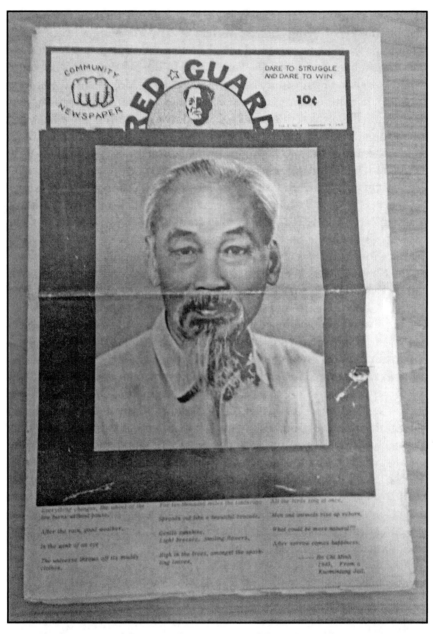

The front cover of the September 1969 issue of the Red Guard Community News.
Image courtesy of Alex Hing.

socialist countries in Asia and protection of the Earth's environment. We worked on health, education, anti-gentrification, and international solidarity with other progressive forces in the community and set up Black Panther style community survival programs. Poster-sized portraits of Ho Chi Minh and Mao Zedong hung from our storefront windows. The response from the KMT and police was furious, and we did our best to rally progressives and defend ourselves.

David Hilliard was running the BPP while most of the other Panther leaders were in jail or exiled. He contacted the Red Guard about joining a delegation to North Korea with Eldridge Cleaver. The Red Guards selected me to be their representative. The Panthers were in crisis at the time. They were being subjected to the FBI counterintelligence program (COINTELPRO), which spread false information; fanned divisions within the group and the Black Liberation Movement; and even assassinated people based on lies by police informers and agents. Meanwhile, new Panther chapters were springing up spontaneously by the hundreds all over the country.

David had his hands full. The task of organizing the delegation fell to Eldridge's colleague, Robert Scheer who, as editor of *Ramparts* magazine, was instrumental in promoting Cleaver through his prison memoir, *Soul on Ice* (1968), resulting in his release on parole. Elaine Brown, Chair of the Panther's Los Angeles chapter was to co-lead the delegation. Seven other activists were selected, and we gathered in Paris. Unlike most other U.S. antiwar activists at the time, the purpose of our delegation was to visit North Korea. Therefore, we did not meet with Madame Binh, the head of the Provisional Revolutionary Government of South Viet Nam (PRG) delegation at the Paris Peace Conference. Eldridge joined us in Moscow and from there we entered Pyongyang through Siberia.

From Korea to Viet Nam

In Pyongyang, the Koreans asked us what activities we would like to include on our itinerary. We all wanted to visit the Vietnamese Embassy to show our solidarity. During our visit to the Embassy, the Vietnamese invited us to Ha Noi to celebrate the 25th anniversary of the founding of the Democratic Republic of Viet Nam (DRVN). It was an offer we couldn't refuse. In order to get to Ha Noi from Pyongyang we had to go through China, and the Chinese also invited us for an extended tour of their country. In this unplanned way, we became the "U.S. Peoples' Anti-Imperialist Delegation to Socialist Asia." In all three countries we were treated as foreign dignitaries. We were people's diplomats who represented peace-loving people in the United States as opposed to the criminal imperialist U.S. government.

We were in the Democratic People's Republic of Korea (DPRK) initially for three weeks with another few days in transit back to the West. We were in the People's Republic of China (PRC) for a week total, traveling to and from Viet Nam and in the DRVN for three weeks. Our delegation also spent time in Moscow and Algiers, and met with the Laotian and Cambodian liberation governments. During this time, the U.S. government banned travel by U.S. citizens to these countries.

At the time, North Korea was a highly industrialized nation, exporting locomotives and tractors to the developing world. Their chemical industry developed a synthetic fabric from domestic mineral sources. They paid a lot of attention to the collective care and education of children to repopulate and rebuild the country after the War. We were taken to several sites and museums where the U.S. military committed nothing less than genocide during the Korean War. During that war there was virtually no opposition, so the U.S. government was not concerned about managing public opinion. The North Korean leadership is not "crazy" as depicted by Western propaganda. Their nation was subjected to unimaginable brutality during a war that has never officially ended. The United States was the first country to introduce nuclear weapons into the Korean peninsula, and every year conducts some of the largest military exercises in the world with the South Korean military. To make sacrifices and preparations in order to protect one's country is understandable. Calling the North Koreans "crazy" only serves to dehumanize them, making it easier for the U.S. government to target them. The goal of the U.S. people in this situation should not be solely that the DPRK change its stance, but primarily to demand that the U.S. government stop its provocations and vilifications and make genuine attempts at understanding and reconciliation.

Seeing Vietnam

Going to Viet Nam was the heart of our trip. I felt that culturally, the Vietnamese were more akin to people in the United States than to the Koreans or the Chinese. Maybe this was because Viet Nam is in the semitropics where people are more easygoing, or because French colonialism layered Western influences on Vietnamese culture. Perhaps, in the midst of a brutal war, everyone dispensed with formalities, and it was easier to connect. In any case, we were treated with genuine warmth. The only time I felt uncomfortable was at an assembly of Party members in Ha Noi. Our delegation was on stage and we were each greeted with applause. However, when I stood up and was introduced as being from the Red Guard in the

United States, the whole auditorium erupted in laughter, which was totally unexpected. I thought about it, but I never did find out why I was so funny.

As in Korea, we witnessed heartbreaking evidence of barbaric war crimes perpetuated against the civilian population by the United States. We also learned about the history of Vietnamese resistance to foreign domination, lessons in organizing different sectors of the population to engage in the resistance, and their strategy for winning the War. The main lesson was that hard work and sacrifices were made by Workers Party cadre in organizing the entire population against the United States and the Thieu puppet regime in the South in different phases of their protracted people's war against the United States. Time and again it was stressed that Marxism-Leninism practiced by the Workers Party of Viet Nam guided their successes and that in spite of being a very poor country, they were defeating the richest, most powerful nation on Earth. We attended a state reception on the 25th anniversary of the founding of the DRVN. While among other diplomats from many countries, we were invited aside into a small courtyard and had an audience with the legendary General Vo Nguyen Giap, who drove both the French and the United States out of Viet Nam. He was eager to greet us. He told us that our work would be long and arduous, but that ultimately, "You will win." And we all toasted to our common victory.

The Vietnamese used an international strategy to win support for their demands at the Paris negotiations and to isolate the United States. The U.S. antiwar movement was a key part of that strategy. If the antiwar movement continued to grow, eventually the government would have to consider public opinion in order for the politicians to stay in power. One of the problems was that very little information was available to the U.S. public about what was going on in Paris or what the demands of the PRG were. Returning war veterans brought information about the U.S. conduct of the War, but visits to the PRG in Paris and Ha Noi by antiwar activists were also critical. Support for the PRG's demands for an immediate U.S. ceasefire and total withdrawal of U.S. troops had to be intentionally mobilized. While battlefield losses and casualties were the main reasons for ending the War, the justness of the Vietnamese cause and hence, the correctness of their demands had to be presented to the U.S. public.

While our ability to see the country was limited because of the War, we still registered important things about the people and the land. At the Lake of the Restored Sword in Ha Noi, many people were exercising in the morning, including practicing tai chi. I was training in karate at the time and thought it would be nice to return someday and do tai chi at the lake. I was surprised to see young men hold each other's hands or drape their arms around each other's shoulders affectionately walking down the street. An outing at a beach with white sand and gentle waves was marred only by antiaircraft firing at a U.S. drone. On a trip to the countryside, a flooded river unexpectedly forced us to stay overnight at a schoolhouse rather than risk an evening crossing. Our hosts found us bedding, opened their meager larder, and prepared a simple meal of rice and local vegetables. We noticed that our hosts themselves did not eat. At the hotel in Ha Noi, we were served mainly French food, but outside, we had simple Vietnamese fare such as pho and spring rolls. The countryside had red earth and crops were growing everywhere. Our rooms had mosquito nets over the beds as well as ceiling fans, and you could see little things moving in the water when you filled the sink. A gecko or two would be hanging around on the walls or ceiling. It seemed that the Russians were everywhere, but I got to talk through an interpreter with the Ambassador of Mongolia in the hotel lobby. I became fascinated with the monochord, a traditional one stringed musical instrument that, when electrified, has the mournful sound of a blues guitar. We were presented with gifts made from recycled U.S. airplanes that were shot down: sandals made from tires, combs and rings from the aluminum bodies.

The Vietnamese were such wonderful people: humble, resourceful, courageous, kind, and beautiful. Yet they were being subjected to cluster bombs, helicopter attacks, tiger cages, the burning of their homes and forceful relocation to concentration camps, destruction of their crops and livestock, and Agent Orange. The U.S. military used some of the most evil methods of torture and killing ever devised because the Vietnamese wanted to determine the destiny of their own nation. The trip made it clear: U.S. imperialism had to be destroyed. Our delegation made this vow.

Going to China, the Motherland

From Viet Nam, we proceeded to China. For me, as a Chinese American, being in China was a dream come true. China was standing up to the West and building a bright future through socialism. For Chinese in America who felt demeaned by racism, connecting to the ancestral homeland meant connecting to greatness. For some of us, this greatness was not just in the past, but also in the present and future.

Our stay was brief. Huey Newton, the BPP leader, had been released from prison while we were there and Eldridge was eager to get back to Algiers to deal with Party matters. En route to Viet Nam, we learned of Jonathan Jackson's armed attempt to free his brother, George. George Jackson, BPP member and author of *Soledad Brother* and *Blood in My Eye*, was going on trial for murdering a prison guard. Now it was an open police war on the Panthers. We met with young people at Tsinghua University, birthplace of the original Red Guards. The Cultural Revolution was still going on and most of us supported Mao's idea of mobilizing China's youth to rid the Party of "capitalist roaders" in order to advance socialism.

I was disturbed, however, when we visited the Summer Palace. Walking along the famous Long Corridor, a breathtaking covered walkway nearly 3,000 feet long with more than 14,000 panels of exquisite paintings on the ceiling and beams, I asked our guide why some of the panels were white-washed. He replied that the Red Guards did that because those panels had scenes glorifying the feudal class. I thought of that as vandalism. I was glad someone stopped them, otherwise the whole corridor would have been destroyed based on that criterion. The delegation was treated to a banquet at the pavilion atop Longevity Hill in the Summer Palace overlooking Kunming Lake. It was essentially three 13-course meals back-to-back. Our delegation, a year before the U.S. ping-pong team, was the first U.S. delegation to visit Beijing since the 1949 revolution. Looking back, I felt it was a dress rehearsal for the latter event, which eventually led to normalizing relations between the two countries.

Back Home in the United States

On our way home, I was singled out at the DPRK–USSR border by Soviet customs agents. I was wearing a Mao jacket and had some literature from China in my handbag. The police pulled me into a room and strip searched me, saying I was bringing contraband into the country. I asked them what they were afraid of, all the while thinking to myself, *Pigs are pigs, the same all over the world.* We made the long flight to Algiers and got to swim on the North African side of the Mediterranean where we ate spit-roasted swordfish, freshly caught at a seaside café. I was in a fever the whole time in Algiers, but it was probably an emotional state of withdrawal from social-ist Asia. When we arrived in New York, customs agents went through our bags looking for contraband—letters to family from U.S. POWs in Ha Noi. Upon my return from Asia, the Red Guards of Chinatown dissolved and we merged with New York based I Wor Kuen (IWK) to become a national organization of Asian-American revolutionaries. Eventually, IWK achieved a series of mergers with other primarily U.S. Third World Marxist–Leninist organizations to form the League of Revolutionary Struggle (M-L), which disbanded in 1990.

The Red Guard had a legal apparatus to deal with the criminal justice system, so some of us formed the Asian Legal Services in a storefront of the International Hotel. Besides criminal services, we did immigration service, income tax, and draft counseling. Our draft counseling was well known: Anyone who did not want to go into the military would not be drafted. We processed approximately 1,000 cases, even obtaining conscious objector status for four active Asian-American servicemen. Through the draft counseling, we formed the Bay Area Asian Coalition against the War (BAACAW) in close relationship with the Union of Vietnamese. BAACAW was a grassroots organization representing Asian Pacific communities throughout Northern California to support the PRG's demands at the Paris Peace Conference. In antiwar marches, the BAACAW contingent would snake dance and chant, "One Struggle, Many Fronts!" We believed the slogan "Bring Our Troops Home" was racist because it applied only to the U.S. troops without consideration of the Vietnamese who bore the brunt of the war suffering. At one antiwar demonstration in San Francisco, a group of Asian women from BACAAW took over the stage to promote the PRG's 7 Point Peace Proposal to the applause of many in the audience. One of the people I worked closely with during that period was Nguyen Van Lui, a Vietnamese cook who was in touch with the PRG and kept us up to date. After the War, he was assassinated in Texas by a gang of anti-communist generals who fled Viet Nam. This gang committed a number of assassinations of progressive Vietnamese in the United States, but no one has ever been prosecuted for any of these crimes.

During this period, I became involved in the U.S. labor movement. As a night porter, janitor, and dishwasher, I eventually got a job in a union hotel. At my very first union meeting, when the agenda reached Good and Welfare—the part of the meeting that precedes adjournment, according to Robert's Rules—I made a motion that the union go on record opposing the War. I was ruled out of order by the president, a member of the Communist Party, U.S.A. When the hotel and restaurant craft unions merged to form Hotel Employees and Restaurant Employees Union (HERE), I participated in building a rank-and-file movement for democracy within the San Francisco local. The rank-and-file movement for democracy eventually captured the union's local leadership. In the process, we led a six-week-long citywide hotel strike that achieved huge economic advances for the membership, including: a paid half-hour meal break; Martin Luther King's birthday as a paid holiday; and translations of the contract and grievances in Chinese and Tagalog.

In the hotel where I was working, a gardener from Germany who was imprisoned at the end of WWII asked me one day to come with him to one of the roof gardens he tended. He had planted the colors of the NLF flag in the center of the garden; a rectangle of flowers, red on top, blue on the bottom, and yellow in the center. He told me that he clipped newspaper articles about the Vietnam War every day and had several scrapbooks full. He did that because, when he was a prisoner of war, he was told that he was personally responsible for the atrocities perpetuated by the Nazis. But there was no free press at that time in Germany, so ordinary people did not know about the crimes that were being committed by the Nazis. However, everything about the Vietnam War could be found in U.S. newspapers so, as far as he could tell, people in the United States had no excuse for participating in or supporting the War.

Today, with one foot in the community and the other in the rank-and-file, I continue to organize for a voice for immigrants, women, people of color, LBGTs, and rank-and-file workers in the labor movement. I am a founder of the Asian Pacific American Labor Alliance (APALA) and a trustee of my local union in New York, which is a part of the New York Hotel Trades Council. I also became a sous chef. I am honored to be in the same profession as Ho Chi Minh, who worked as a baker in Boston and joined our union in the early 1900s.

Musings on Revolution and Martial Arts

I was always a fighter, but in the late Sixties, I decided to become more scientific about it. I began training in Okinawan karate at the Chinese YMCA, under Grandmaster Richard Kim, a legend in karate circles. Kim was very political and supportive of Viet Nam and China. He was also into some of the more esoteric aspects of the martial arts, dealing with the mind and energy. As a Marxist–Leninist, I was not completely open to ideas that were not purely "scientific," but I was also not closed, having seen and experienced some amazing things in training. When I got older and moved to New York, I started to train in tai chi under another legend, Grandmaster William C.C. Chen. Tai chi is based on directing internal energy with the mind in order to defend oneself. The Vietnamese used tai chi principles in their fight against U.S. imperialism, and a lot of Mao's thinking, I realized, was putting Taoism, which is the philosophical basis of tai chi, into a Marxist–Leninist context.

Today, as I continue to practice the martial arts, I experience life through ancient Eastern understandings. I am no longer ideological because ideology is too rigid and I am arriving at an understanding that the principles of self-defense and non-violence are not contradictory, though not in the ways that Mahatma Gandhi or Martin Luther King advocated. Self-defense is natural and if one is really at peace and not aggressive, the violent energy of an attacker is merely returned by naturally redirecting it and not by using force. The Vietnamese did not return anywhere near the violence perpetrated on them and they approached the War understanding that its end would be based on their steadfastness and on the justness of their cause. The whole world supported their fight for freedom and independence. One could say the Vietnamese were victorious because guerilla war meant they were always running away from a fight, while at the same time holding their ground.

As I continue my study and practice of tai chi, I now understand that everything in life can be understood as self-defense and that the goal of struggle is to resolve conflict. I am clear that U.S. imperialism must be destroyed or it will destroy the world and that it will take a revolution of the people of all nations to accomplish this, but I now see a spiritual component to this struggle and personal transformation as being integral to building the movement.

Sorting through Contradictions

On my return to Viet Nam, I was asked what I wanted to get out of the visit. I wanted to know how the people are doing now that the War is over; get to know the people in our delegation; eat some inspiring food; and possibly see some Vietnamese martial arts. I would just be a tourist. "You cannot fill a tea cup unless it is first empty." On all those points, the trip was a success. The main thing I learned was that a lot of us during the War put our hopes and desires for a better world onto the Vietnamese and attached our issues onto their struggle. The Vietnamese were fighting primarily for independence and unification, and the socialist countries were their main supporters. It is apparent to me now that they were not necessarily fighting for socialism because I don't think anyone today can define what socialism is or provide a clear example of it. While in Viet Nam, our delegation asked about the Vietnamese formulation of "socialist oriented market economy" and the former ambassador to the United States shrugged his shoulders and laughed when asked about socialism. His colleague, another high-ranking party official also laughed and said he didn't know what socialism was either. I personally use the term "post-capitalism" rather than "socialism" to describe where revolutionaries should be heading. However, I did talk with a retired party member who was very discouraged about the way things are going. He was the only one who asked about how the Black Panthers are doing now. It seems that he was trying to reach out and reconnect to a period when revolution and defeating U.S. imperialism was the main order of the day.

Decades after the War, a lot of things are in free fall in Viet Nam and there are a lot of contradictions. That's okay because it is Western thought that divides things into two parts and demands that we take sides. Life is too complex for that. The War legacies of unexploded ordnance, Agent Orange, and Vietnamese MIAs need to be addressed by the United States. However, there is a palpable attraction of the Vietnamese to their former enemies. At first, I thought this was mainly due to the need for U.S. investment to help their economy grow along capitalist lines. Viet Nam is a poor country, yet it has the fifth tallest skyscraper in the world. At a Tet party, I met several English-speaking youth and almost all of them were business administration majors. They had the latest iPhones and motorbikes, which they could not possibly afford.

As I see it, behind Viet Nam's rapprochement with the United States is a wariness of an expansionist China. I am hopeful that Viet Nam will deal with this delicate dance in a way that favors them. In any case, it should be clear by now that nobody is going to infringe on their sovereignty. Our hosts asked me what I thought would happen if Viet Nam and China were to go to war. Nobody wanted that and everyone thought problems with China would eventually be worked out. One thing that puzzled me: as a Chinese American, most of the cultural things I saw in Viet Nam seemed to be Chinese. I could not see any major difference between Chinese and Vietnamese culture, as in Korea or Japan, for instance. The Vietnamese have self-determination, a sacred unity of their people with the land, and it is that which defines them rather than external trappings that may be incorporated into their culture. The Vietnamese have also adapted French and Japanese culture into their national character.

One of the things I tried to impress upon our hosts is that they have to change their view of "American" culture if they want to understand the United States. The year 2012 would be the last time that the majority of U.S. voters would be White when a president was chosen. When members of our delegation were interviewed by national television, it seemed the Vietnamese reporters would only interview the White delegates. I was the only person of color who was a part of the group we affectionately called the "Ha Noi 9." Yet my interview was cut off in mid-sentence as soon as it began when the crew ran off to interview former U.S. Attorney General Ramsey Clark. They never returned to me even though I saw them several times afterward.

Yet on another level it seems that Vietnamese do understand how racism works in the United States. I pointed out to our hosts and to our delegation that Blacks participated in the antiwar movement but not by demonstrating in the streets. Instead, Black Americans participated by organizing within the U.S. military and delaying deployment; deserting the military; sabotaging military equipment; and "fragging" (killing) their officers. The U.S. military drafted Blacks in disproportionate numbers compared to Whites. When Black G.I.s returned home, many joined the Panthers. I spoke with a few Vietnamese who studied in the United States, including our interpreters, and they all described direct encounters with racism. In fact, as a result of racism, Vietnamese anti-communists who fled to the United States are now a little more open to working with progressive forces in the Vietnamese-American community.

When we were in Quang Tri, we visited two cemeteries, one for fallen DRVN soldiers and another for NLF guerillas. The Vietnamese government counts as war casualties only those who were killed fighting for their side and not those who were killed fighting for the Army of the Republic of Vietnam (ARVN) in the South. Given the deeply ingrained Vietnamese tradition of ancestor worship, this needs to be addressed. As there is no reconciliation for the dead, there has been no formal reconciliation between the former combatants in Viet Nam even though families were often split apart as sons were drafted into one side or the other depending on who visited them first. We were told that some people would like a Truth and Reconciliation Commission such as in South Africa.

The question of human rights is always linked to the conditions in a "Communist" country, but it is rarely applied to the United States. When the Ha Noi 9 had lunch with David Shear, the U.S. Ambassador, he mentioned human rights in Viet Nam as a concern. Another member of our delegation, Steve Whitman, angrily pointed out that the United States also violates human rights by keeping the largest prison population in the world, the vast majority of which is Black and Latino. Whitman and his wife, Nancy Kurshan, spent many years organizing against "isolation unit" prisons, facilities built specifically for the solitary confinement of inmates. I pointed out that the Vietnamese General Confederation of Labor was revising the country's Labor Code to include more rights for workers, while the U.S. government has consistently eroded the right to join a trade union, a right that is protected under the Universal Declaration of Human Rights.

While we were in Viet Nam, Facebook was closed because it was being used to organize anti-Chinese demonstrations, but it was back online after four days. Also, when we were there, the Vietnamese government gave 10-year prison terms to advocates of what the U.S. is calling a "multiparty system." The Vietnamese government said that those people were trying to establish an independent Buddhist state in Central Viet Nam; in their words, committing treason, a crime punishable by death in the United States. I am not criticizing Viet Nam here but want to point out that Viet Nam has a right to protect itself from treason, as does the United States. I will never forget that my former union president explained to me one day that "the only people who talk about democracy are the people who lost the election." The role of the state is to suppress dissent. This is an objective fact. While the right to dissent is enshrined in the U.S. Constitution, almost everyone in our delegation had been jailed at one point or another for opposing U.S. foreign policy in Viet Nam. Rights come through organizing people for power and pigs are pigs the same all over the world. This is why we are ultimately fighting for a world without states.

About the War, the Vietnamese do not see that they won it. "In war, nobody wins," is what we heard time and again, followed by personal stories of families torn apart, deprivation, and suffering. Their empathy towards U.S. veterans seemed genuine and deep. The changes in Viet Nam since the War sometimes came as a shock. We admired the strong women soldiers we met during the War. But these women are now back in their traditional position at home taking care of their families. It seemed that ordinary people, especially the young, do not want to talk about the War, they would like to leave the past behind and build a modern country with a modern economy. For many reasons, this is going to be a very big challenge.

In Da Nang, we stayed at an unfinished seaside resort that was being built mainly for foreign tourists. However, much of Viet Nam is at sea level and with rapid climate change, many are concerned that much of the country will be permanently under water in the coming decades. The Central coastal areas and the Mekong Delta, the country's rice basket, already have a long history of severe flooding, and this will surely get worse. Ha Noi is totally polluted. I could not put my backpack down anywhere without it coming up dusty. In all the cities we visited, a plethora of motorbikes dominate the streets, sometimes the sidewalks, and even indoors.

In the countryside, there are problems behind the plush vegetation we saw. The defoliation caused by Agent Orange is ongoing. In areas such as near the Da Nang airport where Agent Orange was dumped, the land will be sterile, if not toxic, for generations. In the Central and Northern Highlands, primitive slash-and-burn farming methods are destroying huge amounts of rainforest and NGOs are working there to educate farmers on soil conservation, plant selection, more efficient livestock, and other ecology friendly agricultural methods. And, there is pervasive corruption. In a meeting with a former national legislator who now runs a private university, she described how corruption began with retired generals who received very small pensions even though they were heroes who suffered much during the war. Once their corruption was tolerated, however, it soon became widespread.

Global Crisis, Global Change

In other words, Viet Nam is now like the United States. It is a modern country with modern problems. The challenges Viet Nam faces are the same ones all nations on Earth face. The central issue is when will people wake up and see the essence of a global crisis? Our problem is not nations, ethnicities, religions, political convictions, or any other artificial divide. Our basic problem is the neglect of our natural environment. Human-created carbon emissions are causing rapid climate change, and we will soon be unable to feed ourselves among other catastrophic events. The Earth has been bled dry for thousands of years and this has accelerated drastically since the Industrial Revolution and the introduction of capitalism. We extract from the earth, but don't recycle. Instead we dump, spill, and spew toxic waste into the water, air, and land, subjecting nature to the design of humans for commodities and profit. This results in food scarcity among other things due to the rapidly diminishing supply of fresh water and fertile soil.

Regional conflicts based on the availability of oil are being replaced by conflicts over water. Egypt and Syria are the clearest examples. Unless people there deal with having enough water and soil to grow food and feed the people, no government will last. The good thing is we already have technology to solve our food crisis such as through state-of-the-art urban vertical farms as well as technology to power local economies on renewable energy sources.

Within our delegation, Rennie Davis often proposed high-tech solutions to clean up Agent Orange and locate landmines. Our hosts were receptive to these ideas. In my opinion, the problem lies in the execution. This leads us back to capitalism. As long as profit is the engine that drives the economy, technological resources will not be put to the use of the people and the global economy will continue running on fossil fuels at full speed. Karl Marx's dialectical and historical materialism explains that society will change when a technological breakthrough creates the means for a new mode of production and distribution of resources. It is clear that the computational power of the microchip and the Internet are that breakthrough. I believe that the socialist revolutions of the twentieth century were premature in that we did not have the technology that could create a new economy yet. The goals and ideals of revolutionary socialists were spot on, but unless we had the material basis for the transformation of the economy, we habitually resorted to capitalism. The capitalist class is trying to control the deployment of the new technology, but the capitalist system itself is failing and people are organizing against it locally and globally. How can anyone own information that is broadcast digitally over the World Wide Web? Julian Assange, Chelsea Manning, and Edward Snowden are our new revolutionary heroes. "Anonymous" is a new model for a revolutionary organization, along with local grassroots organizations. Bits of the new society are beginning to pop up. Detroit is now bankrupt and poor people are denied drinking water; however, vast tracts of abandoned lots in that city are being used to grow crops collectively for distribution to the poor. In addition, vertical farms are in operation from Brooklyn to Singapore.

Inspired by the Vietnamese People

In the course of my adult life, whenever I have faced difficulties, I looked at how the Vietnamese conducted themselves during their struggles for liberation. I have been riding a bicycle for decades as my main mode of transportation. Whenever I pack a big load of groceries and the weather is bad, I think about how the Vietnamese used bicycles to transport war material from the Chinese border to the hills around Dien Bien Phu to defeat the French, or along the Ho Chi Minh Trail through the jungle to defeat the U.S. imperialists. Because of the Vietnamese example, I believe any obstacle can be overcome through persistent effort. I very rarely become discouraged.

Lately, though, I am learning how to stay calm. There were a few occasions during our trip when the Vietnamese calmly took care of situations that would have had Americans tearing their hair out. During a national television broadcast, Ramsey Clark's translation equipment failed and a couple of technicians tinkered with it for several minutes until it finally worked, I looked at one of the producers and she did not even look at her watch. The same thing happened with the sound system at a Tet party. People just took their time, fixed the problem, and resumed the show. Nobody panicked. When I went to breakfast at the hotel after my tai chi practice by the lake in Ha Noi, the buffet was not yet set up although the restaurant was open. Even though I was a VIP guest, nobody was running around. This was really cool. I determined that when I got back to work at the hotel in New York, I was going to apply what I learned from the Vietnamese.

Returning to Viet Nam after 43 years made an enlightening circuit on my continuing path along the Way. Unlike the mythical Chinese Monkey King who journeyed to the West, my journey was to the East, beginning with the U.S. Peoples Anti-Imperialist Delegation led by Eldrige Cleaver of the Black Panther Party. I guess I started out, like Monkey, seeking scriptures from another land only to realize that the truth is inside oneself and seeing life as it is in my ongoing quest for justice and world peace. How else can the invasion of Cambodia by Viet Nam in 1978, followed by China's invasion of Viet Nam, and the subsequent persecution of ethnic Chinese in Viet Nam be explained? These were the countries that guided my thought during a period of turmoil in the United States and the mistrust of a thousand years carries on today. Still, I continue to learn from Viet Nam, and the spirit of the Vietnamese will always inspire me.

THE PEOPLE'S PEACE TREATY

JAY CRAVEN, DOUG HOSTETTER, AND BECCA WILSON

In December of 1970, the three of us went to Vietnam—to make peace.[1]

We were part of a 15-member delegation of American student leaders who traveled to wartime Vietnam to meet with our Vietnamese counterparts, to explore and confirm common and agreed-upon terms for peace. The trip came about under the auspices of the U.S. National Student Association (NSA) which, following the U.S. invasion of Cambodia in late April 1970, fielded interest from the Saigon Student Union to explore the idea of a "people-to-people peace treaty." Our delegation consisted primarily of student body presidents and college newspaper editors; though racially diverse, the group included just two women.

Despite grave risks to their own safety, the South Vietnamese students asserted that the U.S. war on Vietnam must stop, and felt confident they could identify necessary conditions for a just peace: the total withdrawal of U.S. troops and the end of the U.S.-imposed government in South Vietnam. They believed that the government in South Vietnam, led by President Nguyen Van Thieu and Vice President Nguyen Cao Ky, had been installed by the United States, did not represent the people of Vietnam, and had no interest in a negotiated peace. The U.S.–backed Thieu-Ky regime banned protests and brutally suppressed dissent; it had jailed not only hundreds of opposition leaders, but tens of thousands of ordinary people it considered dangerous subversives. Most of these political prisoners were routinely tortured. In spite of this highly repressive political atmosphere, the South

*The National Student Association delegation poses with
Prime Minister Pham Van Dong, 1970.
Photo courtesy of Doug Hostetter.*

Vietnamese student leaders proposed to conduct discussions with students from North Vietnam, the National Liberation Front for South Vietnam, and the United States to demonstrate the shared conviction that a negotiated solution was possible.

The South Vietnamese students were not alone in thinking that continued war offered only prolonged suffering and division. The American war in Vietnam had been raging since the massive deployment of U.S. troops in 1965, but its roots actually went back nearly two decades to the French neocolonial occupation of Vietnam, which the Truman and Eisenhower administrations bolstered, advised, and helped finance.

U.S. support for the French persisted right through the decisive battle of Dien Bien Phu, when the French were defeated by forces loyal to Ho Chi Minh, the Vietnamese leader whom American officials knew would be elected if the terms of the 1954 Geneva Accords ending the French occupation of Indochina were ever implemented. The Accords called for a temporary North–South division of Vietnam pending elections in 1956 to reunify the country, terms the U.S. opposed, but had agreed to abide by. Indeed, the Pentagon Papers reveal how U.S. operations to undermine the Geneva Agreements began within 10 days of their signing, through cross-border operations, infiltration, and a massive propaganda campaign, using leaflets to frighten Vietnamese and drive them south. U.S. Senator Wayne Morse, an early opponent to the war, spoke of how, at a 1956 Senate committee briefing, U.S. intelligence officials testified that Ho Chi Minh was expected to win 80 percent of the vote if the elections promised in Geneva were held. So, with the silent assent and active covert support of the Eisenhower administration, Ngo Dinh Diem, the new U.S.–backed prime minister of South Vietnam, refused to hold the elections promised in Geneva.

Over the next 15 years, the U.S. gradually stepped up its military involvement in Vietnam, beginning with sending advisors to train Diem's army and conduct espionage, subversion, and covert actions. Soon after taking office in 1961, John F. Kennedy approved counterinsurgency plans for Vietnam, and sent in 1,300 additional advisors. In 1962, the U.S. Air Force began using Agent Orange to defoliate areas used by insurgent forces. By the time of JFK's death in 1963, 16,000 U.S. military advisors and Special Forces personnel were operating in South Vietnam.

The war quickly escalated during the Lyndon Johnson administration. On August 4, 1964, Johnson assured Congress that the U.S. had "no military, political, or territorial ambitions in the area," and that "we still seek no wider war." But the very same day, he ordered the bombing of North Vietnam in retaliation for what turned out to the fraudulent claim that its navy had attacked U.S. ships in the Tonkin Gulf.

By 1965, LBJ had deployed 200,000 troops to Vietnam, and authorized a massive bombing campaign that would continue for the next three years. That same year, the first campus teach-ins on the war were held at U.C. Berkeley and the University of Michigan. Within a few years, the war had become hugely polarizing issue in the United States. By 1968, half a million American soldiers were fighting in Vietnam—and the U.S. antiwar movement had grown exponentially larger and broader, with veterans now a visible presence in most protests. The war had been brought home.

By 1970, the year our peace delegation traveled to Vietnam, the U.S. occupation of Vietnam had not succeeded—in spite of America's legendary military supremacy and the lethal power of its high-tech arsenal. Indeed, despite its determination and publicly stated confidence that the United States would prevail in Vietnam, the Johnson administration suffered a major shock to its public relations image during the 1968 Tet Offensive, when National Liberation Front and North Vietnamese soldiers overran many provincial towns and even made substantial incursions into the major South Vietnamese cities of Hue and Saigon, where insurgents even breached the walls of the U.S. embassy.

The Tet Offensive was followed by a concerted push by the U.S. peace movement to get American politicians to negotiate an end of the war that would withdraw all U.S. troops. Peace activists were optimistic and felt the time was right to bring the war to an end. In April 1967, Martin Luther King had declared his strong opposition to the war in a powerful speech at New York City's Riverside Church. In 1968, U.S. Senators Eugene McCarthy and Robert Kennedy declared their candidacies for president and attracted a tidal wave of support for their promises to quickly end the war.

But within just a few months of the January 1968 Tet Offensive, Martin Luther King and Robert Kennedy were assassinated and Eugene McCarthy's candidacy foundered in the chaos resulting from the killings and Lyndon Johnson's announcement that he would not seek re-election. The Democratic Party closed ranks around the candidacy of Johnson's loyal and equivocating vice president, Hubert Humphrey. Fed up with LBJ's repeated lies, and angered by the Democratic Party's failure to commit to quickly ending the war, peace activists staged demonstrations that resulted in a police riot at the 1968 Democratic Convention in Chicago. Activists were then blamed for the Chicago conflagration, and the subsequent showcase trial of the Chicago 8 gave further fuel to the frustration of American youth who were being drafted to fight a war in which few of our generation had faith. And, on the Republican side, presidential candidate Richard Nixon's declaration, during the 1968 campaign, that he had a "secret plan for peace" resulted in an escalation of the air war. Although he managed to withhold this information from Congress and the American people for several months, soon after taking office in 1969, Nixon launched intensive B-52 carpet bombings against Cambodia, an immense air assault on mostly civilian areas that would continue for the next four years.

The growing exasperation of young people found a potent outlet during the fall of 1969 when millions of people came together for widespread antiwar actions and mobilizations. Teach-ins and demonstrations took place across the United States in October 1969 and, just a month later, nearly half a million people converged on Washington, D.C., for a march organized by the Vietnam Moratorium Committee. This march became the largest antiwar protest in American history.

Nixon publicly claimed he was indifferent to these massive protests, but later revelations demonstrate this was untrue. "Pentagon Papers" author Daniel Ellsberg first revealed in 1974 his conviction that the massive peace protests in the fall of 1969 had halted White House discussions about plans for an unprecedented late 1969/early 1970 escalation of the war, code-named Operation Duck Hook—an escalation that would have entailed intensive bombing of the North's population centers and its extensive dike system, plus the mining of its rivers and harbors. Also under consideration was a ground invasion of North Vietnam and use of nuclear weapons. (In support of his assertions, Ellsberg cited a variety of sources, including Nixon White House aides Jeb Stuart Magruder and Dwight Chapin.) Moreover, government documents released in recent decades confirm, according to historian Tom Wells and other scholars, that the antiwar movement "exerted a critical influence on Nixon's decision to forgo Operation Duck Hook, thereby helping prevent bloodshed and human misery in Vietnam on an unspeakable scale."[2]

But antiwar leaders would remain unaware of their movement's impact for quite a few years. In the meantime, many activist leaders grew increasingly demoralized, as it appeared our large, highly visible movement was having little effect on the course of the war. Nixon talked tough and called out police and National Guard troops against demonstrators, while building his enemies list and increasing surveillance and harassment of people in all walks of life who opposed the war. Then, in late April 1970, Nixon expanded the war into Cambodia, triggering massive and immediate student sit-ins and demonstrations at colleges and universities across the country. These actions then intensified into an unprecedented U.S. national student strike in response to the May 1970 killings of student protestors— four students gunned down by National Guardsmen at Kent State (Ohio) University, and two students killed by police and state troopers at Jackson State (Mississippi) University. At least 450 campuses were shut down by strikes and protests involving more than four million students.

By this time in May of 1970, the negotiations between the U.S. and the Vietnamese in Paris had been going on for two years, but had only reached agreement on the shape of the table and the composition of the negotiating teams. These talks were intended to find a resolution for the war among each of the warring parties: The United States and its ally, the Republic of Vietnam (RVN), led by Thieu and Ky, controlled part of South Vietnam. On the other side, the Democratic Republic of Vietnam (DRV, or North Vietnam) and the Provisional Revolutionary Government (PRG), which represented the National Liberation Front (NLF) of South Vietnam, controlled large parts of the countryside in contested South Vietnam. It was this group, the NLF/PRG, which the U.S. disparagingly called the Viet Cong, or V.C., that constituted the chief enemy to U.S. forces, since they led the resistance to the American occupation and controlled much of South Vietnam. The central U.S. military policy of "pacification" was aimed at driving Vietnamese people out of these NLF-controlled rural areas into refugee camps in the heavily-fortified coastal areas, which the Americans and their South Vietnamese allies controlled.

It was against this backdrop of static peace talks, intensive war in South Vietnam, and escalation of that war into Cambodia that, during the summer of 1970, the U.S. National Student Association (NSA) Congress decided that if the adults in government would or could not negotiate a peace treaty with the PRG and North Vietnamese, we students would take steps to do what we could. Meeting in August at Macalester College in St. Paul, Minnesota, the NSA Congress overwhelmingly approved a resolution endorsing bold antiwar action in the fall and declaring that "if the war is not ended by May 1, 1971, NSA will commit itself to a concerted expansion of massive non-violent action including civil disobedience at the local, regional, and national levels."

Shortly after the resolution passed, the Congress voted that NSA would send a delegation of U.S. student leaders to Vietnam, to discuss terms for peace with Vietnamese student leaders from the South (both the U.S.-supported Republic of Vietnam and the National Liberation Front) and the North (Democratic Republic of Viet Nam).

The suggestion of a student-drafted peace treaty was initiated by the Saigon Student Union and the South Vietnam National Student Union. These groups consisted of elected student leaders from Saigon and other urban areas controlled by the U.S.-sponsored Thieu regime. Eventually, as anti-Thieu sentiment in South Vietnam grew more widespread and open, the student unions allied with other South Vietnamese peace groupings, including Buddhist leaders, trade unions, and the Women's Committee for the Right to Live, led by prominent South Vietnamese lawyer and writer Madame Ngo Ba Thanh.

At first, NSA discussions focused on the idea of a peace treaty conference of student leaders that would meet in Geneva, to draw attention to the aborted 1954 Geneva Agreements. But organizers faced logistical roadblocks, as it was soon apparent it would be nearly impossible for student leaders to get official permission to leave South Vietnam for this kind of meeting. Some consideration was then given to meeting in Bangkok, Thailand, but, again, logistics proved impossible. Finally, organizers decided to send U.S. student leaders first to Saigon and then Hanoi—to more fully experience conditions in Vietnam and to facilitate a communications bridge helping to link South Vietnamese student activists with student leaders representing the DRV and NLF.

In the months following the NSA Congress, veteran U.S. peace activists, including Chicago 8 defendants Rennie Davis and Dave Dellinger, had several discussions with Vietnamese diplomats in Paris that addressed the planned "people's peace treaty" trip. Saigon contacts were handled by the NSA from their office on S Street in Washington. Initial trip-related tasks were coordinated by newly elected NSA president David Ifshin[3], former student body president at Syracuse University, and NSA communications director Frank Greer.[4]

Within a few weeks of the NSA Congress in St. Paul, Ifshin found himself increasingly engaged with the NSA's fraternal counterpart in South Vietnam—the activist Saigon Student Union (SSU), which had recently become increasingly bold and militant. In early June, just weeks after the nationwide campus strikes in the U.S. sparked by the Kent and Jackson State killings, South Vietnamese student leaders chanting, "we die for peace, not for war," led a march following the funeral of a Buddhist nun who had immolated herself as a "torch for peace." In early July, Saigon student leaders for the first time issued a public statement demanding immediate withdrawal of U.S. troops, an end to U.S. support for the Thieu regime, and asserting that only the Vietnamese people themselves could decide the terms for peace. Three days after the student proclamation, President Nguyen Van Thieu publicly vowed to kill those demanding immediate peace, saying, "I am ready to smash all movements calling for peace at any price because I'm still much of a soldier.... We will beat to death the people who are demanding immediate peace."[5]

At dawn on September 20, the U.S. NSA office received a call for help. Saigon was on the line. A Saigon Student Union representative told David Ifshin that when the SSU's Fourth National Conference had convened on August 30, police had arrested 117 students as they rallied peacefully to protest U.S. Vice President Spiro Agnew's visit to Saigon. Men in U.S.-made helicopters had hurled tear gas at the crowd, and police had brutally clubbed scores of fleeing protestors. Although most of those arrested on August 30 had since been released, four popular student leaders, including SSU President Huynh Tam Mam[6], remained in prison and had been repeatedly beaten and tortured. They feared being killed. The caller said SSU activists had launched a hunger strike "to the death" to bring attention to the plight of the four imprisoned leaders, and that students all over South Vietnam were fasting with them. The caller asked if the NSA would issue a general appeal to American students for expressions of solidarity with the four, and bring pressure to bear to get them released.

Three days after the phone call, Ifshin and 25 student body presidents launched a 10-day NSA solidarity hunger strike and vigil in Lafayette Park, across from the White House. Two days after the NSA fast ended, the four Saigon student leaders were released.

In October, once our Vietnam contacts and travel plans began to gel, NSA officers met with State Department officials who assured them that the U.S. government would facilitate our obtaining visas from the RVN for our travel to South Vietnam to meet with the Saigon Student Union and South Vietnam National Student Union. Discussions with North Vietnamese diplomats in Paris also yielded assurances that visas would be provided by the DRV for travel to North Vietnam to meet there with students from the North Vietnamese Student Union and students representing the NLF.

Most members of the People's Peace Treaty delegation began arriving in Washington, D.C., during the third week in November. NSA leaders and delegation members were elated and encouraged that, for the first time, civilians representing each of the warring parties could be joined in common cause. We were pleased by the assurances of travel access to South Vietnam, but also mindful that in advocating U.S. withdrawal as well as peace and reconciliation with people from North Vietnam and the NLF-controlled areas of South Vietnam, South Vietnamese student leaders were risking their very lives.

During pre-trip briefings with scholars and U.S. peace movement leaders who had recently travelled to Paris and Saigon, our delegation learned that a dramatic political transformation was underway in urban South Vietnam. Not only students and Buddhists, but war veterans, teachers' groups, trade unions, prominent professionals, even formerly anti-communist or neutralist Catholic leaders and politicians were speaking out for peace and forming coalitions. Most unprecedented, these new alliances were in agreement that peace could only occur once (1) all U.S. forces withdrew from the South, and (2) the U.S. ceased its support for the Thieu–Ky regime.

Rennie Davis gave us a rundown of a significant turning point: In late September, only a day after the NSA had received the distress call from the Saigon Student Union, a conservative Catholic member of the South Vietnamese National Assembly, Ngo Cong Duc, had sent shockwaves across Saigon when he held a press conference to reiterate the demands first made by the South Vietnamese student unions: immediate withdrawal of all U.S. forces, an end to U.S. support for the Thieu–Ky regime, and political settlement based on negotiations between all Vietnamese warring parties. A wealthy Mekong Delta landowner and editor-publisher of Saigon's largest daily newspaper, Duc had been elected just three years earlier on an anti-Viet Cong platform. And now he was not only publicly acknowledging the existence of a popular revolt against the Thieu–Ky regime, he was tacitly admitting he supported it; and he was presenting a formal peace proposal in harmony with the latest offer from the PRG side of the Paris Talks, which outlined a roadmap for negotiated settlement between the NLF/PRG and the broad anti-Thieu forces that Duc represented.

On the logistical side, our delegation's hopes for a seamless peace expedition were soon dashed. Although the initial response of the State Department was very positive, their tone suddenly changed once they learned that North Vietnamese diplomats in Paris had welcomed the NSA initiative, and had assured our contacts that visas would be provided for our delegation. Just several weeks before our group was to leave, the State Department informed NSA officers that the visas for student delegation to travel to South Vietnam could no longer be taken for granted. Then travelers returning from Southeast Asia informed us that everyone who listed "student" as their occupation on visa applications was now being denied a visa to enter South Vietnam. It was clear. Our travel to South Vietnam would be blocked.

National Student Association leaders suddenly faced the dilemma that the entire purpose of the Vietnam trip, to forge a peace treaty with representatives from each of the parties to the war, was now in jeopardy. The question was how our mission could still be advanced. After extensive deliberations, organizers decided we should try to send New School graduate student Doug Hostetter into Saigon. Doug, a Mennonite and conscientious objector, had worked as a development and literacy aide in Vietnam and he spoke fluent Vietnamese.

We weren't confident this idea would work—but in the end, Doug accomplished his mission. He managed to slip into Saigon undetected, and met with South Vietnamese student leaders to discuss and ratify the Peace Treaty.

After Doug's rounds of meetings and a peace treaty signing in Saigon, on December 12 he joined the rest of our delegation in Hanoi, where we and our Vietnamese counterparts met to review, and sign, the slightly revised Saigon-initiated document. The first phase of our mission had been accomplished. We were thrilled—and deeply moved.

Still, the NSA delegation was worried about how the U.S. government would react to our announcement that we had signed a People's Peace Treaty between students in the U.S., Saigon, Hanoi, and even students who were living in the parts of South Vietnam that were controlled by the National Liberation Front of South Vietnam.

The exact genesis of the treaty is difficult to reconstruct. But we are fairly certain that ideas for the content of the treaty had first been articulated in communications between the Saigon Student Union and NSA leaders, and later during discussions between U.S. antiwar leaders (including Rennie Davis and NSA officer Larry Magid) and Vietnamese diplomats in Paris. But the actual treaty language evolved gradually, as each of the student entities weighed in. Jay Craven remembers first seeing draft language prior to our departure for Hanoi, in a document provided by former Cornell University professor Bob Greenblatt who indicated it had been written by well-known essayist, cultural critic, and political philosopher Dwight MacDonald, best known for his early work at *Time* magazine and *Fortune* and, later, at *The New Yorker*, *The Partisan Review*, and *The New York Review of Books*. Greenblatt said that MacDonald closely followed diplomatic developments at the Paris Peace Talks and had consulted with writer Susan Sontag, who had traveled to North Vietnam in 1969 and written her insightful and thought-provoking book, *Styles of Radical Will*, from which a section, *Trip to Hanoi*, was then published on its own. (It's also likely that the Greenblatt–MacDonald draft was at least partly inspired by Ngo Cong Duc's peace proposal, which had been reprinted in full in the November 5, 1970 issue of the *New York Review of Books*, with an introduction authored by Greenblatt, Rennie Davis, and Richard Falk.)

Revisions to the initial document came about during student meetings on both sides and through further discussion with peace movement leaders and Vietnamese envoys involved with the Paris Peace Talks. While Nixon administration officials called for an unconditional ceasefire and the release of U.S. POWs, American students and peace movement leaders asserted that U.S. POWs would only be released when the U.S. government committed to a firm date for the withdrawal of its troops.

The Thieu–Ky regime opposed participation by the NLF/PRG in any new post-war government, but South Vietnamese students believed build-ing a coalition government should involve all Vietnamese parties sincerely committed to peace and reconciliation. North Vietnamese and NLF/PRG students asked for terms that respected Vietnamese sovereignty and en-abled the Vietnamese, free of foreign influence, to determine the future of their country. (This had been promised by the 1954 Geneva Agreements, after the French occupation had failed, but U.S. obstruction, in the form of overt and covert military intervention, prevented implementation.) The North Vietnamese and NLF/PRG students also asked that the Treaty call for self-determination for all nations caught up in the war, including Laos and Cambodia.

So, while there were many hands and voices that contributed to the final document, the terms of the treaty were not complicated. The People's Peace

Treaty synthesized multiple ideas and concerns into a document that clearly and directly articulated the steps toward peace through negotiation. Each party agreed that it outlined a reasonable path by insisting, foremost and unequivocally, on an end to the U.S military occupation.

Truth be told, the terms finally ratified in the January 1973 Paris Agreement very closely resembled the People's Peace Treaty, which became the diplomatic blueprint for the end of the war. We chose to act when we did because we saw that there was already a basis for this agreement. We simply felt that we could wait no longer.

As students, we were proud that despite considerable efforts by the U.S. and South Vietnamese governments to sabotage our efforts, we had accomplished our task. We had successfully drafted a four-page treaty with students from *all* regions of Vietnam that spelled out agreed-upon conditions for peace in Vietnam. With politicians and diplomats failing to make progress, we demonstrated that it could be done. And we were confident that the document in our hands would become a powerful tool to educate the American people that a just peace was possible.

We decided that the most secure, effective way to announce the People's Peace Treaty would be to present it at a press conference in Paris, on our way back to the United States. To prevent interdiction by the CIA[7] or U.S.-allied police, as Doug Hostetter had encountered in Laos on his way to North Vietnam, we decided to fly to Paris via the Aeroflot flight from Hanoi to Moscow, a 23-hour ordeal on a Russian turbo-prop, with stops in Vientiane, Karachi, Tehran, Tashkent, and other capitals of the Republics of the Soviet Union along the way.

From Moscow we flew to Paris, where we held a press conference, announcing to the world that we had in-hand an innovative and living document, a "people's peace treaty" that had been agreed to by U.S. and Vietnamese students representing each political constituency. Our message to the United States and the world: peace in Vietnam was possible if we could only act on former president Dwight D. Eisenhower's declaration that "people want peace so much that one of these days government had better get out of their way and let them have it."

We returned to the United States with a mission to spread word of the People's Peace Treaty and to seek support and ratification by student bodies at colleges and universities, political leaders, city councils, unions, national, regional and local antiwar coalitions, and anyone and everyone we could meet and engage. We also planned to use the Peace Treaty as an organizing tool for announced plans to petition Congress to accept its terms. If the nation's elected officials failed to do so or to move toward a negotiated end to the war, our plan, in concert with other peace activists, Vietnam veterans, and organizations from across the country, was to stage massive non-violent civil disobedience in Washington during the first days of May 1971. Our slogan: "If the government won't stop the war, the people will stop the government."

The timing for this initiative was perfect, coming just months after the demonstrations against Nixon's moves into Cambodia and the subsequent Kent and Jackson State killings. U.S. colleges and universities were teeming with students who opposed the war and were tired of inaction, as peers continued to be drafted and sent to fight in a war that fewer and fewer Americans supported. The call for massive civil disobedience in May of 1971 struck a resonant chord—that we could and must raise the social/political costs to the Nixon administration for continuing to attack and occupy Vietnam.

Support and mobilization for the People's Peace Treaty began immediately on our return from Vietnam and Paris. By March of 1971, there were People's Peace Treaty offices in 12 cities. City councils, including Cambridge, Massachusetts; Berkeley, California; and Detroit and Ann Arbor, Michigan, endorsed the treaty. Student body presidents at 300 U.S. colleges and universities had signed the treaty and, at 10 schools, there had been campus-wide referenda supporting the Treaty. By April 21, 1971, the national People's Peace Treaty office had received word that 188 more U.S. colleges and universities would vote on the Treaty by the end of the school year.

Peace organizations from across the country also endorsed the Treaty. Among them: The Committee of Concerned Asian Scholars, American Friends Service Committee, Chicago Peace Council, Clergy and Layman Concerned about Vietnam, Los Angeles Peace Action Council, National Lawyers Guild, New University Conference, People's Coalition for Peace and Justice, Women's International League for Peace and Freedom, and Women Strike for Peace.

Prominent members of the U.S. cultural, academic, and religious community also offered their public endorsement, among them Coretta Scott King, Reverend Ralph Abernathy, U.S. Congressman Herman Badillo, civil rights activist Julian Bond, Congressman John Conyers, and black activists Ericka Huggins and Bobby Seale. Supporters also included religious leaders such as Rabbi Belfour Brickner, Reverends Daniel and Phillip Berrigan, Malcolm Boyd, William Sloane Coffin, Robert MacAfee Brown, Bishop Robert DeWitt, Bishop William Davidson, Bishop Paul Moore, Bishop Tomas Gunbleton, Richard McSoreley, Sister Elizabeth McAlister, Father James Groppi, Sister Margaret Traxler, and Sister Joques Egan.

Cultural supporters included folksingers Joan Baez and Judy Collins; cartoonist Jules Feiffer; actors Rock Hudson, Jane Fonda, Donald Sutherland, Jennifer Jones, Roscoe Lee Browne, and Julie Harris; Hollywood producer Bert Schneider (*Five Easy Pieces, Easy Rider*); feminist leaders Betty Friedan, Gloria Steinem, and Kate Millet; comedian Godfrey Cambridge; writers Denise Levertov, Mitchell Goodman, Cleve Gray, Francine du Plessix Gray, Robert Jay Lifton, I.F. Stone, Studs Terkel, Paul Sweezy, and Dalton Trumbo; and activist and baby doctor Benjamin Spock.

Prominent academics included Howard Zinn, Noam Chomsky, Richard Falk, Kenneth Kenniston, Ashley Montagu, Eric Segal, and Nobel Prize laureates George Wald and Salvadore Luria.

Antiwar leaders included Kay Camp, Rennie Davis, Dave Dellinger, Daniel Ellsberg, Richard Fernandez, David Hawk, Tom Hayden, Abbie Hoffman, William Kunstler, Stewart Meacham, Sidney Peck, Amy Swerdlow, Cora Weiss, George Wiley; union activists Abe Feinglass, Henry Foner, Mo Foner, and Patrick Gorman; and Vietnam veteran leaders Tim Butz and Al Hubbard.

By the end of April 1971, U.S. Congressional Representatives Bella Abzug, Herman Badillo, Shirley Chishom, Bill Clay, John Conyers, Ron Dellums, Parren Mitchell, and James Scheuer had introduced into the U.S. Congress a Concurrent Resolution:

Expressing the sense of the Congress with respect to the People's Peace Treaty

Whereas the efforts to attain a negotiated settlement of the Indochina conflict at the Paris Peace Talks have been unsuccessful for many months; and

Whereas a direct equitable solution to the war is now possible; and

Whereas the principles of the People's Peace Treaty form the basis for a just and honorable end to the war in Indochina;

Now therefore, be it

Resolved by the House of Representatives (the Senate concurring),

That it is the sense of the Congress that the People's Peace Treaty embodies the legitimate aspirations of the American and Vietnamese peoples for an enduring and just peace in Indochina.

4/29/71

The People's Peace Treaty became such a powerful presence on U.S. campuses and in communities that, in March 1971, the U.S. State Department felt it necessary to issue a statement on the People's Peace

- 4 -

5) Together with their peoples, the Vietnamese and American students are fully confident that the just resistance of the Vietnamese people will end in total victory . This will be a victory of the two peoples' desire for peace , independence and freedom, a victory of the lasting friendship between them.

Done in Hanoi, on December 17th, 1970

The Delegation of Students from the United States of America :

- RICARDO BERTRAN
- TERRIE EVELYN COOK
- JOSEPH PHILIP CLARK CRAVEN
- JAMES ALBERT DOHERTY
- RONALD LEE EACHUS
- MICHAEL FRANCIS ENG
- CHARLES DOUGLAS HOSTETTER
- DAVID MICHAEL IFSHIN
- RODERICK JOHN MACPHERSON
- KEITH S. PARKER
- JOSEPH NICOLA PICHIRALLO
- MARK M. RASENICK
- ANTHONY ROMAN
- MARK LAWRENCE WEFERS
- REBECCA WILSON

For the Delegation of the South Viet Nam Liberation Students Union :
- NGUYEN THI CHAU

For the Delegation of the Viet Nam National Union of   ents :

- ĐO VAN HIEN

A page from the original copy of the People's Peace Treaty.
Courtesy of Doug Hostetter.

Treaty in GIST, its reference aid on U.S. foreign relations primarily used by government officials.

After a winter and spring of education and organizing across the country, the peace movement's focus shifted to spring actions in Washington, as hundreds of thousands of people converged. This "spring offensive" began on April 16th, when Vietnam Veterans Against the War staged "Dewey Canyon III," five days of actions that were named after two short U.S. military incursions into Laos that were carried out in February of that year.

The seeds for this veterans' mobilization were planted a few months earlier, in Detroit, when hundreds of vets convened at a rented Howard Johnson's for a long January weekend of dramatic testimony focused on their actions as combat soldiers in Vietnam.

Led by Gold Star mothers, more than 1,100 Vietnam vets marched to Arlington Cemetery, where they planned to lay wreaths on the graves of American soldiers killed in Vietnam. But they arrived to find the gates locked. They laid their wreaths at the gates and departed. They performed guerrilla theater, attempted to surrender themselves at the Pentagon as war criminals, and listened to testimony on possible solutions to the war at Senate Foreign Relations Committee hearings that included a provocative round of testimony by Vietnam veteran and former Navy officer John Kerry.

The vets camped on the National Mall where they were evicted through a court injunction that was overturned by the Washington District Court of Appeals—then quickly reinstated by U.S. Supreme Court Chief Justice Warren Burger. Despite orders to arrest the camping veterans, U.S. Park Police refused to do so, and the encampment continued. Then, on Friday, April 23rd, more than 800 veterans assembled in an unprecedented action to, one-by-one, toss their Bronze Stars, Purple Hearts, and other war medals onto the steps of Congress. The nation paused.

On the following day, April 24th, more than 500,000 people rallied in Washington for the largest antiwar demonstration in U.S. history. Thousands remained in Washington for the planned May Day actions, 35,000 of them camped in West Potomac Park until they were dispersed on the morning of May 2nd by a battalion of police in riot gear, tossing tear gas as they cleared the park. Activists retreated to churches, homes, and college dorms—and they set out early the next morning to act on their carefully planned designs for civil disobedience aimed at stopping the normal functioning of Washington government.

Opposed by more than 10,000 troops ordered into the nation's capital, including soldiers airlifted by helicopter transports onto the Washington monument grounds, May Day protestors impeded government operations on May 3rd as police resorted to mass arrests to prevent even more disruption. The White House ordered government employees to report for Monday morning work in waves, starting at 3 a.m., to prevent dense knots of traffic that protestors could more easily obstruct. And the government deployed legions of police who suspended normal procedures to arrest and herd protestors and more than a few innocent bystanders into a fenced holding pen next to the RFK Stadium in downtown Washington. By 8 a.m., more than 7,000 protestors had been arrested.

On Tuesday, several thousand protestors converged on the offices of the U.S. Justice Department, to protest the mass arrests. As Attorney General John Mitchell stood on his office balcony smoking a pipe, more than 1,000 were taken to D.C. jails. And on Wednesday, May 5th, protestors culminated their actions by taking the People's Peace Treaty to the steps of the Capitol and demanding its ratification. Small bands of demonstrators also posted copies of the Treaty on the doors of government and congressional offices. Police took more than 1,000 people into custody, bringing the total number of arrests to 12,614, making the May Day seizures the largest mass arrest in U.S. history.

The May Day actions were creative, fluid, militant, and disruptive, but protestors maintained their commitment to non-violence and no one was hurt. Most of the arrests were determined later to be illegal—and only 79 convictions were delivered against protestors. The government convened a federal grand jury to seek indictments against May Day leaders, but activists they called refused to testify. That, combined with the government's weak case on the mass arrests resulted in the suspension of the grand jury investigation.

White House Chief of Staff H.R. Haldeman discussed the Capitol action with President Nixon in the Oval Office on May 5th, the day the action took place.

PRESIDENT: How's he's do[ing]—great? What was the situation today? Did they have any more actions?

HALDEMAN: Uh, there's gonna be a, they're going to...

PRESIDENT: March on the Capitol?

HALDEMAN: Uh,...be at the Congress at noon when the thing...

PRESIDENT: (Unintelligible)

HALDEMAN: Well, that's the plan, uh, whether they do it never can quite sure. But they, they've followed the plan pretty much up to now. It's (tape noise) the theory is they're gonna...

PRESIDENT: Demonstrate up there, at the Capitol?

HALDEMAN: From twelve noon until the People's Peace Treaty is signed, you see, they're demanding that the Congress sign this. This is this peace treaty that they've signed with North Vietnam. (Laughs)

PRESIDENT: Hmm. (Tape Noise)

HALDEMAN: They've got no (tape noise) special permit. Best estimate is 2,000 demonstrators. Trouble very likely.

PRESIDENT: Good.

HALDEMAN: They've planned two meetings tonight to plan demon...

PRESIDENT: That was last night.[8]

About May Day, then-CIA director Richard Helms is quoted in Joe Allen's book, *Vietnam: The (Last) War the U.S. Lost* (2008), as saying, "It was obviously viewed by everybody in the administration, particularly with all the arrests and the howling about civil rights and human rights and all the rest of it...as a very damaging kind of event. I don't think there was any doubt about that."

It is impossible to know the full and precise impact that the 1970 People's Peace Treaty had on public opinion, the government, or the U.S. negotiators in Paris. We do know that during the first two years of the U.S. peace talks with the Vietnamese in Paris, negotiators accomplished very little. We also know, thanks to now-declassified White House documents held at the Lyndon Johnson Presidential Library, that representatives of the 1968 Nixon presidential campaign worked behind the scenes with the South Vietnamese Thieu-Ky regime to sabotage Lyndon Johnson's progress in the Paris Peace Talks, in order to facilitate Nixon's election. Johnson was apparently close to agreeing to a bombing halt that could create an opening for a ceasefire and a framework for lasting peace, but encountered unexpected resistance from the South Vietnamese. Johnson learned of Nixon's back-channel sabotage through wiretaps, but equivocated about acting on this knowledge, fearing that disclosure of the wiretaps would sully his own reputation. Finally, Johnson was apparently persuaded that to charge Nixon so close to an election that Nixon was likely to win would compromise Nixon's effectiveness as president and damage the overall credibility of the U.S. government. So, the war continued.

An additional complication to the negotiations surfaced during the Nixon administration, when, in debt to South Vietnamese President Thieu for collaborating in his behind-the-scenes maneuvers during the 1968 election, Nixon was limited in how far he could push the Thieu government. This became especially problematic during the final rounds of talks during the summer and fall of 1972, when, according to various authoritative accounts, Thieu dug in his heels and proved intractable to the Nixon team.

It was only two years after the signing of the People's Peace Treaty and the sustained actions of non-violent civil disobedience by returning soldiers, students, and others that the U.S. government finally reached full agreement with the Vietnamese and signed the Paris Peace Accords that led to the end of U.S. involvement in that war. During the spring of 1971, the People's Peace Treaty was distributed as a pamphlet and poster and was republished and summarized in student newspapers as well as underground and alternative publications all over the country. It became the leading instrument used to educate hundreds of thousands of Americans that it was possible to end the Vietnam War on terms that were fair and negotiable. Mainstream media carried a few news stories mentioning the Treaty, but did not report on what the document actually said. According to historian Charles DeBenedetti, the People's Coalition for Peace and Justice promoted the People's Peace Treaty "virtually without media coverage."[9]

It is tragic that the Nixon administration chose to pursue war on Vietnam for those two additional years, rather than heed our call to embrace the People's Peace Treaty. This document, which had the overwhelming backing of the U.S. peace movement, and which earned widespread support among American college and university students, was entirely ignored by the administration. If they paid any attention to it at all, Nixon's right-wing cohorts harassed U.S. student leaders and jailed South Vietnamese students who participated in the innovative Peace Treaty initiative. And they dismissed the Treaty as "communist-inspired." In fact, its contents were entirely compatible with the terms that Nixon's negotiators eventually agreed to in 1973.

In 1971 and 1972, Nixon chose to intensify his high-tech air assaults as he pursued his "Vietnamization" program, which then-U.S. Ambassador to South Vietnam Ellsworth Bunker cynically dubbed "changing the color of the bodies."[10] During the 12-day 1972 Christmas Bombings, alone, the United States lost 43 airmen, killed in action, with another 49 taken prisoner. The Vietnamese government documented 1,624 of their civilians killed. And if you look at the entire last two years of the war, U.S. National Archives & Records indicates that 3,173 U.S. soldiers were killed. South Vietnamese (RVN) government records show that during that same period, 45,688 ARVN (Army of the Republic of Vietnam) soldiers were killed. North Vietnamese and National Liberation Front casualties were estimated at 23,581.

In the four years between Nixon's sabotage of Johnson's 1968 peace efforts and the time, just prior to the 1972 election, when Secretary of State Henry Kissinger declared "peace is at hand," more than 20,000 U.S. troops died in Vietnam,[11] more than 100,000 were wounded, and more than a million Vietnamese were killed. Total American soldier deaths in Vietnam were 58,209. Total Vietnamese deaths during the war are now estimated at three million.[12]

Nothing, militarily or politically, was gained through those final destructive years of the war. And now, four decades later, with the U.S. positioned as Vietnam's largest trading partner, it is worth reflecting on why we fought this brutal, immoral, and costly war. It is also worth considering how the U.S. and Vietnamese student peace movements and the People's Peace Treaty helped show the way forward by breaking through the political obstacles placed in our way by a government that sought to mystify the peace process, distort the motivations of the "other side," obfuscate their own intentions, demonize those pushing for peace, and repress dissent while escalating the killing. Massive bombing attacks and search-and-destroy missions against small villages that returning U.S. soldiers compared to the My Lai massacres (where more than 500 unarmed civilians were slaughtered in South Vietnam by the U.S. army) were routine practice.

The social impact of the war, here and in Vietnam, continues to resonate. More than 50,000 U.S. soldiers deserted during the war, and more than 60,000 resisted the draft by going to jail or fleeing to Canada and other countries. The U.S. government's own National Vietnam Veterans Readjustment Study (NVVRS) estimates that 30 percent of Vietnam veterans—or 800,000 men and women—have struggled with often debilitating Post Traumatic Stress Disorder (PTSD), as a result of their combat experience. At home, the social fabric frayed to the breaking point, resulting in the greatest social and political polarization since the U.S. Civil War—a divide that continues to resonate today.

The People's Peace Treaty sought to simplify the basic conditions and understandings that were needed to move away from continued war and toward peace, independence and self-determination for Vietnam, Laos, and Cambodia—so that the people of those devastated lands could finally be free to rebuild their shattered societies and forge their own futures. It also sought to provide a basis for re-unification at home and a chance to start healing the wounds of war.

At a time when political leaders in the United States and South Vietnam were insisting that only further war could bring peace, the People's Peace Treaty, drafted and signed by Vietnamese and U.S. students, demonstrated that peace was already possible.

A PACIFIST IN THE WAR ZONE

DOUG HOSTETTER

Editors' Note: Part Two of this chapter previously appeared in the Spring 2014 issue of Fellowship *magazine. Reprinted with permission.*

Part One: Journey to the South

I was drafted as soon as I graduated from college in 1966, but coming from a Mennonite family, my draft board granted my request to be classified as a conscientious objector. As most young men my age were being sent against their will to Việt Nam, I decided, as a conscientious objector, to do my alternative service in Việt Nam working for the Mennonite Central Committee. I did community development and literacy work in a small provincial village in Central Việt Nam at the height of the war in the late 1960s. When I returned from Việt Nam, I enrolled in graduate school in Sociology at the New School for Social Research (now the New School) in New York City. One of the organizers of the U.S. National Student Association (NSA) People's Peace Treaty delegation thought it would be very useful to include a student who was fluent in Vietnamese. I was recruited to the delegation just as NSA learned that the U.S. State Department was no longer supporting this trip, and South Việt Nam was already denying visas to all U.S. students. My name was intentionally left off of the list of participants in the NSA delegation to South and North Việt Nam, which was distributed to the press. I had been asked to travel separately a few days before the rest of the delegation planned to leave for South Việt Nam. At the Tân Sơn Nhứt Airport in Sài Gòn I applied for a visa as a sociologist (which I was) on vacation (which I was), and was granted a visa with no difficulties.

On my very first night in Sài Gòn, I had an unsolicited conversation with a cab driver that helped me to realize that the Vietnamese people had a much deeper understanding of their own history, and the futility of the American war in Việt Nam. I copied the eloquent comments of the nameless cab driver in my journal that evening:

> You Americans can do what you want, eventually you will have to withdraw just like the French after eighty years. You can bomb all you want, we will just fill up the holes and continue as before. Bring in all the troops you want. Eventually, you will have to leave and still we will be here. You can bring all the money you want, and you can buy some Vietnamese, but you can't buy their hearts. You might be able to buy a Vietnamese woman for a night. You might be able to get her to marry you, but when you get on that plane, to go back to the States, she won't be on the plane with you. Whatever you do, eventually you are going to have to leave, and we will still be here. In the end, Việt Nam is ours.

I soon made contact with and was warmly welcomed by Huỳnh Tấn Mẫm, President of the Sài Gòn Student Union, and his colleagues at the Sài Gòn Student Union. The Sài Gòn Student Union had initiated the idea of a peace treaty drafted by students, which would outline the path for ending the war. They had previously shared their concept and strategy of a people's peace treaty with antiwar activists visiting Sài Gòn, who in turn had shared it with North Vietnamese, and Provisional Revolutionary Government (the government in the areas of South Việt Nam not controlled by the U.S. or the Sài Gòn government) diplomats in Paris. I met with Huỳnh Tấn Mẫm and four or five of the leaders of the Sài Gòn Student Union in their small Student Union office, far from campus, in one of the poorer sections of town. They were eager to work with us and with the North Vietnamese students to develop the People's Peace Treaty. I also took the opportunity to visit Mennonite friends in Sài Gòn, and return to Tam Kỳ in Central Việt Nam, to visit with Vietnamese friends and colleagues from the years I had worked there with the Mennonite Central Committee. While in Tam Kỳ, I spent an evening in the small fishing village of Kỳ Phú, a few kilometers east of Tam Kỳ, where a few years earlier I had started a literacy class for children from that village. I knew the village well, as one of my literacy teachers, Bửu, had been born and raised in Kỳ Phú, and he was eager to welcome me back to his hometown. My journal entry that night tells the story:

Doug Hostetter (right) with Huỳnh Tấn Mẫm and the Saigon Student Union.
Photo courtesy of Doug Hostetter.

I'll never forget the evening spent at Kỳ Phú. I rode out on Bửu's Honda, the first evening. There was a soft monsoon rain falling as we rode out through the green paddies. We had to wait at the river's edge for about half an hour for the man from the far side of the river to hear us calling and come over and pick us up. Just standing there in the late afternoon and watching the sunset and the rain fall on the flooded fields was almost a religious experience. That night Bửu had invited a group of friends and relatives to come to his house. We all sat around the kerosene lamp and talked about what they thought should be in the peace treaty and how they thought we could make peace in Việt Nam. There were people who had husbands, sons, brothers, or fathers in the north, fighting in the mountains, or fighting in the mountains in the south for the PRG (Provisional Revolutionary Government), and likely some had relatives in the ARVN (Army of the Republic of Việt Nam). But everyone was together in the desire for the Americans to leave and that there be peace in Việt Nam. They were really excited about my going to the north and the idea of a people's peace treaty. They all liked the idea of a people's peace treaty. They all sent greetings to the people of the north.

I returned to Sài Gòn to attend two major student rallies on the theme of Vietnamese national unity and peace. After the rallies, Huỳnh Tấn Mẫm stated that we needed to hold a press conference before I left to announce that the Sài Gòn Student Union had signed the People's Peace Treaty, which called for the complete withdrawal of all U.S. military forces from Việt Nam and for the Vietnamese to resolve their problems internally. I remember responding, "Sure, we could hold a press conference tomorrow, but if we do, when I pass through security at the Sài Gòn Airport the next day for my way to Bangkok, I will be arrested, and never heard from again."

Mẫm responded, "But I know the Sài Gòn and U.S. governments, if we don't hold a press conference with you here, they will deny that you were even in South Việt Nam, or that the Sài Gòn Student Union was involved in drafting and signing this treaty. Government backed media in both of our countries will say that the People's Peace Treaty was completely drafted by the North Vietnamese and signed only in Hà Nội." After some discussion we agreed to hold a "secret press conference" before I left, inviting only a few trusted Vietnamese and international journalists who would all agree to hold the story until I had cleared security and left Việt Nam. I don't recall who the trusted Vietnamese journalists were, but I do remember that the most trusted international journalist in Sài Gòn at the time was Dan Southerland from the *Christian Science Monitor*.

The "secret press conference" went well, and I had no trouble getting through customs at Tân Sơn Nhứt Airport the next day. I had an overnight in Bangkok and left the next morning for Vientiane, Laos, where I was scheduled to catch the once-a-week Aeroflot flight from Moscow that stopped in Vientiane on its way to Hanoi. The one thing that we had not considered was that the CIA would pick up Dan Southerland's report from the wire even before it was printed. When I landed in Vientiane I dropped my luggage at my hotel and headed for the bar in the Hotel Constellation, the press watering hole in Vientiane. There, I had planned to meet a friend from Dispatch News Service. He saw me as soon as I entered and rushed over to tell me that the Lao Police had been at the bar an hour earlier and had approached an American with a mustache something like mine, asking if he was Doug Hostetter. And when that man said no, they asked to see his passport. "They are looking for you, so if you are carrying anything that you would not like them to find, I would recommend that you dispose of it right away." I quickly returned to the hotel, retrieved the signed copy of the People's Peace Treaty, and brought it to my journalist friend. I asked him to keep it secure and give it to me the following morning before my flight to Hà Nội. He agreed, and we had a quick beer and a catch up before I returned to my hotel.

I was back in my room no more than 15 minutes before there was a loud knock on the door and four Lao police were asking to enter and search my luggage for "illegal documents." It was a bit awkward for everyone. I had removed only the People's Peace Treaty, but I still had the peace proposals put forward by the delegations of the various governments (U.S., the North Vietnamese, and the Liberation movement in South Việt Nam) at the official negotiations in Paris. I also possessed an analysis of the Paris negotiations, articles about Việt Nam, and background materials for the trip. My materials were all in English and Vietnamese, and the four Laotian Police spoke only Lao, broken English and no Vietnamese. They had the further disadvantage of not knowing exactly what they were looking for. They explained that we would need to wait for English and Vietnamese translators to help them go over the materials in my briefcase, but they could lock the materials in their safe, and we could all go out to dinner while we awaited the translators. It was a sumptuous dinner in Vientiane's best restaurant. When we returned to the locked safe with my briefcase, I noticed that the materials in the briefcase were not in the order in which we had left them. Among the suspicious documents that they selected to take for further inspection were: the North Vietnamese Peace Proposal, the Provisional Revolutionary Government (the liberation movement in South Việt Nam) Peace Proposal, but not the U.S. Peace Proposal (even the Laotian police knew that the U.S. Government Peace Proposal was not worth further study!), military postcards that I had bought in the PX (commissary) in Sài Gòn, and my copy of Eldridge Cleaver's *Soul on Ice*. After a complete search of my room and luggage—which included taking apart my ballpoint pen to look for a secret message inside—the police lieutenant colonel who was in charge of the investigation stood up and announced proudly in broken English, "We search just like they do in the United States. I was trained in Fort Knox!"

The next day, my journalist friend met me at the airport to return the signed copy of the People's Peace Treaty, as we had agreed earlier. Then in North Việt Nam, the other 14 members of the People's Peace Treaty delegation warmly welcomed me. The group had divided in Washington, D.C. with part of the delegation traveling directly to Hà Nội, while the rest of the delegation was to travel first to South Việt Nam, and then rejoin their colleagues in Hà Nội a week later. The delegation members who had flown to South Việt Nam arrived a few days after me, but were refused entry at the

Sài Gòn Airport, and placed on the next flight to Bangkok. From Bangkok they had then flown to Vientiane and North Việt Nam, arriving in Hanoi a week before I did. We were warmly welcomed by the "Viet–My," the Vietnamese-American Friendship Organization which had been welcoming U.S. peace movement activists in Hà Nội since the mid 1960s, and the Việt Nam National Student Union (North Vietnamese Student Union). The northern students were very excited to see that the Sài Gòn Student Union signed the draft Treaty, and they asked many questions about the Sài Gòn Student Union, and about the peace movement in the Vietnamese cities in the South.

Again from my journal written at the time:

One of the North Vietnamese student leaders asked me about the leaders of the Sài Gòn Student Union. "Did they ask you to help them in any way?" I responded, "They asked for no direct help but asked for support and keeping them informed of what was happening in the American movement." A second question: "Did the South Vietnamese request any other help?" I responded again, "No, they did not." A third question: "Were there special requests of the North Vietnamese students from the students in the South?" I replied: "No, they were interested in building up communication and knowing what was happening in the North. They made no specific requests." They asked for remarks on the struggle of the student movement in the South. I reported that the student movement in the South was not communist. It was nationalist, patriotic, and struggling for independence from the Americans and from the Sài Gòn Thiệu/Kỳ (S. VN President Nguyễn Văn Thiệu and VP Nguyễn Cao Kỳ) government. Question Four, "Can the student movement in the South be co-opted or bribed?" My response: "I do feel as though some of the students had been bought off or bribed already, [but] the group that remained, I think, is firm and solid." Final Question: "How do you feel about the peace treaty that was given by the South?" Answer: "I think the treaty is very good and have no problems with it."

In retrospect it is very clear to me—as it was at the time—that the students from North Việt Nam were trying to make sure that they were dealing with authentic patriotic students from South Việt Nam, not students who had been "bought" by U.S. government or intelligence agencies. From their perspective, joining in the treaty with students from Sài Gòn carried grave risks. If the Sài Gòn Student Union was benefitting financially from their contact with the NSA, their motivations would be suspect, the whole effort would be compromised and the treaty would be meaningless. Before they could move forward in earnest, the North Vietnamese students had to ascertain as best they could that the South Vietnamese students were authentic patriots, truly committed to the terms of the treaty. At that time, students in North Việt Nam had no contact with the non-communist student movement in South Việt Nam. As far as I know, I was the only person who could verify the authenticity and patriotism of the Sài Gòn Student Union. But once they were convinced that the response from the South was real, the North Vietnamese students laid all their cards on the table.

Mai Hiển, the student from Hà Nội responsible for Foreign Relations in the Student Union, said:

> Although the political view of South Việt Nam and the North are different, there is a mutual desire for peace, independence, liberation, and reunification. This is the desire of all Vietnamese. Our life and situation is different, but what we need most is independence, and our war struggle for independence has been going on for a thousand years. We have always struggled against the aggressors—outsiders—and for independence. We will suffer all. All solutions must be viewed from the point of view of independence. This is true of all Việt Nam. The students in the South have made two requests, immediate withdrawal of U.S. troops, a new government in the South. We agree that this is what is needed to bring independence. We place our hope in this treaty. We want you to bring this opinion to the United States. We feel that most common Americans also feel the same way. We will thank you for presenting this to the United States. Your trip will encourage us in this struggle. If Nixon continues aggression in the South, we will continue our struggle.

John Doherty, a representative of the NSA, replied, "We will do our best to inform our people of what we have seen and felt. "

By then it was abundantly clear to me that it was time for U.S. troops to leave Việt Nam and for the Vietnamese to take over securing their own destiny. I had heard that same message from the cab driver in Sài Gòn in the South, and from the fishermen and women of Kỳ Phú in Central Việt Nam. Now, that concept of an independent destiny for Việt Nam had been codified into a treaty signed by students in the South as well as students from the North. All that remained for us as Americans to do was to return home to convince our government that America's time in Việt Nam was over. The Vietnamese were now ready and eager to determine their own future—without our help.

Part Two: The Path of Return Continues the Journey

When I learned that Việt Nam had invited a group of U.S. antiwar activists to come to Hanoi in January 2013 to commemorate the 40th anniversary of the signing of the Paris Peace Accords that ended U.S. direct involvement in the Vietnam War, I realized that it was time for me to return to Việt Nam.

I had first gone to Việt Nam back in 1966, soon after graduating from Eastern Mennonite College in Harrisonburg, Virginia. I had received conscientious objector status from the military, and then volunteered to do my Alternative Service in Viet Nam, at the height of the Vietnam War, working for the Mennonite Central Committee (MCC) in Việt Nam with Vietnam Christian Service (VNCS). VNCS was a joint program in Việt Nam of the Mennonite Central Committee, Church World Service, and Lutheran World Relief, but was directed by MCC. As a Mennonite, I understood that I had no enemies, but I was called to use only the "weapons" of love and truth in the struggle to build a just and peaceful world.

Our Mennonite vision of the world clashed sharply with that of the U.S. government. The U.S. military had designated the North Vietnamese and the guerillas active in South Việt Nam as the enemy. But those guerillas were the same Vietnamese peasants who had fought the French during the colonial era when they were known as the Việt Minh. During the U.S. War, they were called the National Liberation Front (NLF), or Americans sometimes called them the Vietnamese Communists (VC). Having seen the enemy, the U.S. government had deployed a vast array of weapons and troops against them. When I arrived in Sài Gòn in 1966, there were hundreds of thousands of U.S. military personnel already deployed on the air, land, and sea of Việt Nam.

I was the first VNCS volunteer sent to Tam Kỳ, a village in Quảng Tín (currently Quảng Nam) Province in Central Việt Nam, about 100 miles south of the Demilitarized Zone.[1] Two years before I arrived, the U.S. military had lost control of most of the province. With the exception of Tam Kỳ and two other small towns near the coast along Route 1, the NLF controlled the entire province. The U.S. military strategy at the time was to drive the civilian population out of the areas controlled by the NLF and into the towns controlled by the U.S. military and the Sài Gòn government. When I arrived in late 1966, Tam Kỳ was teeming with refugees.

I was surprised to learn that the primary interest of most of the refugee families was for their children to be able to go to school. After the NLF took over the rural areas of Quảng Tín Province two years earlier, the U.S.

military responded by destroying the infrastructure: the clinics, market places, and schools. It was obvious to me that I was ill-equipped to teach Vietnamese children. If I were going to organize classes for these refugee children, I would need to find local Vietnamese to be the teachers. I had started teaching English in several of the high schools in Tam Kỳ while developing my Vietnamese language skills. I was able to use contacts in the high schools to find students who would be willing to work as volunteer teachers for classes of refugee children. We started at first on weekends and summer vacation, and later expanded to year-round classes. By the end of my three years in Tam Kỳ, we had 90 high-school students teaching more than 3,000 refugee children how to read and write in villages all across Quảng Tín province.

Tam Kỳ was in the middle of the I Corps Tactical Zone, the much fought-over northernmost military section of South Việt Nam. When I first came to Tam Kỳ, a CIA briefer explained, "You can go a kilometer east or a kilometer west of Tam Kỳ. Beyond that you are in VC territory. We control Route 1 north and south of Tam Kỳ during the day, but at dusk, that also reverts to VC control." The U.S. government officials and military officers in Tam Kỳ all lived in heavily guarded military compounds, with guard towers, encircling high walls topped with barbed concertina wire and protected by land mines.

I rented a small bungalow in the center of village, just across the street from a high school where I taught. When I first moved in, my landlady told me, "The National Liberation Front often overruns Tam Kỳ. I have only a four-foot wall around the house, but if you get yourself a few rolls of concertina, a sturdy steel gate, and a 50-caliber machine gun for the front yard, you should be able to hold off the NLF until the Marines can come and rescue you!" I explained to her that Mennonites as people of peace do not use weapons or even set up defenses for ourselves. "We try to live at peace with all peoples and trust in God," I said. I did put up a sign with a peace dove, a cross and the name of our organization in Vietnamese so people would know who I was and where I lived. But I never put a gate in that four-foot wall, and everyone knew that I didn't have a weapon.

During my three years in Tam Kỳ, the NLF took over the village about a dozen times. Usually it would be for only an hour or so in the middle of a moonless night after a brief exchange of fire with the local Army of the Republic of Việt Nam (ARVN) soldiers of the Sài Gòn government. During the Tết Offensive in 1968, however, the NLF, with the help of North Vietnamese soldiers, took over and stayed in Tam Kỳ for more than a week. It was always terrifying during a takeover. There would be a firefight in the street and you could clearly hear the ARVN soldiers firing their U.S. manufactured M-16 rifles and the NLF guerillas firing their Russian-made AK-47 rifles. In our houses everyone would crawl into a bomb shelter if they had one, and, if not, they would get on the floor and stay as low as possible. After some time there were usually fewer shots from M-16s, and more from the AK-47s, and finally the M-16s would disappear completely and we knew that the NLF was in control of the streets of Tam Kỳ. The NLF would always then attack the heavily defended armed compounds at the edge of town where U.S. government-related officials stayed: the U.S. Agency for International Development, the Military Advisory Command–Việt Nam headquarters, and the "U.S. Embassy" compound where three or four CIA agents lived.

The VNCS staff were the only Americans in Tam Kỳ who were not in a military compound, but our house was never attacked despite the fact that we lived in the easily accessible center of the village.

Often, fear drives violence. In combat, soldiers often kill out of fear of being killed. When a peacemaker renounces weapons, and even the ability to defend oneself, it can diminish the fear that propels violence. Yet volunteers in Việt Nam knew that commitment to nonviolence was never a guarantee of safety. Three pacifists lost their lives during the Vietnam War: Daniel Gerber, a Mennonite, was abducted in Ban Mê Thuột, Việt Nam, 1962, and never heard from again; Ted Studebaker, from the Church of the Brethren, was killed in Di Linh, 1971; and Rick Thompson, a Quaker, died in a plane crash in Quảng Ngãi, 1973. In the end we knew that our survival depended on common sense, careful planning, and God's grace.

I did feel very vulnerable in Việt Nam. I realized that despite my good intentions, I looked very "American" to most Vietnamese, and I was in the middle of a combat zone in the middle of a U.S.-initiated, ill-fated war against the people of Việt Nam. I was very thankful to have survived during my time in Tam Kỳ, and quite frankly, by the end of my three-year assignment, I felt guilty that I had survived a war that had taken so many friends.

Four years ago, one of the high school students who had been a teacher in my literacy program in Tam Kỳ emigrated to the United States. When he came to New York, he filled me in on what happened in Tam Kỳ when the war finally ended in 1975, six years after I had returned to the United States. I learned of many friends who died, and others who survived, during that long and difficult war. But perhaps the most surprising bit of information was that my best friend in Tam Kỳ had had a few secrets.

Lê Đình Sung, a local artist, had been my closest friend and advisor while I was in Tam Kỳ. His father, who lived 25 miles north of Tam Kỳ had been killed while I was there by South Korean troops working with the

Lê Đình Sung and Doug Hostetter, 1968.
Photo courtesy of Doug Hostetter.

U.S. military. Sung had introduced me to his younger sister and his mother who had fled the violence that had killed his father. When the war ended, neighbors discovered that Lê Đình Sung had an older brother who was a high-level official in the NLF during the war. At war's end, the brother had returned was appointed as a top administrator in the new government in Tam Kỳ, and Lê Đình Sung had been named the new Education Chief.[2]

Through a Vietnamese acquaintance, I was able to get in touch with Lê Đình Sung's family by email. I was saddened to learn from his daughter that my artist friend had died two years earlier, but she and her brothers remembered me well, and invited me to visit them when I was able.

• • • • •

I had been invited to be part of the U.S. antiwar delegation to Việt Nam in January 2013 to commemorate the 40th anniversary of the signing of the Paris Peace Accords, because of the work that I had done with the People's Peace Treaty and Medical Aid for Indochina, after returning from my alternative service work in South Việt Nam. It was a great honor to return to

Hà Nội with other antiwar activists, nine of us having participated in peace delegations to Hà Nội during the war years. We were treated royally by the Vietnamese government. We were honored international guests at a grand celebration of the 40th Anniversary of the Paris Peace Agreement held at the National Convention Center, and a few of us were hosted by Vietnamese President Trương Tấn Sang in the Presidential Palace and invited to participate with him in planting a "peace and friendship tree" in the Hà Nội Peace Park.

In addition to celebratory visits with mayors and provincial officials in many cities, we were also invited to visit the organizations and institutions that are dealing with the legacy of the Vietnam War: Agent Orange and unexploded ordnance. The U.S. military used over 15 million tons of bombs and explosive ordnance during the Vietnam War. Approximately 10 percent of the bombs and other explosives used during the war, failed to detonate on impact, leaving thousands of tons of unexploded munitions scattered throughout the country, on the surface and underground. These deadly explosives have killed or injured more than 100,000 civilians in Việt Nam since the war ended in 1975.

The other significant legacy issue of the Vietnam War is Agent Orange/dioxin. Agent Orange is the name of one of the herbicides and defoliants used by the U.S. military in Việt Nam. Monsanto Corporation and Dow Chemical manufactured Agent Orange for the U.S. Department of Defense. Agent Orange contains dioxin, one of the most toxic compounds known to science. Between 1961 and 1971 the U.S. military sprayed nearly 20 million gallons of chemical herbicides and defoliants in South Việt Nam and the eastern portions of Laos and Cambodia. The government of Việt Nam estimates that 400,000 people were killed or maimed and 500,000 children have been born with birth defects due to dioxin in Agent Orange.

· · · · ·

While in Việt Nam, I also took time to return to Tam Kỳ, where I had worked more than 40 years earlier, and meet two of the children of my artist friend, Lê Đình Sung. It was a deeply moving experience to meet with Phương Loan, who was about 11 when I had left Việt Nam, and her older brother Việt, who had been 15 when I left. They both remembered me well as I had spent much time in their home with their father. They are both grown now, and have children of their own who are the age that they were when I left Tam Kỳ. Phương Loan is a classical musician who plays the 32-string zither with the Đặng Xuân traditional music group in Hội An, the ancestral home of the family and her brother, Việt, is now a building contractor in Tam Kỳ.

Lê Thị Phương Loan and Doug Hostetter, 2013.
Photo courtesy of Doug Hostetter.

We had a wonderful reunion after 43 years of separation, reminiscing about the war years, and the time that I had spent with them as children during the height of the war. When I asked about their father's older brother, I was astounded to learn that Lê Đình Sung actually had four brothers, all of whom fought with the NLF but stayed in touch with their family living on the other side. Two of the brothers were killed in the war. The oldest brother, who had returned to become a senior official in Tam Kỳ when the war ended, was now too old and infirmed to receive guests, but I did meet the other surviving brother who had spent the war years on the other side as a cultural worker with the NLF.

My path of return to Việt Nam was a continuation of my journey to learn peace-building. As I relished renewal of relationships from 45 years ago, I began to comprehend that a critical element of peace-building is authentic friendship—relationships that transcend the national, racial, ethnic, religious, and political boundaries that usually separate humanity. I came to realized that Lê Đình Sung and his family were true friends of a young American who had come trying to live at peace in the midst of a bitter and deadly war. I also realized that on the many occasions when the NLF took over Tam Kỳ while I was there, I had God's protection. But God had some assistance from Lê Đình Sung and his brothers—on the other side.

JOURNEYS TO REMEMBER

JAY CRAVEN

Days before National Guard troops shot 13 students at Ohio's Kent State University and state troopers shot 14 African-American students at Jackson State in Mississippi, I was elected student body president of Boston University's College of Liberal Arts. The students at Kent State and Jackson State had been protesting the Nixon administration's expansion of the Vietnam War into Cambodia. After the shootings, I joined student activists across the United States to stage an unprecedented national student strike that closed universities for the final weeks of the school year. It was 1970 and I was 19 years old.

Later that summer I attended the 10-day National Student Association (NSA) Congress that was held at Macalester College in St. Paul, Minnesota. That's where I first learned about the idea for a People's Peace Treaty. When I arrived on the Macalester campus, the feel of the recent spring turbulence was still reverberating.

The NSA had a fairly long history, having been founded in 1947 after an international student gathering gave birth to the International Union of Students (IUS). NSA leaders sought to animate free speech on campuses and advance their own opposition to McCarthyism, South African apartheid, and college segregation. Starting in the early 1950s, the NSA's international program, where American student leaders met and developed contacts with foreign counterparts, was infiltrated by the CIA. Some NSA officers worked closely with their Agency handlers, gathering intelligence at gatherings in Europe and elsewhere. Other NSA officers were kept in the dark. One such staffer, Michael Wood, learned of the CIA connection and told what he knew to the popular leftist monthly, *Ramparts Magazine*, which blew the cover on NSA's CIA connection in February 1967.

Seeking to restore its legitimacy, reformers set out to create a "new NSA." They increased student services to include travel, insurance, and record-purchasing programs and brought a range of speakers to their annual themed conferences. The 1970 event was focused on "The Crisis of the 70s" and it identified a separate issue for treatment on each of its 10 days. Some days fared better than others. Students turned out in large numbers to hear antiwar speakers. But numbers dwindled on "Poverty Crisis Day," when the meals served conformed to U.S. Department of Agriculture allotments to people on welfare.

Inside the Congress, I heard many speakers and special guests, among them former U.S. Attorney General Ramsey Clark, education activist John Holt, revisionist historian Gabriel Kolko, and civil rights pioneer Fanny Lou Hamer, who gave an electrifying speech about the connections between the Mississippi Freedom Rides and the Vietnam peace movement. She emphasized Martin Luther King's legacy of non-violent civil disobedience and urged our next generation of students to use its power as a lever for change. I knew about Hamer's leadership of the Mississippi freedom delegation at the 1964 Democratic National Convention—I never expected to see her at the Minnesota gathering.

Ex-Kennedy speechwriter Richard Goodwin gave a major talk Tuesday evening. Speaking for the students present, Goodwin warned President Nixon that, "Our freedoms are not yours to decide or dispose of and this is not your country but ours!" Nobody who was listening seemed to disagree.

Outgoing NSA President Charlie Palmer picked up on Goodwin's theme of taking things into our own hands as he talked about his contact with South Vietnamese student leaders who had proposed the idea of a people-to-people student peace treaty. Members of the Chicago 8, Rennie Davis, Dave Dellinger, and John Froines arrived in a flurry and spoke further about the Vietnam War.

Using the May 1970 student strike as a backdrop, Davis spoke persuasively, in a rising cadence, as he proposed a massive civil disobedience action aimed at policy makers in Washington. "We will take the energy and conviction we showed last spring," Davis said, "and we will carry it to a new level focused directly on the seat of power. Because we will bring tens of thousands of students to Washington next May, to mark the anniversary of the Kent State protests and take our movement to the next step, into the streets using a massive display of non-violent civil disobedience to demand an end to the war. Our purpose will be clear. And our slogan will declare, once and for all, that if the government won't stop the war, we will stop the government."

Rennie's tagline was pretty bold—the kind of call to action that could capture the moment and move people to their feet. I figured it could also trigger a new round of grand jury investigations and conspiracy charges. I was immediately intrigued and also a bit scared—by the fresh memory of students gunned down at Kent and Jackson State. What might this look like—this massive effort to shut down the United States government?

Davis needed to light the fuse for his May Day call so he wanted NSA backing. He was used to projecting ambitious actions against the war, since he had been a leader of the potent and influential Students for a Democratic Society (SDS) that spurred seven years of activism on college campuses. But by 1970, SDS had lost steam as it splintered off into the Weather Underground and Progressive Labor Party. May Day represented Davis's most ambitious call that, by necessity, had to mobilize a younger post-SDS student generation.

Formal discussion on the May Day proposal was preceded by an address by that year's Pulitzer Prize–winning journalist Seymour Hersh, who detailed the events of mass murder and rape at My Lai. His speech vividly illustrated the savage brutality of the war. Despite this, not every student leader at the NSA Congress bought into Rennie's call for May Day civil disobedience. Some feared that more students would get hurt. Others calculated that by even voting for the resolution they could get indicted and sent to jail.

I fell in with a group that supported May Day—and we spoke in favor of a formal NSA resolution to endorse Rennie Davis's plan. Debate was fierce and, after several hours of it, the opposition moved to table the discussion for further consideration Friday night.

During the day on Friday, rumors circulated that if the resolution passed, a number of delegates planned to call a press conference where they would suggest that the May Day call for civil disobedience was part of a Communist plot. Some students demanded that delegates vote by name, in the event that conspiracy charges were pressed. Supporters of the proposal became disillusioned after opponents of the May Day resolution cried, "Right on!" after every speech against the bill.

Late Friday night, the vote was finally taken by a roll call of each attending college and university. The vote came to a tie: 140 to 140. A second vote was taken after a five-minute recess. The May Day resolution lost by four votes. Chaos broke out as some delegates hugged each other in joyous celebration. May Day supporters broke out in a mocking chant, "We want Nixon," and on the following day local newspapers and radio stations reported, "NSA delegates support Nixon war policy."

When Saturday night came, everyone purged his or her conscience by passing a modified version of the original May Day proposal. It called for May actions but ruled out civil disobedience specifically aimed at Washington. Even with the compromise, some student leaders moved to pull their colleges out of the NSA.

The Calm after the Storm

I returned to Boston from the NSA Congress and took off with my cool girlfriend for two weeks of camping in the dunes on Martha's Vineyard. A month into the school year, I traveled to Washington to attend another student leaders' congress, this one sponsored by the Association of Student Governments (ASG). I wasn't sure what this event would look like, except that the ASG paid our expenses and put us up at the posh Sheraton Park Hotel. Once I arrived, I got the picture. The conference mostly featured Nixon administration officials speaking to 1,000 student leaders gathered in a huge Sheraton ballroom. The ASG was the Nixon administration's orchestrated alternative to the NSA.

Whereas Lyndon Johnson had pretty much been prevented from traveling to college campuses because of his war policies, the Nixon team decided to bring student leaders to them. Speakers included Attorney General John Mitchell and Secretary of Defense Melvin Laird. Vice President Spiro Agnew did not speak, but he did walk around the lobby and hallways with Secret Service agents flanking him, sawed-off shotguns at the ready.

I came to Washington primed to pose a question to Defense Secretary Laird. The night before I flew from Boston to Washington, I ran into muckraking journalist I.F. Stone at a Cambridge party thrown by his daughter. I told Stone where I was going and his eyes lit up. "I've got a question you can ask Laird," he said. "You see, while Nixon talked about reducing levels of violence on college campuses, after Kent State, the Pentagon got busy shipping trainloads of M-16 assault weapons to National Guard detachments across the country."

"Ask Laird to talk about that," Stone said, eyes sparkling.

I waited for the Q & A session after Laird's long-winded speech to student leaders in the huge Sheraton ballroom. A number of hands went up and a couple of students stood to ask questions about the draft and careers at the Pentagon. I kept my hand raised but Laird ignored me. Then an aide approached Nixon's defense secretary on the dais, to signal that it was time for Laird to leave. Not wanting to miss my chance, I stood and shouted my question, citing I.F. Stone's statistics of hundreds of thousands of M-16s, shipped to National Guard troops just weeks after Kent shootings.

Laird appeared startled, then angry that my question got through. He darted from the stage, but an Associated Press reporter snagged him at the stairs and asked him to comment. He confirmed the allocation of the military assault weapons to National Guard troops. Then the reporter came over to me. A small article appeared on the AP wires and it appeared in newspapers across the country the following day. Mission accomplished.

Back at my complimentary hotel room, I received a phone call indicating that a Mr. Donald Rumsfeld wanted to meet me in the lobby café. I said I'd stop by and took the elevator downstairs. Rumsfeld wasted no time and made me an offer. "It appears by your question at the Laird speech that you've done your research," he said. The words sounded like a compliment but the way Rumsfeld said them didn't.

"We like to be in touch with college students who are up on the issues," he said. "Maybe you'd like to work with us; come to Washington to meet from time to time, to tell us what you think and what you're seeing on campus."

I replied that I wasn't interested—that I knew the stories of government infiltration and co-optation at the National Student Association. I said that I thought people at the Pentagon already knew what students thought and that I had better things to do than making plane trips to Washington to drink soda pop and discuss student politics with Nixon's men. Mr. Rumsfeld nodded and we parted company.

A week after returning from the ASG conference, I received a call from Michael Lerner asking if I could meet up with him for a conversation. Lerner was an assistant professor of Philosophy at the University of Washington and he was one of the activists indicted in the Seattle 7 conspiracy trial. Lerner and others led a militant February 1970 Seattle antiwar demonstration in the wake of guilty verdicts against the Chicago 8 defendants, for disruptions at the 1968 Democratic Party nominating convention. The angry Seattle protests resulted in confrontations with police and 76 arrests. Lerner and six others were indicted as demonstration leaders. He and fellow defendant Chip Marshall had also appeared at the NSA summer event, to support Rennie and publicize their own trial.

I met Lerner on a fabulous fall afternoon at a below-sidewalk café, Le Patisserie Francaise, two blocks from my second floor walk-up in Harvard Square. Lerner got right to the point. "Rennie Davis asked me to meet with you to see if you'd be interested in joining the NSA peace treaty delegation."

I was immediately excited by the prospect. I remembered the peace treaty discussions and the contentious fight over Davis's May Day proposal at the NSA summer congress. I had even shared a blow-by-blow account of the summer events with my history professor, Howard Zinn, and he loved the whole idea of a student peace treaty and civil disobedience planned for

Washington. Zinn had been active in the movements for civil rights and against the war, and he had written a book *Disobedience and Democracy* (1968) that made the case for direct action.

"Sure," I told Michael. "I'd love to be involved in the NSA trip."

"There will be 15 student body presidents and college newspaper editors," said Lerner. "The NSA is developing a list. But Rennie wants to make sure that some of the delegates will work for May Day—and he remembered that you helped move the May Day resolution at Macalaster College."

"I support May Day," I said, liking the idea of an effective action against the war but not really knowing what might actually happen. "And I think we can get Boston students to go to D.C."

"If you go to Vietnam," said Lerner, "you'll need to do more than bring some students from Boston. Rennie will want you on the road to colleges across the country, speaking on campuses and to activist groups. He wants you to help lead this."

Suddenly a lot was in play. "We'd go to Vietnam?" I said. "I thought the NSA meetings were planned for Geneva."

"That's changed," said Lerner. "The U.S. student delegation will go to Vietnam. Some will go to Saigon and the rest will go to Hanoi. Are you willing to go to Vietnam?"

I thought fast. I was a political science major and had become active against the war. But I still thought I'd study law and maybe run for political office, inspired by Bobby Kennedy and Gene McCarthy. I wondered how a trip to Vietnam might affect all this.

"I'd go to Vietnam," I said. "To Saigon."

"I'll tell Rennie," Lerner said.

Rennie and Dave

A few days later, I got a call. "Hi, Jay? This is Rennie." I'd not really met or talked to Rennie Davis but here he was addressing me as his good friend, in an easy, confident, laid back tone of voice. "I'm here in Washington and I was wondering if you could come down and meet a couple of us. We'd like to get to know you a bit and talk about this trip we're pulling together for Vietnam."

I didn't know who Rennie meant by "a couple of us," but I had been to Washington several times and I liked the city. I said I'd make the trip. A few days later I used my Eastern Airlines youth fare card to get a $16 ticket to Washington. My roommate Bobby Noble joined me, interested to see how all of this would play out.

We caught a taxi at National Airport and sped along Washington's broad avenues and narrow tree-lined streets to Rennie's apartment on Lanier Place. As I walked up the three flights of stairs, I felt nervous and still in the dark about who I'd be meeting. I knocked on the door. A slender long-haired guy opened it. "I'm Terry," he said. "Come in."

Terry introduced himself as Terry Becker, founding member of the *Quicksilver Times*, Washington's underground newspaper. Only two others were there—Rennie, with his wide smile and thick glasses, and an older man I also recognized, who introduced himself simply as "Dave." I knew who he was—Dave Dellinger, the lone older activist associated with the Chicago 8. Howard Zinn later told me that Dave drove an ambulance during the Spanish Civil War and spent several years in a federal prison for his resistance to the draft during World War II.

Dave smoked a Cuban cigar and sipped from a snifter of cognac. He briefly stood to shake hands and asked me to take a seat. My roommate Bobby shifted in his straight-backed chair beside me, suddenly unsure of why he had come along. Dave did most of the talking.

"What's your history of opposition to the war?" Dave asked.

"Have you ever participated in civil disobedience?"

"If you are selected to go to Vietnam, will you be willing to devote the next six months of your life traveling and helping to organize May Day?"

"Can you take time off from college to do all of this?"

I don't think I'd ever been so scared. I'd heard Dave speak to thousands of students at two antiwar rallies. And I saw him in the shadows of the NSA Congress in Macalester. Now, here he was, smoking a contraband Cuban cigar—looking every inch the movement's Godfather, two years before the Brando movie even came out. He wanted a commitment.

I shared my history of activism, of how I'd campaigned for Gene McCarthy and Bobby Kennedy but set out for BU thinking I'd join ROTC to help pay for college. Then, two weeks into my freshman year, I joined hundreds of BU, Harvard, and Radcliffe students to provide sanctuary in BU's Marsh Chapel for AWOL solider Ray Kroll, who refused his orders to ship out for Vietnam. I described the round-the-clock teach-ins where I, like many others, spoke from the podium about my opposition to the war. I explained how, after a week in the chapel sanctuary, dozens of police and FBI agents charged in to seize Ray Kroll and take him back to the stockades for court martial.

I described meeting Howard Zinn and taking classes with him—and talked about joining 50 students to protest the presence of a General Electric board of directors meeting on BU's campus. We rallied to object to GE's role as a war contractor and charged the university with complicity for hosting the board meeting at a time when they knew students mostly opposed the war. Then, as we were leaving the vigil, 80 Boston police attacked us, clubbing students and arresting some. I explained how I got caught up in the melee and joined the immediate call for a student strike to protest police brutality and the university's role in calling the cops.

I talked about my participation in the 1969 mobilizations in Boston and then Washington, and said that I'd shot a film about them.

"We're thinking about making a film," said Rennie, in his first real comment of the evening. "We've got some filmmakers from Newsreel and one of them, Robert Kramer, made a feature film called *Ice* that's about a political uprising in the United States, triggered by an American invasion of Mexico. It's gotten a lot of play in France." I said I went to see a lot of films in Cambridge and Boston but hadn't seen *Ice*.

Dave repeated his earlier question about civil disobedience. He wanted to know more about what I had done. I talked about my admiration for Martin Luther King and described how I'd regularly sneaked boys off campus at the boarding school I attended. I felt silly comparing this to Martin Luther King at Selma. Then I remembered the "hot dog cooperative" I'd started at BU and wondered if that might count.

"During the BU sanctuary for Ray Kroll," I said, " an older man named Ted Moynihan with a kind of hippie spirit showed up on the student union plaza to sell hot dogs. He'd grill them over big steel bowls and iron grates he'd set up on top of shopping carts. When he wasn't grilling the wieners he'd play a harmonium and recite poetry. People liked him and bought his hot dogs—until the university had him arrested for competing with the University's food service."

"The cops took Ted to jail and he got off by agreeing to stop selling. So, I contacted him and said I'd pay fifty bucks for his shopping carts and grates. I re-opened the concession as a hot dog cooperative, charging "members" 25 cents for a Xeroxed black-and-white strip of paper that I called their membership card. For your quarter you were entitled to three charcoal-broiled all-beef frankfurters and an assortment of condiments that included chopped onions, relish, mustard, ketchup, and wheat germ."

Dave looked amused, so I continued.

"My argument was: 'This isn't a business; we're not making money; we're just feeding ourselves.' Within a week, I was selling 2,500 hot dogs a day with lines of students and faculty snaked around the block. The university didn't know what to do. But then they cited me for trespassing—and I got hauled off to the police station. Professor Zinn immediately showed up at the station to offer his support, and he got me a lawyer to negotiate my way out of it. As a result of all this, I was elected president of my freshman class at BU."

I looked at Dave, then Rennie and Terry, not sure of their reactions. This was hardly an anti-imperialist movement that I'd started, selling hot dogs in Boston. "Does this count as civil disobedience?" I asked.

Dave smiled and took another sip of his cognac. "I think it might," he said. "Did anyone help you with this or did you cook all the hot dogs yourself?"

"There was this exotic art student and photographer. Her name was Sonia. She helped me some and made a flag with a white on black symbol she designed. It showed a clenched fist holding a hot dog."

Dave looked at Rennie, who smiled. "I'd say you're in. We'd like you to join the NSA delegation and go to Vietnam. And we want to work with you for May Day. Are you sure you're ready to make this commitment?"

I wish Rennie hadn't asked if I was "ready" because it reminded me of what I already knew—that there would be risk involved here, especially if I ended up being sent to North Vietnam, which would pretty much ruin any chances I had for going into politics. Or maybe, I thought, it would be another way of going into politics, which didn't involve kissing babies or getting gunned down like Bobby Kennedy and Congolese Prime Minister Patrice Lumumba or the Yves Montand character, Greek politician Grigoris Lambrakis, in Costa-Gavras's film, Z (1969). But then I thought about Martin Luther King and Malcolm X and Emmett Till, Medgar Evers, Cheney, Goodman, and Schwerner—and others. I decided to stop thinking for a while.

After what felt like a pretty intense hour of questioning and dialogue, I was excited, not sure what was happening, and scared stiff. Then Rennie lit into a graphic discussion of the current situation in Vietnam, including a blow-by-blow account of Nixon's escalation of the air war. He was even more worked up than Seymour Hersh had been at the NSA Congress, talking about My Lai. "We believe," said Rennie, "that the war has reached a point where Vietnam's actual survival could be in jeopardy."

After Rennie's half-hour litany of horrors in Vietnam, Dave finally said something funny. Thank God.

I said I would do everything Dave and Rennie asked me to do that night—and I did. That night changed my life and prompted me to face the fears that I felt at the prospect of this kind of bold activism. The evening in Washington marked the beginning of an extraordinary journey that would not have been possible without that turn of events.

"Saigon Gets Iffy. How About Hanoi?"

I traveled to Hanoi in December 1970, even though I initially hoped I'd go to Saigon. But the United States and Saigon governments wouldn't allow us into South Vietnam, so I went north with the rest of the People's Peace Treaty delegation (only one student, Doug Hostetter, managed to slip into Saigon). I'd gotten over my concerns about wrecking my future career prospects through

Theirrie Cook, Jay Craven, and Becca Wilson in Hanoi, 1970.
Photo courtesy of Becca Wilson.

a trip to Hanoi. At this point I was thinking about May Day and civil disobedience pretty much day in and day out. I'd read Noam Chomsky's dense analysis, "At War With Asia" and Susan Sontag's "Trip to Hanoi," so the impending expedition north seemed urgent and fit into what I saw as an emerging narrative.

I still wanted to go to Saigon, but I saw it just wasn't in the cards. I liked that it was South Vietnamese student leaders who initiated this people-to-people diplomacy to highlight their call for an end to the U.S. military occupation of their country. I knew that even though the United States was allegedly supporting the South Vietnamese in the name of "democracy," the Saigon students' actions to make a peace treaty would trigger worse repercussions than any of the rest of us would suffer. Jail, torture, or even death at the hands of the repressive Thieu–Ky regime were real possibilities. Knowing that these South Vietnamese students wanted to take this risky and heroic stand, favoring peace and reconciliation among all Vietnamese parties to the war, seemed like the right idea at the right time.

We were banned from Saigon by the U.S. State Department and South Vietnamese government because we also planned to meet students from North Vietnam and the National Liberation Front of South Vietnam. Once we were blocked from the South, I wondered whether our travel to North Vietnam might also be stopped. Trips to North Vietnam were officially outlawed; it said so just inside the front cover of my sparkling new passport.

I did some research and discovered that Supreme Court Associate Justice William O. Douglas, playwright Arthur Miller, and civil rights pioneer W. E. B. DuBois had their passports confiscated when they set out to travel to prohibited countries, which then included China, Cuba, North Vietnam, and North Korea. But I also learned that DuBois had successfully challenged the travel ban, winning a 1958 Supreme Court case where the Court declared that "Congress had never given the Department of State any authority" to restrict travel for political reasons. I suddenly felt that I was on more solid ground. We had our visas to Hanoi. I appreciated the irony that I could get into the banned country, North Vietnam, but was blocked from going to visit America's most high-stakes ally, South Vietnam.

I had never traveled outside the United States except for a snowy romantic interlude in Montreal and Mont Tremblant, Quebec, where I fell for a Philadelphia schoolgirl who became my very fun high school sweetheart. Now I was headed to a war zone and was told that our plane from Vientiane, Laos, to Hanoi could be shot at by Laotian Pathet Lao resistance fighters who faced constant American bombardment. Or maybe we would encounter problems with American air fighters—they were constantly in the sky. I knew from my research that there had been ICC (International Control Commission) flights, in particular, that had to take evasive action flying this route.

So I felt a sense of intrigue, mystery, and a little danger as I peered out the window of our Aeroflot propjet to Hanoi. I looked at the rugged mountains and gnarly countryside of Laos and imagined how a person could get swallowed up in these dense forests and tangled mountain passes that constituted the area Americans called the Ho Chi Minh Trail, where thousands of Vietnamese, under constant air attack, guided bicycles laden with supplies headed to the war zone in the south.

It was early morning when the mountainous Laotian countryside yielded to a patchwork of irrigated rice paddies below us. As we floated lower, toward our Hanoi landing strip, I picked up more detail. Narrow dirt banks divided the paddies and peasants in conical straw hats tended rice shoots. I was immediately struck by how tidy and organized everything looked. Every square inch of land appeared to be either cultivated or studded with well-kept huts and outbuildings.

On the Ground: History Comes Alive

We landed safely at the airport outside Hanoi and piled into a small bus for the trip over rough dirt roads that ran next to the paddies and fields where peasants toiled oblivious to us. I hadn't been in a Third World country before—and I was struck by the poetry-in-motion of people's hard work. Guided by a willowy teenaged girl wielding a thin switch, a water buffalo pulled a simple cart stacked with twisted branches used for firewood. Other carts hauled bolts of cotton or bamboo.

A pair of women irrigated a rice paddy by rhythmically swinging small wooden water buckets hanging from a long pole resting on their shoulders. Our guide, an astute former diplomat and music composer, Xuan Oanh (pronounced like "Swan WAN") pointed out bomb craters that pocked the countryside.

"You probably wonder why the U.S. aircraft would bomb a field," he said. "We wondered that, too."

Oanh looked carefully at the members of our group to see who, if any, picked up his irony. Several did. He smiled.

"When we saw them start to bomb our fields, we scratched our heads and said, 'There's no military value in a field.' But, of course, a bombed field can't produce food. The crater draws all the water into it, enticing mosquitos, eroding the soil, and making it impossible to cultivate rice."

Oanh sneaked another curious look at the members of our group. "We needed to do something. And we saw that the craters looked like small ponds, so we decided to breed fish."

Again, Oanh smiled. "The B-52s make the biggest holes. For more fish."

As I got to know him during our trip, I learned that Oanh loved to tweak us with vivid tales of Vietnamese ingenuity, history, and culture. He was fluent in seven languages and had served in a variety of respected government positions, including at the Paris Peace Talks. He spoke of his love of Hemmingway, Steinbeck, and Jean Genet.

Xuan Oanh wrote the national anthem of his country and he translated foreign periodicals and books, including *Star Wars*, Jeffery Archer's *Kane and Abel* (1979), and Jacqueline Susann's *The Love Machine* (1969). When I asked him what American he would most like to meet, he replied, "Babbit," the character from Sinclair Lewis's eponymous 1922 novel that satirized American middle-class culture and was widely credited with helping Lewis win the Nobel Prize for Literature. "And I'd like to drive an Oldsmobile," Oanh added, with a chuckle.

Our other Vietnamese hosts, older men like the very serious Mr. Quat and calm and wistful Mr. Mai, were friendly and they kept us on schedule and on task. Oanh emanated dry wit and keen intellect. He was irresistible. And fun.

Still in our small bus, we traveled across the wide Red River by way of an improvised wooden floating bridge that swayed a bit against the force of the current. Travel at river level across the floating bridge was snail-like, but the reasons for our impeded movement were clearly evident. Looming high above us to the south we could see the twisted steel of the Long Bien Bridge, repeatedly bombed by U.S. jets, then repaired, due to its crucial role in bringing supplies into the city by road and rail, then bombed again.

The bridge had been built in 1899 during the first French occupation—and it was designed by Paris's Eiffel Tower architect, Gustave Eiffel. A less well-constructed bridge would have crumbled under the impact of so many air assaults, but the bridge endures to this day, albeit mostly for pedestrians, mopeds, and slow-moving trains. The Long Bien Bridge stands as an indelible reminder of the American war, evident through still-visible bomb damage.

The bridge also stands as a testament to Vietnam's long history with France, reaching back to the eighteenth century when missionaries set up operations and intervened in local culture and social practice. Wars with France date back to the Napoleon III–ordered attack on Danang in 1858, when Vietnamese pushed back against growing western religious and political influence, and the French Catholic insistence on monogamy that threatened the status of Vietnamese courtesans.

From 1884 until 1954, the French played a continuing role as occupiers and colonizers. Insurrections against French rule started in 1885 and continued, without much success. During World War II, France's Vichy government ceded its influence to Japan which, in March 1945, moved to fully occupy Vietnam.

Vietnamese nationalists and communists, led by Ho Chi Minh, fought the Japanese, who relinquished their hold at the end of the war. Ho Chi Minh used the end of this war to claim independence for Vietnam but intense machinations among the French and Chinese forces loyal to Chiang Kai-shek caused a new round of intense fighting that persisted until May of 1954 when Ho's Viet Minh decisively defeated the French at Dien Bien Phu.

After its war with Vietnam, the French agreed to the terms of the 1954 Geneva Agreements, which promised independence to Laos and Cambodia and promised speedy elections to unify Vietnam. The U.S. disliked the agreement but agreed not to interfere—although U.S. forces began immediately to sabotage the Geneva Agreements, through anti–Viet Minh propaganda and psychological warfare, cross-border and covert operations in the North, and support for the militantly anti-communist Diem regime being established in the South to oppose and prevent the promised elections from taking place.

France, to its credit, became a friend to Vietnam after its Indochina war, working behind the scenes to host the Paris Peace Talks between Vietnam and the United States. And, according to close Kennedy advisor Arthur Schlesinger, Jr., writing in his Robert Kennedy biography, *Robert Kennedy and His Times* (1963), French President Charles DeGaulle acted as part of a multinational diplomatic effort to advance a political settlement prior to the war's escalation.

An excellent and detailed account of this effort can be found in Working Paper #45, produced by the Woodrow Wilson International Center for Scholars. It shows how DeGaulle's effort complimented a series of extensive discussions, already in motion, that started as early as Kennedy's 1961 Vienna meeting with Soviet Premier Nikita Khrushchev and continued through back-channel negotiations involving Indian, Russian, French, Italian, and Polish diplomats, along with the U.S. Ambassador to India, John Kenneth Galbraith. Kennedy's hope, according to the Wilson Center report, was to implement a negotiated settlement for a South Vietnamese coalition government similar to his Laos Agreement of 1962.

According to the Wilson Center working paper, progress was being made and, by the summer and fall of 1963, initial agreements were taking shape for economic, postal, and cultural exchanges between North and South Vietnam that included trades of South Vietnamese rice and beer for North Vietnamese coal. The assassination of crisis-plagued South Vietnamese President Ngo Dinh Diem, in November of 1963, and the JFK assassination, three weeks later, appeared to put an end to the most promising of these diplomatic moves that, according to Arthur Schlesinger, Jr., and others, represented a missed opportunity to prevent the looming U.S. escalation.

At the time of the Diem assassination, a hot and politically divisive debate was roiling the White House, especially about the impending coup against Diem that resulted in his death on November 2, 1963, one day after the coup began. The coup occurred with support from U.S. Ambassador Henry Cabot Lodge, the CIA, and, apparently, with approval from JFK's roving ambassador Averill Harriman. Indeed, the anti-Diem conspirators were handed $42,000 in American cash by CIA operative Lucien Conein on the morning of the coup.

Now-released White House tapes and documents from the days preceding the coup show Attorney General Robert Kennedy, on October 29th, arguing hard against it and Kennedy insisting, hopefully, that if he wished to call it off, he could. But pro-coup advisors dominated the discussion and discouraged Kennedy's wishful thinking, saying instead that "the train was already moving" against Diem and the U.S. surely wanted to be on board.

But I digress.

Into the City

Driving into Hanoi from the airport, every new sight felt intoxicating. Low-slung faded-yellow buildings showed the influence of the country's years under French colonial rule. Thousands of people rode bicycles along wide boulevards, even in the damp chill of December. I felt a refreshing change from the congested traffic of Boston and New York. During a visit many years later, however, I had to dodge the dense swarm and thick blue-gray exhaust of non-stop motorbikes moving like a school of fish along every city street in Hanoi and Ho Chi Minh City (Saigon). I wished for those earlier days.

Our time in Hanoi was spent in meetings, museum visits, sightseeing, and symbolic activities like a day spent helping students at the agricultural university haul rocks to lay the foundation of a research building they were building under the cover of a forest, in order to shield the planned building from American air attacks.

We stayed at the ancient Hoa Binh (Peace) Hotel, a French stucco structure with large tile floored rooms and four-posted beds where elegantly draped mosquito netting created the feel of nineteenth century colonialism. One night, we were roused from our sleep by the sound of air raid sirens. An American F-11 fighter jet attacked a site on the edge of the city. We weren't in any danger, but the Vietnamese clearly took no aircraft incursion for granted.

Floating to Haiphong

One day, as we crossed the Haiphong River on our way to the monkey-infested mountain islands of Ha Long Bay, Xuan Oanh brought out a silver pipe and a leather pouch. He took of pinch of *thuoc lao*, a potent herb that contains nine times the nicotine as regular tobacco. Oanh lit the pipe and passed it around as members of our group inhaled and coughed, eyes watering. None of us had dared to bring marijuana on this long trip, so Oanh figured his thuoc lao would create a cultural bridge to the young Americans. I think each of us tried it—and we got a slight buzz—the kind you get from an unfiltered Camel, if you're not used to smoking.

Drifting across the Haiphong River, we passed the pipe while Oanh slipped out his clunky Russian-made cassette machine and pushed the play button. Bob Dylan's "Subterranean Homesick Blues" filled the air as we crossed on the ferry. By playing Dylan's song, Oanh showed his interest in all things American, including Dylan's politically themed music that talks about activists getting their phones tapped. I wondered whether he knew that Dylan's line, "you don't need a weatherman to know which way the wind blows," inspired the name taken by the Weather Underground that targeted U.S. buildings they felt represented the war.

Oanh smoked some *thuoc lao* and turned to speak two or three of us. "The music of Bob Dylan takes me back to my life as a child in the rural countryside," he said. "It reminds me of the first sounds of Vietnamese music that floated through my window."

I had a tape player, too, a small SONY rig that a guy from CBS News had brought to JFK airport just before we left New York. CBS wanted me to record interviews and shoot film with the high-end Super 8 camera they also supplied. I shot footage of babies who had been born to mothers in affected areas of South Vietnam, sprayed with Agent Orange. But when I showed it around after returning, no one was interested in broadcasting it.

I also grabbed beauty shots of Ha Long Bay that I gave to the Newsreel filmmakers, Robert Kramer, Ellen Ray, John Douglas, and Peter Biskind. These were the filmmakers that Rennie had told me about in Washington. They were making a 16mm antiwar documentary called *Time is Running Out* that I and other organizers played at hundreds of college and community venues, to drum up support for the planned May Day actions. I got to hang out with them, the first "real" filmmakers I'd met, and they used my footage for a lyrical interlude amidst intense shots of the war and the May Day call to action that followed on-screen displays of our Peace Treaty provisions.

I didn't use the CBS tape recorder for much, but it came in handy in moments like this when, after Oanh's Dylan song rolled out, I switched on a tape I'd brought of the Jefferson Airplane's "Volunteers." We continued ferrying across the wide river to the strains of Grace Slick and Marty Balin.

I'd used "Volunteers" as part of the musical score for my first film, a Super 8 epic in which I mixed footage of thousands of people marching in the fall 1969 Boston and Washington moratoriums with shots of five-year-old boys playing football with their dads, and Bergman and Antonioni–inspired images set against a steel-blue cornfield in late fall and the industrial wasteland of Dupont's 1400-acre Chambers Works Plant, where, over the years, workers manufactured smokeless gunpowder, explosives, and radiological materials used for the atomic bomb. I slipped "Volunteers" in to score the final section of my film, shot during the huge Washington march, as militant protestors broke away, late in the day, to charge police at the Justice Department.

Now, floating across the Haiphong River, I was playing the song on my tape recorder. I thought my song would complement Oanh's Dylan tune, but

I suddenly felt self-conscious, like the American college kid I was, trying to link Dylan's poetic meditation with the Jefferson Airplane's self-admiring 1960s call to action. I thought about the two different worlds and sensibilities represented in the music. "Subterranean Homesick Blues" felt universal while being specific to an American time and place. "Volunteers" felt a bit generic, a pop culture anthem about a "revolution" that was fun to imagine but never came even close to being realized.

Vietnam had embarked on an actual revolution under Ho Chi Minh and, decades later, the monumental effort and tragic cost of it persists. Their struggle seemed endless and, no doubt, tiring. Ho, himself, didn't live long enough to see the end of war. Perhaps the U.S. military failed in its goal to establish lasting political control over Vietnam but it certainly exacted (and paid) a terrible price. I felt this as we crossed the Haiphong River and I've re-visited and elaborated on this feeling many times since then—including during my two subsequent trips to Vietnam.

On both of these trips I got this sinking feeling of how much is demanded of those sent to the front lines to fight any war. Of course, this applied to the Americans as well as the Vietnamese on all sides of the conflict. In his book *The Sorrow of War*, peddled on Hanoi streets alongside *The Ugly American*, Vietnamese writer Boa Dinh expressed this phenomenon well, saying, "Each of us carried in his heart a separate war. But we also carried the immense sorrow of war."

I and most of the people I knew who opposed the war had friends who fought in Vietnam, but our experiences were a world apart from U.S. soldiers in Vietnam, let alone the Vietnamese. I and many others didn't want to fight in Vietnam because we felt that the U.S. military occupation was illegal and unjust. What had these people done to us?

Indeed, Ho Chi Minh's forces advanced U.S. interests during World War II, working closely and extensively with Americans in the Office of Strategic Services (OSS) to fight the Japanese, gather intelligence, and help retrieve downed American pilots. Ho wrote a telegram to President Harry Truman, on February 28, 1946, begging for the Americans to oppose the return of French colonialists to Vietnam and honor what Ho felt were Roosevelt's promises of the Atlantic and San Francisco Charters, to support Vietnamese independence after the war. But Roosevelt was dead—and the Cold War was getting started. Truman backed the French effort to re-take Vietnam.

Vietnamese Voices from the War

I've made two trips back to Vietnam, but not until 2003 and 2013. In 2003, I met with a leading poet, Le Minh Khue, a deeply reflective woman with a permanent sadness etched in her thoughtful and handsome face. She talked to me about her experience working for some 10 years along the Ho Chi Minh Trail, starting as a teenager, detonating unexploded bombs and filling in the gaping craters left by American bombs, so that supplies could move to the front.

Khue remembered her time during the war as one when she gave everything to the epic fight for national salvation. By 2003, she felt bypassed by the vision of revolution that had inspired her selfless commitment for all those years—with so many pressures, sacrifices, and intense pain. But how could the nation's leaders have delivered on the high expectations that people inevitably needed to fuel the sustained fight—especially given such heavy losses? Added to this weight of history is the simple truth that the nation's leaders advanced because of their ability to mobilize and fight a war. They were not necessarily positioned to lead a visionary peace.

Vietnam scholar Dana Sachs writes about Khue's dilemma in her fine essay, "Small Tragedies and Distant Stars—Le Minh Khue's Language of Lost Ideals." In Khue's short story "The Distant Stars," writes Sachs:

> Three teenage North Vietnamese girls detonate unexploded bombs and...theirs is an uncertain existence. Explosions bury them in rubble. Bombs drop dangerously close to their hideout. But the young women approach their duty with good humor and a love that is "selfless, passionate, and carefree, only found in the hearts of soldiers." War, as seen through the eyes of these young women, becomes the noble struggle of people who fervently believe in its goals.[1]

Sachs points out that in Khue's early story, one of her teenaged characters expresses her feelings during the time of the war: "I loved everyone, with a passionate love, a love beyond words, that only someone who had stood on that hill in those moments, as I did, could understand fully."[2]

In 1990, when she was 41, Khue published her story, "A Small Tragedy." According to Sachs:

> Once again, Khue presents an image of three girls at war, but this image is not a positive one. An important political official orders thousands of young people to fill bomb craters along a riverbank during the middle of the day. Although precautions might have been taken, none were, and when American AD6s fly over and drop bombs on the young people, many are killed. As one witness describes the scene, "I've never seen so many people die like that. They were empty-handed, puny, running like ants on the naked riverbank. I tried to dig into one depression to pull out three young girls but they died in such a tight embrace I couldn't even untangle them."[3]

"Although this description sounds horrifying," Sachs writes, "its language is devoid of emotion. The closest the witness comes to articulating his horror is that same statement 'I've never seen so many people die like that,' which seems almost clinically detached in comparison with the passionate engagement of the earlier story. The effect of this understatement, however, is to increase the story's emotive power. By refusing to describe an emotional reaction, the author forces us to imagine the scene for ourselves."

Sachs points out how Khue's earlier apparent optimism seems to have faded after the war, replaced with a helpless sense "of three girls martyred for no reason whatsoever. In thematic terms, war, which once seemed like a valiant fight for freedom and self-determination, becomes an enterprise in which the powerful rule over the lives—and the deaths—of the powerless."

Khue was not alone in her reconsideration of the war. Other Vietnamese writers, starting in the 1980s, also began to examine the war from a critical perspective—not to suggest that the fight to expel the Americans was wrong—but that war did not lead to the dream of social and economic transformation that sustained so many people during the long war that cost some three million lives.

During my 2013 trip, I met Danh, a former NLF guerilla, over coffee at a café in Hanoi. He was a poet and had been a documentary filmmaker, too, in his life after the war. But Danh had been in bad health since his days of fighting and was now dying from his exposure to Agent Orange. He, too, felt bypassed by time and history and the reality of what could be accomplished in his country after the end of the long and costly war. Before he died, he said, he had one request: "I feel that the American soldier who came here feels sorry for what he did," he said. "I am sure of it. It's all I need to know before I die. That the American solider understands and that he is sorry."

I am sure that Khue and Danh also carry an experience of what we call Post Traumatic Stress Disorder (PTSD) from the war—although Vietnamese to whom I spoke know nothing of PTSD, its diagnosis, or possible treatment. Their experience adds to my sense of the destructiveness of war. It hardly matters what side you're on when it comes to the lingering impact—the life sentence that is conferred on those who must fight.

Back to the River

Maybe it was the *thuoc lao* we'd smoked, but, drifting that day across the Haiphong River, I suddenly felt what should have been obvious from the start: how different our worlds were. Our antiwar experience in America charged and defined our time and culture. It gave us meaning, as we worked to stay the hands of Johnson, Nixon, and Kissinger, who were forced to react.

They escalated the war with impunity but they also had to yield, at certain key junctures, to the pressures activists mounted through opposition and resistance.

We were able to suspend business as usual—and to increase the price the government would have to pay to continue the war. Draftees resisted; students marched; Gold Star Mothers joined hands to oppose further killing; radical Catholic clergy including the Berrigan brothers, Philip and Daniel, broke into draft boards and poured blood on draft files; Yippies mocked the establishment through political theater; and soldiers returned home to testify to war atrocities and throw their hard-earned medals onto the Capitol steps.[4] More than anyone, Vietnam veterans exposed the war's brutality and futility to anyone who was listening. And, through a combination of actions, Johnson was pressured to withdraw from politics and Nixon was forced to stop the war.

For the Vietnamese, the war was simply a matter of life and death, of the right to self-determination, and of national salvation. Whole generations had to postpone their lives in order to resist foreign occupation. And when they prevailed against the Japanese, the French took over. And when they decisively defeated the French, the Americans took over. And, even after that, the Chinese got into the act, in 1979, when Chinese forces invaded Vietnam in retaliation for Vietnamese actions in their conflict with Pol Pot's Kampuchea (Cambodia).

War and thwarted revolution were simply a part of everyday life. As we saw during our trip, people everywhere were intimately aware of the country's long history of resistance to invaders. As we drove from Haiphong to Ha Long Bay, Oanh described how the Vietnamese had repelled subsequent waves of Japanese and French invaders during the nineteenth and twentieth centuries. And he took particular relish recounting their 30 years of resistance to Mongol invaders from 1258 to 1288 A.D. In one battle, the Mongols landed to find Vietnamese forces mounted on battle elephants. The Mongols were ordered to fire their arrows at the elephants' feet, causing the animals to panic and retreat.

During the climactic final battle with Kublai Khan, in 1287 and 1288, the Mongols attacked with a huge force, "the last invader who brought 500,000 troops to occupy Vietnam," Oanh explained. "The Mongols landed in 500 vessels which the Vietnamese destroyed by outflanking them in an intense and bloody sea battle."

"We had to build the Mongols a new navy to send them home," Oanh said, wanting to make clear that the Vietnamese would never accept defeat and that they would be gracious to their former enemy, even in victory.

Final Days in Vietnam

During our relaxing trip to Ha Long Bay, we cruised among a cluster of small mountain islands in an open boat. We got off at one of the islands and climbed toward caves where we saw birds and monkeys. Back at our hotel along the beach, our lunch on the open-air patio was interrupted when our waitress, dressed in the traditional Vietnamese flowing tunic, the *ao dai*, approached our table calmly. She carried a World War I–vintage single-shot rifle and a pith helmet.

"Please," she said. "Take these and stand under the stairs. You will be safe there." I walked toward the stairway carrying the rifle and helmet, and I heard the Vietnamese waitress's voice. "Sir," she called. I turned and she made a gesture, as if putting the helmet on her head. "Put it on," she said. "We can't be sure where the bombs will fall."

We followed instructions and, within a few minutes, we returned to our tables to finish eating our prawns, rice, and spring rolls that we seasoned with pungent Vietnamese *nuoc mam* sauce. Our waitress returned to collect my hat and rifle. "We believe the jets were attacking the coal mines nearby—a favorite target," she said.

During our final days in Vietnam, we met with students to conclude our discussions about the Peace Treaty—and we were introduced to a group of doctors and women, with their young children, who had been exposed to Agent Orange during U.S. defoliation missions in South Vietnam. The children showed a range of severe deformities that the doctors said resulted from their exposure to the chemical defoliant. They presented charts that showed chromosome damage and the women gave statistics indicating how long they had lived in sprayed villages, how much contaminated water they drank, and how their children immediately showed signs of distress. Some babies, they said, died.

I used the Super 8 movie camera that had been provided by CBS news to film the women and doctors. I didn't film much else—the Vietnamese resisted color film and photographs, which they said could be used by the U.S. military to target bombing raids. Black-and-white still photos were considered generally OK. But I did film the children and their mothers, along with footage at Ha Long Bay. Back in New York, I gave my footage to filmmakers making the May Day documentary.

When I arrived back home in Cambridge, I also sought out the eminent Harvard geneticist and molecular biologist Matthew Meselson, to show him what I brought back and ask him to speak out against the use of Agent Orange. Meselson had been a resident at the U.S. Arms Control and Disarmament Agency where his particular interest focused on biological and chemical weapons, which he believed had little military value but could cause long-term damage. He was influential and, in 1984, he received a MacArthur "genius" award.

Meselson agreed to meet with me and I told him what I saw and heard from the Vietnamese doctors. He dismissed what I had as being insubstantial and inconclusive "propaganda." I was discouraged when I left his office but, years later, I discovered that he had been instrumental in arguing for the termination of herbicide spraying in Vietnam. In fact, he had been to South Vietnam just before we traveled, to begin a pilot study of the ecological and health effects of the military use of herbicides.

I realized later that what I perceived at the time as Dr. Meselsen's indifference was probably just due to the fact that he was working with far more detail and substance. It seemed to me that he disbelieved and belittled the Vietnamese doctors we met and the information I brought for him to review. I now believe he played a substantial role in the ultimate termination of the U.S. military's application of Agent Orange, which was used from 1961 to 1972 and resulted in the spraying of 19 million gallons of herbicide over 4.5 million acres of land.

The impact, of course, has deeply affected hundreds of thousands of Vietnamese and probably just as many U.S. soldiers and their families. Battles still rage, in and out of court, where Vietnam veterans argue that the effects of their exposure includes everything from rashes and muscular dysfunction, to birth defects, cancers, leukemia, and a range of psychological disorders.

In 1979, a class action suit, on behalf of 2.4 million veterans who were exposed to Agent Orange, resulted in a settlement with chemical companies amounting to $240 million. The Vietnamese say that half a million children were born with birth defects related to Agent Orange and that two million more people are suffering from herbicide-related cancers and other maladies. In 2004, a group of Vietnamese citizens filed a class-action lawsuit against 30 chemical companies, many of them the same ones that settled with the veterans. In March 2005, a federal judge in Brooklyn dismissed the suit; another U.S. court rejected the final appeal in 2008.[5]

As we drove toward the airport on our final morning in Vietnam, I took a last look at the legions of people on bicycles, going to work or school or wherever they needed to be. I thought about how the streets were teeming with people, unlike the time Vietnamese had to be evacuated from the cities during Lyndon Johnson's air war, Operation Rolling Thunder, which ran from March 2, 1965, to November 2, 1968.

During this extended period, people throughout North Vietnam experienced heavy bombardment—as the U.S. mounted its most extensive and challenging aerial assault of the Cold War. All told, the U.S. Air Force, Navy, and Marines flew more than 300,000 bombing sorties against North Vietnam. Official goals of the campaign were to boost the sagging morale of the Saigon government and convince North Vietnam to abandon its support for the NLF insurgency against the South Vietnamese government. Targets included bridges, railroads, roads, factories, and air defenses, although there were also plenty of bombed hospitals, schools, and homes.

I remember seeing the "personal fall-out shelters" on every street, six-foot deep holes, lined in concrete and with a concrete lid. During the heaviest times of bombing, people would take shelter in these individual hiding places. The argument: more people will survive if they are each in their own protective space. If they assemble in mass shelters, a bomb could kill 300 people. This way, it might only kill five or six.

Heading Out

As we arrived at the airport to head to Paris and then New York, Xuan Oanh asked me what I'd do when I returned to Boston. I said I'd work to circulate our People's Peace Treaty and organize people to go to Washington in May to commit civil disobedience.

"Will you go to jail?" he said.

"Probably," I replied.

"I have been in jail," he said. "During the fight against the French. It's bad but you'll be OK."

I smiled and extended my hand. Oanh handed me a folder of papers. In it was the diary of an American soldier who had been killed in battle in South Vietnam. I had been told, before I left New York, that such a diary might exist in Hanoi, since it was believed that NLF soldiers fighting in the South had found it on the battlefield. I asked about the diary when I first arrived but got no answer and no promise that anyone would look into it.

Surprised and grateful, I thanked Oanh and said I would make sure that the diary found its way into the hands of the soldier's family. Oanh nodded and hugged me. Then he said his good byes to others in our delegation and dipped his head, in a sign of farewell. He winked and flashed a two-fingered peace sign.

"Keep the faith," he said.

Our other Vietnamese hosts also offered parting words. Then we took off from the airport. As we lofted into the sky, the now-familiar rice paddies grew smaller and clouds fluffed the sky, leaving us in our private thoughts about all we'd experienced during our two weeks in Vietnam.

A Soldier's Story

As we gained altitude, I turned to the soldier's dairy in the folder Oanh had handed me. The young man, Buddy Anello, was three years older than I was. His mom had died when he was four years old and his father, apparently feeling overwhelmed, sent him and his three brothers to the Milton Hershey school for orphans. I'd grown up around Philadelphia, too, and when I was 12 years old, I landed a job on the grounds crew of a Pennsylvania boarding school. I found a mentor there, Tom, a Milton Hershey grad who had also served in Vietnam but got discharged from the Army because of his tendency to get into fistfights. I was the only kid on the crew and Tom liked me well enough to show me the ropes and tell me a few hair-raising stories about life at Milton Hershey.

As we cruised high above the Ho Chi Minh Trail and on to Vientiane, Laos, I read Buddy Anello's diary intently—taking in every word and placing it into the context of the immersive experience I'd been through with Vietnamese from the north, south, liberated zones, and, now—an American soldier drafted into the Army and sent to Vietnam. Here are some excerpts, published with permission of Buddy Anello's dad, in the May 15, 1972 issue of *Win Magazine*, and used here with permission.

> **October 16, 1967.** It all starts in the San Francisco Bay. Feelings are the color of the ship. Gray. I look at the night and the city lights and remember all the beautiful things I've done there—and I have to turn. I look at the bridge with the many people traveling their happy way, but not knowing the ship below carries a load of deep thought. And the lights play on my mind. So I have to turn. Just three miles away, behind the old smoke stack. You can't see it. But that's where I live. I know it's there, but they don't know I'm here, and I have to turn. I turn to the faces whose thoughts are just like mine and only seem to make the ship grayer. And the stars offer me no help cause now I look at them alone. So I turn for the last time and walk away with my eyes to the ground.

> **October 18.** Tomorrow we pass under the Golden Gate Bridge and everyone will say, "Isn't it beautiful," and I'll say, "Yes, wasn't it." But hopes are always there, for it's not a terrible long time, It's just an eternity.

> **October 23.** Finally arrived. We had to wait for General Westmoreland to give his welcome speech, salutes, and all that flag waving jazz. Meanwhile, my weapon was strangling me and my duffle bag was trying to pull my arm off my shoulder. Then, of all

things, we had a parade. All I could remember from training was "don't bunch up." General talked to the guy next to me, but to have him tell it, it's like he got kissed by the Pope.

October 24. Still waiting for supplies before we move out. I was told I'm supposed to be a tunnel rat. My platoon sergeant likes me (sarcasm).

October 27. Left for another place today. Duc-Pho. It's finally back to C-rations again. It rained all night. A trio of misery: cold, scared, and hungry.

October 28. Why are we here? A question always on my mind...I think and stink a lot more... I think about what I'm going to do after I serve my two-year sentence for being an American citizen and what's Mary, Brother Don, Al, Bill, Papa Joe, Gwynne, Moreen, and the bus driver who left me off in Harlem and said good luck, thinking or doing right now.

October 29. A hell of a night. Definitely. I went out to take a piss and someone whips a grenade my way. One leap and I was back in the bunker. Call me Jack-be-nimble.... Two men killed last night.

October 30. Hot as hell. A perpetual steam bath. My feet are two big mosquito bites at the end of my ankles. I could care less about the war. Just leave me alone and I wouldn't bother you.

October 31. 6 A.M., I get up and I read the obituary column and if I'm not listed, I go eat breakfast.

November 2. The hardest day so far. Close to 80 pounds of shit on my back, raining like hell and we're tramping through the rice paddies. A man got blown up last night by our own artillery. Who can you trust?

November 19. The helicopter couldn't make it in so that meant no cigarettes. The hell with the food.

November 21. Lost respect for a bunch of people today. For no reason, they tore down this hootch, burnt it, tramped down their garden, ripped out their trees and there wasn't even any suspected enemy. I told him I hope someone kicks in his TV tube while he's over here. Like he said: "Just to let them know we're here." Really made me sick but what am I to do? Stand and watch and forget.

November 25. Back to hoofing and humping again. Froze last night. But how do you write it? It's hard to explain the cold to someone who's warm.

December 6. When will it ever end? You can't fight what you can't see. Yet we walk like we're in a shooting gallery. The Major sits at his desk smelling of starch and saying, "There's a lost regiment out there somewhere. Search till you find them. And I ask, "How do we find them?" And he says, "Wait until they shoot at you." Yet we walk, fools that we are, because it will never end.

April 4. It seems that the latest fad is to build up a kill record. Since our platoon got in that battle, we killed 45 V.C. The other platoons are jealous so now they kill any body just to match our record. I've seen—skip it. I'll write about that later. I can say I've seen brutality to the utmost. Grossness, ridiculous and senseless killing. And no conscience whatsoever. I get the usual statement handed down since from the days of the cavalry and the Indians. "The only good gook is a dead gook."

April 6. Now back to what I've seen. The grossness of character. One guy walked up to this old man, asked him for an I.D. card. The old man didn't pull it out fast enough for him. So he blew him away. Then to add to it, he lit a cigarette and put it in the bullet hole in his head. People out in the fields running, so they mowed them down. When they went to check, it was an old woman and children. "They should know better than to run," was their excuse.

Another old man asked for a cigarette. They gave him one, put it in his mouth, then busted his jaw. Rat patrol at night. Things I've heard: Rape at bayonet point. One guy made a woman blow him while she was holding a kid in her hands. Walk into a hootch and just blow them all down. Record it as a kill.

And they wonder why the war is taking so long. Why should anybody want to be V.C. Yes, America—we have power, we have strength. We fight for freedom, the name of peace. The name of God. And to me it's all in vain.

May 2. Walking on point today. Saw a man about 20 years old, so I yelled "La day" (meaning come here). He turned and saw me. His eyes went big—and he tore off running. So I shot him. He ran a hundred yards down some trails with his guts in his hand.... The thought of what I did made me sick. I'm not proud of what I did.

May 8. I feel kind of funny, knowing I'm going on leave and all my buddies are stuck in Dragon Valley. I'd be a fool to turn it down. But I just can't get over the feeling that I'm letting them down. Of course if I was there and some dude cancelled his leave just to help out—I'd be calling him a fool, too. I only hope nothing happens while I'm gone. It's a strong wish-due to circumstances. But I wish!

The End Game

After he wrote this final passage in his diary, Buddy Anello left for five days of R&R in Taipei. When he returned, he told stories of his time away to his G.I. pal, Dave Lang. Lang says he talked about the days and nights Buddy spent in Taipei with a bargirl. He talked about choosing the girl, who was sitting in a corner, away from the line-up of girls being paraded for G.I.'s to select. Lang wrote that Buddy liked that she seemed uncomfortable with the bar scene and that she was only there because her family had problems and needed the money. Buddy told Lang how he had to sign the girl out of the bar, like he would at a library.

Buddy told Lang of things he did in Taipei, like buying bouquets of flowers that he and his bargirl companion would give to unsuspecting people in the city, running up and down the streets. When people were astonished or startled, Buddy would turn around and use his camera to shoot a picture of them, even though his camera had no film.

Buddy told Dave Lang that, after his five days of R&R, he had a hard time getting on the plane to return to Vietnam. Lang wrote that Buddy said, "Toward the end, I really didn't want to go back."

"And he told me it was really hard getting on the plane. And he threw in a comment about an MP when he was getting on the plane saying, 'Hey, trooper, your hair's a little bit too long.' And Buddy said, 'Forget it, pal, I'm not even going to listen to you.'"

"He said he had these three nightmares. He was walking up a hill. It was green elephant grass. He was the only one there. He was walking by himself. And he said he kept walking and walking and walking. And he just couldn't get out of Vietnam. He was trying to walk out of Vietnam and he said he just couldn't do it. He said, 'There I was left. I couldn't get out of Vietnam. For the rest of my life that's where I'll have to stay, just trying to walk.' He said he had this dream three nights in a row. This was his premonition of dying."

Buddy Anello was killed in action on May 31, 1968, during a nighttime firefight. During his time in Vietnam, Buddy was awarded the Purple Heart, the Silver Star, the Military Merit Medal and a marksmanship citation. He was also given, posthumously, a medal from the Army of South Vietnam. When he died in Dragon Valley, Vietnam, Sgt. Bruce Anello was 20 years old.

FROM HANOI TO SANTA BARBARA

BECCA WILSON

Part One: Hanoi, December 1970

Below are excerpts from an essay I wrote in 1971, in diary form, about the December 1970 People's Peace Treaty trip to Vietnam. A longer version of this article was published on February 5, 1971 in El Gaucho, *the University of California at Santa Barbara student newspaper, which I edited during the prior 1969–70 academic year.*

December 2

The city of Hanoi is an ecologist's dream. During our bus ride from the airport to the city, we passed through the "suburbs": trees, vegetable gardens, small huts clustered among banana trees, weeping willows, and stands of bamboo. But even in the city itself, where most of the houses are two and three story French colonial style villas and mansions, there are hundreds of trees, parks everywhere, and several beautiful lakes. The city is vibrant, alive, but serene. People stroll down the streets or ride their bicycles. The only noise is an occasional blaring horn from one of the few cars as it as it warns the crowds to clear the way. [Young male] soldiers walk down the street holding hands; old women in black blouses and pantaloons squat in circles on the street corners, selling fruit and vegetables; children giggling and screaming run along the sidewalks in packs.

In our hotel today (named Hoa Binh, which means peace) we met with our guides and interpreters from the Committee for Solidarity with the American People. We gave Mr. Quat, the chairman of the Committee, a list of what we wanted to see and the people we wanted to meet and he assured us that every request would be granted.

As an introduction to our stay in Vietnam, Quat gave us an account of the history of Vietnam and the present political situation as it is seen by the DRV (Democratic Republic of Vietnam, what we call North Vietnam). Quat began by explaining that the Vietnamese see their history as a long struggle against foreign invasions and for national independence. The Vietnamese people's first victory came in the thirteenth century over invaders from Mongolia. Next in line were the Japanese, then almost a century of French colonialism. This history of struggle against foreign domination, we soon learned, is in the blood of every Vietnamese. It is passed on from generation to generation.

Quat's own personal life is testimony to this national consciousness: now in his late 40s, Quat moved to the North in 1954 when, in accordance with the Geneva Agreements, all forces resisting the French agreed to relocate north of the 17th parallel. National elections, promised in 1956 to reunify the country after the temporary division, were never held, and Quat has not seen his family for 16 years. Just recently he received word that his wife's two brothers, having heard about the renewed bombing of the North, joined the NLF.

December 7

Our bus journey to Linh Binh province today was long…. We had to pass over several makeshift one-lane floating bridges built by villagers to replace steel bridges destroyed during the four-year air war, from 1964 to 1968. The original structures will not be rebuilt, I suppose, until the people are reasonably sure that there will be no more bombing.

On the way to Linh Binh province we passed a large field, torn up and full of rubble. One of our interpreters explained that this was where the village of Phu Ly had once been. During the air war, every hut in the village had been destroyed by bombs, and many of the villagers had been killed. Occasionally, in other villages that we passed in our bus, we saw crumbling remains of homes and buildings along the road; we could see individual manhole-type bomb shelters, bunkers, and trenches. But generally, despite these sights, we found that we had to remind ourselves that we were visiting a nation in a state of war. There really is an uncanny serenity about this land—no cars on the road, and no one is in a hurry.

Young women and soldiers ride along calmly in the rain on their bicycles; children squatting under trees wave and point as we drive by; little boys sitting on a water buffalo watch their elder siblings plow; families wade in the rice paddies, building irrigation canals out of chunks of mud or harvesting the last of the season's rice crop.

The slogan most popular in Linh Binh is "The Song Can Overcome the Bomb," the province chief told us with a giggle. Before inviting us to lunch, the chief, a small, sturdy, intense man of about 55, talked about the effects of the four years of bombing on Linh Binh province. The 500,000 people in the province are mostly peasants, he said, and 10 percent are Catholics. During the "air war of destruction," as the Vietnamese call the four years of U.S. bombing, over 10,000 tons of bombs were dropped on the province. Out of a total of 123 villages, 113 were attacked. Several townships were completely razed.

"They claim the targets are military, but without exception they strike at the people—at hospitals, schools, dikes, markets, churches, pagodas," the province chief calmly declared. "They even attacked our cemeteries. Even the dead cannot have peace." He gave us many concrete examples of churches being bombed, of schools being attacked as classes were going on, of open-air markets being bombed in broad daylight.

Large crowds of people of all ages gathered around us as we surveyed the ruins of three churches that had been bombed in 1968. At the first two churches only the walls were still standing. Bomb craters, some as large as 100 feet in diameter, now filled with water, circled the ruins.

The villagers, who had been told we were Americans, smiled and waved at us; never did we see signs of hostility—only puzzlement and curiosity. We witnessed bitterness only once, when we spoke to a 75-year-old nun who had been one of the few survivors of a bombing raid that demolished several buildings in the church compound including part of a chapel and the entire nuns' dormitory. Twenty-eight people, including five nuns, 11 children, and five pregnant women, were killed; 31 persons, including 15 children, were wounded.

The old nun said that the attack came suddenly at 11:30 one morning; without any warning, the planes came flying low and dropped eight bombs. All she remembers is a thunderous explosion. While she was talking she stared past us, unable to look at us in the eye. A younger nun came in the room while the old nun was talking; she didn't want to talk about the bombing, saying that her mind "wasn't too good" ever since she was injured in the bombing. But she nodded approval when the older nun asked us to go back to the United States and demand that President Nixon send reparations for the damage done to the church. "As Christians, we will do all we can to fight against the United States imperialists, but we want reparations," she said right before we were about to leave.

I'm still haunted by the despair in the nuns' faces. All of us were deeply affected by the experience. We couldn't talk too much for a while. We were tense and sullen on the bus ride back to Hanoi, but our mood was transformed when we got out of the bus to wait while a flat tire was being changed. Our presence immediately drew the attention of bicycle riders, passers-by, villagers, and people working in the nearby fields. Within about 10 minutes, we were surrounded by a crowd of about 100 people. They asked the interpreter who we were, and he said we were American students. Immediately, smiles lit up on all the faces.

Some of the people walked up and warmly shook our hands. Then they sang us a song, the song of unity. We sang them "Where Have All The Flowers Gone?" They watched us with affection and excitement in their eyes, and applauded wildly when we finished singing. A young man in his 20s leaned over on his bicycle and said earnestly, "I hope that when you go back to America, you will tell the American people the reality of Vietnam and the destruction caused by the United States imperialists. I am sure that if the American people know the truth, they will try to end this war." We promised him that we would do as he'd asked.

December 8

They teach their children not to hate American people. The children know the difference between the American people and the American government. Their mothers and fathers and schoolteachers call those who come to bomb and maim "U.S. aggressors" or "U.S. imperialists." Rarely do they call them "the Americans."

It's difficult to understand how and why the Vietnamese are capable of making this distinction. But apparently, it's an integral part of their culture and history. Tri, one of our guide-interpreters, a small, gentle middle-aged man who often laughs wryly and wistfully as he talks, gave me an example today: when the Vietnamese defeated the Mongolian invaders back in the thirteenth century, they built them a whole fleet of ships, loaded them up with food and provisions, and sent the remaining Mongolian soldiers off to their homeland.

We met some children today while we visited Hoa Xa collective farm, about two hours by bus from Hanoi. As we walked by the farm's kindergarten class, the children were singing a song. We stopped to watch them and asked the interpreters to translate the lyrics. It was a song the children sing to help them to learn how to count: the child asks his mother, "Mommy, mommy, how many bombers do you see in the sky—one-two-three-four-five-six-seven-eight-nine-ten?" "Dear child," the mother interrupts, "there are too many bombers for me to count."

December 10

I've often had the feeling, since we've been in Vietnam, that I'm watching a play whose characters are larger than life. Today was different. We weren't just visitors, observers, but we became participants and we shared a day in the life of a group of Vietnamese people.

Our visit to the campus of one of North Vietnam's two agricultural universities started with the kind of meeting we had become accustomed to: the school's director proudly discussing the institution's achievements, the determination of the students to keep studying "under the rain of bombs," their brave attempts to protect from United States aircraft the buildings they had built with their own hands....

As with other meetings we had had with the Vietnamese, we learned a lot, but felt like outsiders. Our lives touched our hosts'—and vice-versa—only in the abstract. But a few minutes after the meeting, it all changed. A group of students took our arms and ushered us into the school's combination cafeteria-meeting room-dining room. We sat among the school's entire student body, who had gathered to sing songs for us and with us. They sang us a few songs, joyous and hopeful in tone. We sang them the only two songs all of us knew ("If Had a Hammer" and "Where Have All the Flowers Gone?"). Then, together we all sang the Vietnamese song of unity. And you could really feel unity in the air.

Most of the students went back to their classes, but a group of them stayed to show us around the campus. Clusters of one-story mud and clay buildings with thatched roofs, surrounded by fields in various stages of cultivation, serve as classrooms, dormitories, and labs. Walking around we also noticed several lakes, but were informed that some of the bodies of water we were seeing were not lakes but bomb craters now filled with rain water. The students walking with me, their arms in mine, said that before the bombings, they used to swim in the lakes; but today they are filled with unexploded bombs and mines, making swimming too dangerous.

At lunch in the school cafeteria, we ate the delicious, fresh, non-chemical food that the students produce themselves, and exchanged talk about our schools and hometowns. During dessert, the students disappeared somewhere. A few minutes later, we saw the whole student body marching in the campus's main quad, single file, carrying banners and red flags with bright gold stars (the flag of the DRV). Some of them—even the women—wore helmets and leafy camouflage and carried rifles.

What we were witnessing was a demonstration organized that day in every school of North Vietnam to protest the shooting, a few days before, of a 12-year-old South Vietnamese high school student by an American G.I. As the students marched in the quad, heads held high, faces serious and intense, they alternated curt chants with raised fists. We were invited to join in. We stood in the rain with them, wearing conical straw hats like theirs. Two students gave passionate speeches about the feelings of solidarity between the people of the North and the South on their common struggle for independence and freedom. Two of us spoke, about our feelings of solidarity with them, about our promise to try to end the war when we got back home. When David Ifshin got up and burned his draft card, the students applauded wildly; some of them had tears in their eyes.

The demonstration was over within a few minutes. Just as serious and disciplined as when they earlier filed into the quad, the students marched away, back to their afternoon's activities. One group's task was to build an outdoor stage for plays and other cultural activities, and the American delegation was invited to help out. Armed with shovels and spades, our job was to cut up the moist, compact earth into cubic chunks, put them into straw baskets hanging from a bamboo pole to be swung over the shoulders and carried to another part of the field. It wasn't easy.

Even those of us who had done manual labor before (including the 6'2" men) found it difficult. Our interpreters, city dwellers who never work in the fields and most of whom are under 5'3", made us look like oafs. We discovered that carrying the baskets full of earth not only takes strength, but also grace and coordination.

The contrast between the big, muscular Americans and the frail, small Vietnamese at work made everyone hysterical with laughter. We were sweaty within 10 minutes and stumbled all over the place while carrying the baskets. After 20 minutes, the Vietnamese became concerned about our health and made us stop working. To refresh us, they had especially brought to the field a large thermos of green tea. They toasted us for our efforts as most of us were still laughing at our own ineptness.

The symbolic nature of sharing manual work moved us all. But, to the Americans, the contrast between us and the Vietnamese—our brute strength, their skillfulness and grace—was also chilling. It seemed a perfect metaphoric vignette of the war: the United States's inability to win, despite tremendous technological and military superiority.

Another vignette later on in the day was a basketball game that some of the men in our delegation played with a group of Vietnamese students. Those of us who watched couldn't help but see the same arrogance and aggressiveness in the American team as we have associated with brash military men. The American team, from the start, was really trying to win, their faces anxious, their movements rough. It began as just an enjoyable game, but soon the competitiveness of the Americans rubbed off on the Vietnamese team, and then both sides were bent on winning. The game ended up a tie, fortunately.

The Vietnamese relied on swift maneuvers and finesse in their movements. Our side took advantage of being taller and stronger to make points. The audience, I'm sure, wasn't especially aware of this particular symbolic aspect of the game. They clapped just as enthusiastically for both teams. But the players—even if unconsciously—were. Both teams sat down together after the game for a drink. And for the first time in Vietnam the atmosphere was unmistakably tense.

Those of us on our delegation who'd been watching the game saw in ourselves—young Americans who like to think we are part of a new culture—the same offensive, aggressive qualities that make Americans disliked all over the world. Perhaps we were exaggerating the game's symbolic value—out of our guilt, our inability to accept love and praise from the people our country is killing and maiming. Perhaps we saw more in the game than was really there. In any case, one reality that all of us have been aware of throughout our experience in Vietnam is that if we young Americans want to build a new world, we've got a lot to recognize and overcome in ourselves. It wouldn't hurt us to be "Vietnamized" a little.

December 12

We had our second meeting with the National Students' Union today. By the time of our first meeting with the students on our fifth day here, we had already discovered that there would be nothing for us to "negotiate" with them before signing the peace treaty. Like the Vietnamese students, it is obvious to us that the United States must immediately and completely withdraw from Vietnam, Laos, and Cambodia. The rest is up to the Vietnamese to solve and decide. But all of us on the delegation strongly support the eight-point peace proposal of the Provisional Revolutionary Government.

The Vietnamese students asked us about plans of the antiwar movement in the United States. We explained that the movement has been silenced, that people are intimidated, frustrated. (The North is being bombed again, but where is the protest?) We also told them about plans to revive the movement around May 1. Major antiwar groups behind the idea of "people-to-people peace" are calling May 1 the "people's deadline to end the war." If by that time Nixon has not announced his intention to withdraw all troops, massive protests will take place nationwide.

Thereafter, besides massive demonstrations and non-violent civil disobedience, an intensive educational campaign will attempt to inform the American people about the Vietnamese proposals for peace and try to awaken them to Nixon's real intentions of continuing the war with a smaller number of troops, but a larger number of bombers. The students were heartened by our words. They thanked us, as they had before, for "waging such a courageous struggle."

Quat, our host from the Solidarity Committee, was also at the meeting. He tried to explain the depth of feeling that the North Vietnamese have for their compatriots fighting in the South: "No words can express our sentiments," he began in a quivering voice, "We feel very strongly, from the bottom of our hearts, when we hear of massacres against our people in the South. It's not just a political feeling, it's deeply personal, because no one in the North does not have some relations in the South."

"Some people think that all students in the North are communists and that those in the South are nationalists—as a matter of fact, not all the students sitting here today are communist. It's not a question of communism or non-communism. The reality is that we all face the calamity of United States aggression."

December 13

Our hosts really don't want us to suffer too much. They are always sure to schedule intense meetings preceded or followed by relaxation or entertainment. Today they prefaced the meeting we had requested with the Committee for Investigation of United States War Crimes with a morning of rowing in one of Hanoi's beautiful lakes. I guess they knew it was going to be a heavy experience for us.

We were given a documented discussion of the kinds of weapons used by the United States in Vietnam: the dozens of different kinds of "anti-personnel" bombs designed to kill and maim people dropped daily for four years in the North, and now dropped daily in unimaginable quantities in the South; the pacification program, which drives people out of their villages with defoliants, explosive and anti-personnel bombs and into "strategic hamlets," or refugee/concentration camps where they can be controlled and isolated from the NLF. The statistics and details are so staggering that they lose their meaning after a while. We were literally numbed at the end of the presentation.

We were then introduced to three people who had been victims of the weapons we had heard about. (This was also at our request: We wanted to be sure to get at least one visceral glimpse at the war's horrors.) First we met Phan Thi Thiem, a woman age 22, wounded on March 28, 1970, by a pellet bomb. Such bombs explode into fragments so tiny that they can't be removed. She and her co-workers in the state store in Nghe An heard the planes coming and ran to a shelter. One bomb fell right on the shelter, wounding her two friends. One died a few minutes later. Another pellet bomb exploded above the shelter, piercing Thiem in the neck, shoulders, arms, and thighs. All of the pellets are still in her body. She took off her blouse to show us the pellets. Just that movement was excruciatingly painful. So is walking outside on a windy day. Or taking a bath.

The second victim we met was Nguyen Duy Luy, age 25. We could hardly look at him. He had been disfigured by a phosphorous bomb on Sept 21, 1969, while he and his team were working on their rural cooperative's land. Today, after six plastic surgery operations, he still looks almost ghoulish. The planes had come and dropped two phosphorous bombs as they passed over his field. Luy's three co-workers died on the spot. All he remembers is seeing a big fire. Then the fire ate him up.

Bui Van Vatt, age 20, was the third victim. He looked normal except for bandaged hands and a five-inch long scar around the front of his neck. He had been wounded (unlike the two others) in the South on March 14, 1970. Artillery was being fired into his village; he ran to a bomb shelter. Two planes flying very low spotted him and released a phosphorous rocket. His hands and chest were hit. He was given first aid at the village, then four people started transporting him to the hospital. On the way there they met 12 American G.I.s, who killed the people transporting Vat with machine guns, then cut off their heads with knives. The G.I.s weren't sure whether Vat was dead or not, so they kicked him a few times; he pretended to be dead. They kicked him again and then slit his throat.

Colonel Ha Van Lau, the chairman of the Committee, stood up after Vat left the room and said, "The G.I.s are directly committing these crimes, but the real criminals are the United States imperialists who make those boys into murderers. We always remember what the mother of Meadlo, one of the G.I.s in the My Lai massacre, said to Nixon, 'I have given you a pure boy. You have given me back a murderer.' We are sure that when the American people know the truth, they will want to stop this war."

We wondered: Hadn't most Americans heard about such atrocities? Are we all a nation of Good Germans?

December 14

This morning was our second session with the War Crimes Committee [Committee for Investigation of United States War Crimes]. And [it was] just as horrifying as the first. Two doctors, specialists in chemical warfare who devote all of their time researching the effects of toxic chemicals used in Vietnam by the United States, spent two hours with charts, formulas, and photographs scientifically proving to us that one of the defoliants used in Vietnam causes genetic abnormalities.

One of the deadliest of the chemicals is a defoliant called 2-4-5-T. It is considered an agent of biocide, in that it has the capacity to kill everything that is living—plants, animals, and human beings. According to testimony by Jackie Verret to the 91st session of Congress, the doctors said more than 40 million pounds of 2-4-5-T were sprayed over a period of nine years over an area of 5 million acres in South Vietnam.

Then we met three young mothers who, while pregnant, had lived in areas where 2-4-5-T is used. They carried their deformed babies in their arms. One of the babies, a year old, has a shrunken head about the size of a grapefruit. Doctors say he "almost has no brain." He can't hold his head up, has no muscle coordination, and cries constantly. The other two children, ages 2 and 3, look bizarre but not deformed. They can't walk, sit, or stand, are mentally retarded and have chromosomal abnormalities.

We had been furiously taking notes; outside we snapped a few pictures. Afterwards, we apologized to the mothers for submitting them to such cold, clinical treatment. One of them answered that she didn't mind, since the information would go back to the American people. "I'll do anything to prevent this from happening to another person."

· · · · ·

During the first week, we had been caught up in a kind of euphoria, being treated with such touching warmth by everyone. The horror of this war hadn't really struck us until yesterday. We began, too, realizing the strength it takes the Vietnamese to be able to sing and laugh amidst this atrocity. We began to understand what self-control it takes for a group of people whose families and friends have just been bombed by the plane they just shot down to be able to take the pilot away to a prison camp without laying a hand on him.

December 15

We're now in Ha Long Bay, staying at a resort hotel deserted most of the time except when foreign visitors are taken here. Nixon's press conference announcing his intention to renew bombing of the North if any more reconnaissance planes are shot down took place only five days ago. But the people, even in this beautiful seaside resort area, are getting ready. On the way here in the streets of Hanoi, we noticed that the people have started cleaning out the man-hole type shelters along the streets; the first few days we were here, they had been full of garbage and dirt. We crossed Haiphong Harbor on a ferry on the last stretch of our trip to Ha Long Bay. Aside from gigantic Russian and Chinese tankers looming over the water, we saw dozens of small, hand-built boats with sails that resemble fans—the same kinds of boats the Vietnamese used to fight against the Mongolians. Today they don't do much good against the United States, but at least they help the people to stay alive; they're fishing boats.

The countryside after we left Haiphong resembles the coast of California. In the woods and forests and fields we drove through along the seaside, we saw groups of people about our age squatting in circles, climbing up hills, marching in line. Oahn, one of the interpreters, said that the people were in military training. We weren't too surprised, until we kept passing throngs and throngs of people—we must have seen 2,000 to 3,000 people, all under 30 and half of them women, in maneuvers. When we got to Ha Long Bay, the province chief informed us that after the call of the Workers' Party for the people to renew their preparedness (in response to Nixon's threats), 10,000 young people in the province had volunteered to join the militias or the army.

Aside from the doctor who accompanies us every time we go to the provinces, this time we have each been given a metal helmet to bring along for protection. Some of our interpreters wear pistols on their hips. We never really thought we'd be needing the helmets, but we were wrong. Just a few minutes after we'd gone up to our rooms for our naps, a 16-year-old girl carrying a machine gun excitedly pointed at our helmets on the chair and gestured for us to go downstairs. We ran down the stairs and were told to stand under a doorway. Trembling, we asked what was going on. It was an air raid—radar had picked up a group of U.S. planes from the 7th fleet coming in our direction.

The machine-gun toting girl and the other young girls who work at the hotel scurried up on the roof, ready to shoot. By this time our group was nearly in a panic. The Vietnamese, of course, were as calm as always. They said we'd have to wait five minutes to find out if we'd have to go to the shelters. It was a hell of a long five minutes. We had already accepted our (at least honorable) deaths by the time the hotel manager ran up to say everything was alright—the planes turned out to be reconnaissance planes, flying 60 kilometers away from here.

Aside from that scare, the stay here has been rest and relaxation all the way. At least for us, it has. But for many people in this province, it's time to prepare for escalation of the war. Even after dinner, as a group of students and workers sang us songs, we could hear military chants in the distance.

December 17

We signed the treaty today. And this morning had our last meeting with the North Vietnam National Union of Students; we were joined by representatives of the Liberation Students' Union of the NLF, who had heard about the treaty while visiting Hanoi and wanted to sign it. Toward the end of the meeting, Nguyen Thi Chau,[1] a member of the central committee of the Liberation Students' Union, got up to sing us a song.

Chau cried tonight, as she signed the treaty with us under the blinding lights of movie cameras. She started to talk about the deep feelings she had for her comrades in the North, but couldn't finish. Tears streamed down her drawn face. When it came time for Hien (the North Vietnamese students' representative) to say a few words, he too, was crying—and too moved to speak.

We were more affected by that silent communication than we ever could have been by the symbolic act of signing a peace treaty with our supposed enemies. Our presence was irrelevant to this passionate expression.

Our country had created the pain we were seeing. Our country had perpetuated the artificial division of Vietnam, the separation of families from families, of friends from friends. Our country had invaded their country, devastated its countryside, killed and maimed its people, created the birth of monstrously deformed children.

We had just signed a piece of paper that, in effect, had disassociated us from what our country had done. But our hearts were not full. Right as we stood there watching the pain and suffering of two Vietnamese people, one from the North, the other from the South, the war went on only a few hundred miles away, on the same soil we were standing on.

Leaving this land and these people would not be truly sad; what would be sad would be for us to come back to the United States without feeling a human duty to fight to stop the horror and pain. It would be sad if we left remembering the pain without the songs, the songs without the pain.

December 19

On our way home, I wasn't really sad to leave. It was like saying goodbye to your parents before going off to war, trying to show you're strong and not afraid, knowing you may never see them again.... I'll never forget what

Premier Pham Van Dong told me yesterday as we said goodbye after a warm encounter. He picked each one of us a rose from his garden, and each of us shook his hand and said goodbye. I told him that I hoped we'd meet again on the day of the common victory of the American and Vietnamese people. Fatherly, serious and tender, he said the struggle would be long and hard but added, "You will need courage, courage, courage. The rest will come by itself."

Part Two: Santa Barbara, 1971

January

Santa Barbara, California, my hometown at the time, took up the People's Peace Treaty more swiftly and enthusiastically than I'd anticipated. In January 1971, soon after I returned from Vietnam, I and a small group of friends launched an organizing campaign around the Treaty. Most of our early success grew out of the outspoken support we received from Tom Tosdal, newly elected student body president of my alma mater, University of California–Santa Barbara (UCSB). Tom had not been active in the loose New Left coalition on campus that I identified with, which had spearheaded antiwar and student power protests and allied with black and Chicano activists. In fact, because Tom had defeated a candidate more closely tied with these movements, I was surprised and immensely grateful when he became the Treaty's main champion on campus. After Tom asked his student government colleagues to support the Treaty, the student council not only enthusiastically endorsed it, they decided to turn it into a referendum to be placed on the next student elections ballot. It was ratified by an overwhelming majority.

February and March

In early February, four friends and I crammed into a car for a marathon round-the-clock road trip to Ann Arbor, Michigan, to attend the national People's Peace Treaty conference, aka the Student and Youth Conference on a People's Peace. At this exciting gathering, which attracted nearly 3,000 activists from all over the country, we devised plans for an educational campaign based on the People's Peace Treaty, and for a series of May Day demonstrations, primarily in D.C., but also in major cities and college towns nationwide. Nixon had just invaded Laos a few days before the conference began, and because of our large numbers, attendees at first had been tempted to stage an instant demo. Instead, we decided nearly unanimously that it made more sense to spend our precious moments together getting down to work. The organizing slogan for the conference, which Rennie Davis was instrumental in coordinating, was "Peace Is Coming—Because The People Are Making The Peace." We explored ways to reach out to activists from the veterans, labor, and Black, Chicano, and women's liberation movements. And because the conference agreed to endorse the No Business as Usual (aka "Ghandi With a Fist") tactic, we also learned the basics of civil disobedience. As one of my friends later wrote in the UCSB student newspaper soon after the conference, "Other actions will take place across the nation, which whenever possible, will follow the model of disruptive but non-violent tactics.... Marches have been ineffective. On the other hand, there are many people who do not approve of street fighting and yet are sincerely opposed to the war. Civil disobedience can involve large numbers of people and at the same time force the government to respond."[2]

Over the next couple of months, I and my friends (mostly students and recent ex-students) forged an alliance with the newly formed local chapter of the Vietnam Veterans Against the War (VVAW) and began working together to bring the Treaty to the older generation activists, traditional peace groups, pacifists, and progressive ministers in town.

Our UCSB-based student peace and anti-draft movement had primarily focused on exposing the university's complicity with the war, opposing ROTC, and challenging the right of Dow chemical and other corporations profiting from the war to recruit on campus. We'd rarely done this kind of local community outreach, primarily because just as antiwar sentiment was peaking, in late 1969 through early 1970, other campus issues took center stage and events began spinning out of control. (In early 1970, our campus experienced unprecedentedly large, peaceful but militant demonstrations protesting the firing of a young anthropology professor and countercultural icon. Several weeks of protest culminated in a massive sit-in blocking the doors of the administration building. In response, for the first time in campus history, administrators called in an army of outside police. Sheriffs from three counties descended on campus and clubbed several students, drawing blood—also a first. In Isla Vista, the student community [aka ghetto] adjacent to UCSB, the next four months brought a student shot and killed by police, three riots—two of which were police riots—the Bank of America burned to the ground, hundreds of arrests, and scores of injuries.)

Our group also brought the People's Peace Treaty to the Isla Vista Community Council (IVCC), a new entity established in the wake of the bank burning. After polling local residents, who overwhelmingly backed it, the Council later endorsed the Treaty, and an IVCC rep became one of the most vocal leaders in efforts to get it ratified by Santa Barbara city and county officials. And within a month the IVCC unanimously passed a motion to erect ornate signs at all entrances to Isla Vista proclaiming, "This town is at peace with Vietnam."

Among antiwar activists in my circle, the mood during this period was mixed. The Treaty did revive our movement's morale, but battle fatigue and despair were still plaguing us. The following excerpt from an article published in March in the student paper captures some of the local zeitgeist. It was written by my friend Bob Langfelder, an early leader of the Santa Barbara chapter of the Resistance, the first nationwide draft resistance group, founded in 1966. In 1970, Bob was falsely accused and wrongly convicted of taking part in burning down the Isla Vista branch of the Bank of America. He lost his appeal and did a year in jail:

> I just figured out it has been over 2,000 days since my first protest march against the war. 2,000 days of failure. 2,000 days of marching, picketing, vigiling, writing leaflets and letters, leafleting them, petitioning, reading, talking to all kinds of people; getting married, going into VISTA, getting un-married; turning in my draft card, refusing induction, counseling others to, waiting to be prosecuted, but after a year and [a] half, they make me 1Y; talking to more people and even rioting a little; being indicted, tried, convicted, sentenced to a year for inciting and participating in a riot that I didn't really participate in.
>
> It all adds up to failure. And it hurts even more now that it appears the Vietnamese could lose everything they have struggled for. I'm guilty of not doing as much as I could have for them. It's like we who have opposed the war have won all the arguments, but we—or I—have found myself unable to repeat all the arguments like a daily tape recording.
>
> As Noam Chomsky said, "Continued mass actions, patient explanation, principled resistance can be boring, depressing. But those who program the B-52 attacks and the 'pacification' exercises are not bored. And as long as they continue their work, so must we."
>
> So now I can sign the People's Peace Treaty and clean my hands of the whole mess; so I wish. As I talk to people about the Peace Treaty, I sense among some a subtle feeling of antagonism toward the apparent arrogance of radicals, as if to imply one becomes and stays a radical because of the easy self-assurance such conformist non-conformity may offer and the easy answers we have to all problems.
>
> What such people ignore is that the radical temper is often turned most radically upon oneself. Maybe what has been written here serves as an example.[3]

April

In early April, our Santa Barbara Peace Treaty Committee and the student government co-hosted a statewide People's Peace Treaty conference at UCSB. We held a teach-in on the war and the recent invasion of Laos featuring Bob Scheer and Banning Garrett, showed films, and broke into smaller constituency-based and regional work groups to develop ways to promote the Treaty and to plan coordinated protests in May. Much to my exasperation, the gathering was marred by an infuriating outbreak of factionalism sparked by a Trotskyist sect called the Workers' League, who condemned the People's Peace Treaty based on their ideological disagreements with the National Liberation Front of South Vietnam. My vague recollection is that the Workers' League dogmatists dismissed the NLF as "bourgeois nationalists."

In the course of archival research to refresh my memory of those days, I was delighted to discover *Deep Cover*, a memoir by former FBI undercover agent Cril Payne, who had once been assigned to spy on antiwar activists in Santa Barbara. Payne, one of the first agents out of the regional Los Angeles FBI office to grow a beard and long hair and adopt a sartorially plausible hippie-freak persona, claims in the book that he and three fellow agents (nicknamed "The Beards" by the FBI's LA office) "participated in just about every demonstration held in Isla Vista or Santa Barbara that year [1971]." They also cultivated and trained "Arlo," a strapping young local they hired as an informant. In one passage, Payne recalls one of the Beards' first assignments:

> The first statewide meeting we attended in Isla Vista was the People's Peace Treaty Convention. The purpose of the convention was to 'ratify' a peace Treaty negotiated by a group of American antiwar activists with representatives of North Vietnam. It was hoped that overwhelming support from students could ultimately force the United States government to accept the Treaty. A noble though highly impractical cause.
>
> After attending dozens of conferences, conventions, meetings and workshops, we observed that the only factor common to every gathering was that the participants could never reach agreement on anything. The various political groups were fiercely dogmatic... and fought constantly for influence.... Participants would argue for hours over whether the students or the workers would bring the revolution. I had a difficult time understanding why the Bureau was so concerned over the threat from the so-called "New Left."[4]

A recent Gallup poll showed:

73% of the people want all our troops home by the end of this year.

Can you imagine what would happen if they all spoke up?

You can speak up.
Sign the:

Joint Treaty of
Peace Between the
U.S. and
Vietnamese People

(A copy of the treaty is printed on the next page.)

In March 1971, the Santa Barbara People's Peace Treaty committee produced this poster-size leaflet and distributed it locally and to West Coast antiwar groups. On the reverse they reproduced a full-page ad published in the New York Times *including a 3-point summary of the Treaty and a list of prominent endorsers.*
Image courtesy of Becca Wilson.

My recollection is slightly different: In spite of the tedious, tendentious harangues and debates conference attendees were forced to endure, we did succeed in agreeing to a timetable for a week of protests in May. We also created an initial structure for local organizing and decided on ways to disseminate and seek ratification of the Treaty by a wide range of entities, from unions and churches to elected officials. At the conclusion of the conference, we sent a telegram of solidarity and support to the Saigon Students Union, who at that time were suffering a new round of vicious repression for their continuing, incredibly courageous work opposing the U.S. military presence in South Vietnam and U.S. support for the Thieu-Ky regime.

Working groups created at the conference each took on different tasks and/or agreed to coordinate all activities for one of the days of action planned for the first week in May. After the conference, many of us, especially those wanting to help coordinate the disruptive "no business as usual" actions, decided to break into smaller "affinity groups" or collectives so we could more safely guard against the undercover FBI agents and informers that we were certain were lurking in our midst. My feisty little tribe took responsibility for planning an action in front of a local plant engaged in war-related research and development.

Sometime during this period, I was approached by Keith Dalton, a reporter for the mainstream newspaper in town, the *Santa Barbara News-Press*. Though Keith was the paper's police reporter, he sympathized with some of the Isla Vista/UCSB New Left activists frequently targeted by the cops. He warned me that according to his sources, the FBI was tailing me everywhere. I wasn't a bit surprised, but having my apprehensions confirmed creeped me out and racked my already rickety nerves.

May

Here are the actions we managed to pull off in May:

Saturday, May 1: A Festival of Life with music and food is held in Isla Vista. Around 3,000 people march down State Street, the main street in Santa Barbara's downtown, with many marchers passing out educational flyers about the People's Peace Treaty and the war to people on the sidewalks. Probably two-thirds of the marchers are students and young people, but there is also visible participation from businesspeople, clergy, local unions and the Central Labor Council.

At a rally in a local park, after the usual passionate speeches, plus guerilla theater skits lampooning Nixon and his generals, a VVAW leader leads a solemn, silent ceremony. He lays his metal field helmet on the grass, and he and a group of fellow veterans cover it with medals and ribbons. The pile explodes into huge hot flames after someone douses it with homemade na-palm: gasoline, liquid detergent—and a match. Later, about 50 protestors hold a vigil outside the county jail, in support of 100 inmates (about one-third of the total) who have gone on a hunger strike in support of our week of peace protests.

Sunday, May 2: A day of dialogue in Santa Barbara's progressive and liberal churches, featuring the Treaty and the war.

Monday, May 3: A group of veterans in uniform pickets the Draft Board office. Activists pack the county Board of Supervisors meeting to speak out on an agenda item a member of our May Day coalition had suc-ceeded in placing on the official agenda: consideration of the People's Treaty and a suggested resolution urging that a date be set for withdrawal of all U.S. troops from Vietnam. An IVCC representative, antiwar vets, and oth-ers address the Board. Although a couple of the county supervisors say they agree the Vietnam War is "tragic" the Board refuse to take a stand, claiming they "lack jurisdiction." Pointing out that plainclothes police officers were in the audience, a *Santa Barbara News-Press* article quotes one supervisor as saying the federal government is doing its best to "get us out of Asia with honor," and another as saying, "I support the President."

Tuesday, May 4: Veterans picketing at the Draft Board continues for a second day. Declaring that "the Vietnamese people are not our enemies," activists flood the chambers of the Santa Barbara City Council, and urge it to endorse the People's Peace Treaty. An IVCC representative says polls indicate 73 percent of Americans favor December 31, 1971 as the deadline for troop withdrawals and "the last day of dying and killing." In addition to leaders of traditional peace groups such as Women's Strike for Peace and Peace Action Council, several members of VVAW speak out. Underscoring the demoralization of the troops that was increasingly in the news, veteran John Lenorak (who would later become my boyfriend and much later, my brother-in-law), tells the Council that as early as 1966–67, when he was in Vietnam, he saw fragging incidents, fellow Marines addicted to heroin, and whole platoons refusing to go out on patrol. Another vet cites links between South Vietnam's General Ky and the heroin trade. Pro-war folks also testi-fy. A building contractor claims a majority of Americans "don't want sur-render." A woman reads a letter denouncing our May 1 peace march from a group called Tax Action, claiming that aspects of the protest constitute "treason," such as marchers carrying Viet Cong flags or displaying the U.S. flag ripped or upside down. In the end, the City Council votes unanimously to deny our request for a resolution supporting the Treaty and asking Nixon to set a date for withdrawal of all U.S. forces. In its unanimous motion to deny our request, the Council adds a statement deploring the "desecration of U.S. flags" during the May 1 march. As he's walking out of the council chambers, one of my buddies turns and yells out, "See you at Nuremburg!"

Wednesday, May 5: At dawn, around 350 of us stage a very lively and disruptive demonstration in front of the General Motors AC Electronics plant in the town of Goleta, a couple of miles from the UCSB campus. When we arrive, a large phalanx of sheriffs is already there to greet us. Our research indicates that this facility has received more than $2 million to research and facilitate production of cluster bombs and rocket launchers. (For once, it appears the authorities agree with us. Asked by a *Santa Barbara News-Press* reporter why protestors singled out this plant, a Sheriff's Lieutenant is quoted as saying "they are responsible for making weapons of genocide.")

The mischievous collective I'm part of stages a "stall-in" to block traffic on the street outside the plant. In the middle of the busy boulevard, I and several of my friends suddenly stop our cars, jump out, and throw open our hoods, pretending that we've broken down (our vintage vehicles do in fact fit the part). Meanwhile, our comrades begin milling in the street and in the plant's driveway, handing out flyers and copies of the Treaty to employees entering the plant by foot or car. We succeed in creating delightful pandemonium and quite a traffic jam, but not for as long as we'd hoped. The California Highway Patrol shows up, and officers on motorcycles do eventually manage to force us off the roadway. Awhile later, Sheriff's Deputies in full riot gear use their two-foot-long billy clubs to shove our large crowd across the lawn fronting the plant, and into an adjacent parking lot. Eight people are arrested, among them several of my friends. My girlfriend Susan is slapped with felony assault on a police officer after throwing an orange at a guy we suspect is an undercover cop.

In downtown Santa Barbara later in the day, as other "no business as usual" events are unfolding, older members of Women's Strike for Peace fan out on State Street. Dressed in mourning outfits and carrying flowers, they pass out flyers and copies of the Treaty to pedestrians and in stores. Other less polite actions that day include a sit-in in the middle of an intersection in downtown Santa Barbara, during which several hundred demonstrators succeed in halting traffic for nearly an hour. And down the street 50 protestors block the sidewalk in front of offices of General Electric Tempo, a "think factory that thinks the unthinkable—nuclear weapons, the arms race, the genocide against the people of Indochina. Over half of GE's production is war-related," says the leaflet that we distribute to passersby. When yet another group of bold demonstrators moves to block traffic on the 101 freeway, the state's major north-south artery, an angry guy in a pickup truck guns his motor, speeds into the crowd, and narrowly misses several youths forced to leap backwards to avoid him.

July

A shocking turn of events: One day, a postman shows up at my door with a certified letter. It's from the District Attorney's office, informing me that I've been charged with three misdemeanors as a result of my participation in the May 5 demonstration outside the G.M. plant in Goleta—disrupting traffic, participating in an illegal assembly and resisting the lawful order of a police officer. Once I secure a lawyer and show up for the preliminary hearing, we meet with the prosecuting attorney and he shows us his evidence: several proverbial 8" × 10" glossy group photos of the protest with my face circled in red marking pen.

The short version of this long saga: I plead guilty to disrupting traffic. In exchange for this plea, the D.A. offers me the choice between either 45 days in jail, or two years' probation, terms of which are that I'll be instantly slapped with three months in jail and a hefty fine if I take part in any demonstration involving or resulting in illegal acts. I choose the jail term. In the *Santa Barbara News-Press*, the D.A. claims I'm playing the "martyr." The paper quotes me as saying I don't want anything to interfere with my constitutional right to continue protesting the war.

Doing my time in the Santa Barbara County jail is weird on more than one level. For one thing, all of the political prisoners—my friends arrested during our week of protests in May—have come and gone. I'm now the only one. One of my cellmates in our large group cell is Valeta, a heroin addict doing a year for sales of heroin.

Because of her "good behavior," Valeta has been made a trustee, and much of her time is spent doing clerical work in the guards' office. One day Valeta takes me aside to whisper a secret in my ear: the guards have instructed her to Xerox all of my incoming and outgoing mail, and send it to the FBI.

1972

A year or so later, I'm now co-editing an alternative weekly newspaper that I and a small collective of friends have created to counter the hegemony of the *Santa Barbara News-Press*. One day, my colleague Jim comes in to the office bearing a hot story—a personal account of espionage, Santa Barbara style. A few us gather around as Jim spins his amazing tale: one day, he and a couple of friends overhear a young woman they've been hanging out with talking on the phone. Something about her end of the conversation leads them to suspect the woman—her name is Valeta—may be working undercover. They confront her. It doesn't happen overnight, but eventually, Valeta cops to the charge; she admits she's getting heroin from the police in exchange for information about local antiwar and New Left activists.

Valeta!? I'm flabbergasted.

But the tale doesn't end there: Valeta and her boyfriend Jimmy, also a junkie, insist they're actually working as "double agents"—they're feeding the cops harmless stuff about we rabble-rousers, while gathering truly useful data for us about police activities. Jim and company cautiously go along, but soon it becomes quite obvious that they're being royally conned.

And now, it appears the best solution is that good old lifeblood of investigative journalism: an exposé. We need to publish a photo of Valeta and Jimmy, exposing them as two-bit snitches who pose a serious threat to The Movement.

For a few moments, Pham Van Dong's parting words return for another sweet visit: "It will take courage, courage, courage. The rest will come by itself."

THE MAKING OF A PEOPLE'S DIPLOMAT

JOHN McAULIFF

It started when I was a senior at Carleton College in Minnesota. A seminar gave me the chance to do a research paper on Vietnam. At that time, war in Vietnam wasn't in much of anybody's awareness in the United States. Nevertheless, in the spring of 1964 I was reading Bernard Fall's perspective in the *Saturday Review*.

Then I led a delegation from Carleton to participate in Mississippi Freedom Summer. Soon after the summer was over, I joined the Peace Corps. At that point, volunteers could get complimentary copies of the *New Republic* and the *New York Times* "Week in Review." So, through '65 and '66 I was following the escalation of U.S. involvement, making analogies between villages in Vietnam and Peru, where I was living with Quechua speakers in the Urubamba Valley.

When I got back to the United States in September 1966, I knew I was against the War. I was 24 years old and classified 1A, which was red meat in the draft system. I filed immediately for conscientious objector (CO) status. I wrote in the application that I would have participated in World War II, but because of the nature of the Vietnam War as an interventionist war, I would not do so now.

That draft board was in Noblesville, Indiana. The only CO applications they had dealt with were from Seventh Day Adventists. So the Board, probably thinking it was a good compromise, gave me 1AO, which is non-combatant military status.

By then I had a history of civil-rights and the Peace Corps. So I guess they gave me credit for a certain level of sincerity. But I had read the handbook published by the Central Committee for Conscientious Objectors front-to-back. I realized that the moment they recognized me as "1AO," they had lost the option of denying me a full non-military alternative service exemption. So I appealed and received 1O, meaning I could perform alternative service in lieu of being in the military.

But then a different series of events started. I was a graduate student at the Institute for Policy Studies in Washington when co-director Marc Raskin was indicted by then Attorney General Ramsey Clark for encouraging resistance to the draft. Clark directed the same charge against Dr. Benjamin Spock, Mitch Goodman, Bill Coffin, and Michael Ferber. I turned in my draft card at a demonstration at the Justice Department (this was one of the things people were doing—either burning them or turning them in). Legally that meant I was non-cooperating, refusing to do the alternative service required of COs. I learned this the hard way when I was arrested at a demonstration in New York. The police discovered there was a federal hold on me because of my draft-card action. The feds obviously hadn't made a big effort to find me because it would have been easy to do. I spent an extra 48 hours in the Tombs, the old holding jail in New York City, while my "crime" was sorted out.

I decided finally to do alternative service on the premise that actively working against the war was more productive than symbolically sitting in prison. By then I was the first national president of the Committee of Returned Volunteers (CRV), an organization made up mostly of alumni of the Peace Corps who came together to oppose the war. I represented CRV in the executive committee of the national antiwar coalition and led a large group of members in the demonstration at the 1968 Democratic National Convention in Chicago.

My alternative service assignment was in the print shop of Goodwill Industries in Indianapolis. With the approval of the shop manager, I used free time to print out discussion papers for the coalition. In 1970 I was literally going out the back door of Goodwill to fly to Sweden while the FBI was coming in the front door to talk to the head office about me. Not long after, Goodwill fired me. The way the alternative service system worked, as long as you did not refuse another assignment, the clock continued ticking on the two years. Selective Service never came up with a new job, so I spent the rest of my time editing and selling the *Indianapolis Free Press*, the city's "underground" newspaper. I also continued to organize statewide participation in the People's Peace Treaty and the May

Day civil disobedience demonstrations in Washington. I was detained for three days in the Washington Coliseum but, like everyone else, was released without charges because of the way arrests were mishandled.

I went to Sweden as part of a peace coalition delegation to a Stockholm conference and met, for the first time, representatives of North Vietnam and of the National Liberation Front in the South. As important, I discovered soul mates in the progressive Swedish Social Democrats who led the conference, several of whom were members of Parliament and went on to be ministers in the government of Sweden. That helped me gain confidence that one could maintain U.S. political values and practices while respecting the different assumptions and experiences of communist revolutionaries.

In 1972, I began work with the American Friends Service Committee (AFSC) for an Indochina summer project. A main focus of my work was opposition to the U.S. bombing of the dikes that protected Hanoi from the Red River, an international war crime. We took posters about the campaign onto the floor of the Democratic Convention that nominated George McGovern. My summer job turned into a life-changing experience that lasted more than 10 years during which I created and directed the Indochina Program in the Peace Education Division of this extraordinary Quaker-led organization.

The antiwar movement entered a new phase starting in 1973 when U.S. forces were withdrawn from Vietnam. There were no longer news stories of U.S. casualties. U.S. POWs came home. The air went out of the balloon in terms of a mass U.S. peace movement. Nevertheless, while there were no more big demonstrations, there was still broad sentiment against the war. The Indochina Peace Campaign (IPC) led by Tom Hayden and Jane Fonda—in association with AFSC, the Mennonite Central Committee, Church World Service, and other religious and progressive organizations—worked to transform that sentiment into focused successful pressure on Congress to end aid to South Vietnamese dictator Nguyen Van Thieu.

We became a different kind of peace movement that paralleled the activism of the McGovern wing of the Democratic Party. This was a good fit for me. I have always been most comfortable at the intersection of mobilization activism, antiwar politics, and finding vehicles for actually influencing policy.

Vietnam, 1975

I arrived in Hanoi on the day the war ended: April 30, 1975. It was the last of several trips organized by IPC, and my first time in Hanoi. I accompanied an AFSC staff member from North Carolina and three grassroots activists from IPC. Literally, we arrived in Hanoi within hours of the U.S. ambassador's evacuating Saigon. We were in the homeland of the victorious "enemy" for the first two weeks after the end of the war.

As soon as we arrived, our host Do Xuan Oanh said, "Forget about your program. Nobody you were going to see is available now."

We told our Vietnamese hosts they should be with their families on this historic day, not with us. They were pleased to agree. Left to ourselves, we walked from the Thong Nhat Hotel (later modernized as the Metropole) and immediately separated into the crowd. The Vietnamese were celebrating with family groups and coworkers—tens of thousands of people, including the Hanoi Conservatory orchestra—simply walking around Hoan Kiem Lake, the Lake of the Redeemed Sword. In the midst of the crowd, I was hauled up into the back of an army truck. They spoke no English and I knew no Vietnamese. I rode around the lake with them, fortunately recognizing the Post Office clock tower when I completed the circle. It was mostly not vehicles on the street, just people. It was powerful.

We had joined a very Vietnamese response to the end of the war. I remember talking with a European journalist who was surprised that local people had not been happier about peace. What he had in mind was "VE Day" or "VJ Day," where folks got drunk and celebrated noisily. Even the fireworks display that night was absent the component of explosive sound, perhaps because memories of Nixon's Christmas bombing were too raw.

In the days and weeks following, we spent a memorable evening with the editor of the Communist Party newspaper, *Nhan Dan*, reflecting on his and the country's difficult history since declaring independence in 1945. We visited agricultural communes, villages and urban locations that still showed evidence of U.S. bombing, including Bach Mai Hospital. During our travels we witnessed many overt signs of the war. There were still overturned railroad cars next to tracks that had been targeted. We saw filled-in personal shelters along streets of downtown Hanoi as well as large bomb craters, especially on the outskirts of the city. It was not hard to find people who could relate their experiences during the "Christmas bombing" of December 1972 (Operation Linebacker II).

We went to Ha Long Bay. Back then, it was a two-day trip via the port city of Haiphong, a harbor mined a few years before by the Nixon

Hanoi postwar celebration viewed from the back of a truck, April 30, 1975.
Photo by John McAuliff.

administration. We returned to Hanoi for the formal celebration of the end of the war and for the reunification of the country held in the national stadium. It was like what you see in current May Day marches in Vietnam: people come from different workplaces, artistic and sports groups carrying signs and parading through the stadium, the whole thing not very ideological or militaristic.

Being there at that significant moment in history solidified my interest in Vietnam and the consequences of the war. When I arrived in Vietnam, I had worked with AFSC for three years. The Quakers were already addressing the humanitarian consequences of the war in both North and South Vietnam. Once I was actually in Vietnam, I began to obtain a deeper perspective on Vietnamese history and culture and the personality of the Vietnamese people. I had more access to this history and culture than was common in the antiwar movement. Antiwar activists knew more than the general public, and apparently U.S. government knew the least of all.

In 1975, Americans, whether pro or antiwar, still had the image of the Vietnamese and Chinese as "big buddies." Although I understood intellectually that this view was inaccurate, I was still a bit startled during our drive to Ha Long Bay. We stopped and saw an immense permanent mural. We were told this is where Vietnamese forces put the logs in the river at low tide. The Chinese invaders came in at high tide. When the tide went out their boats were sunk by the pointed logs that were under the water. The point of this mural is that conflict with China is not just textbook history. For the Vietnamese, conflict with China is a lived reality. This illustrates one of the fundamental flaws of U.S. thinking with regard to the purpose and goals of the War. By characterizing the Vietnam War as "containment" of China, it is clear that Cold War policymakers did not know, or at best misunderstood, Vietnam's historical relationship with China.

The Campaign for Normalization

That was 1975. During the ensuing seven years, I continued working for the AFSC. That period put me into the process of trying to deal with postwar issues within peace and religious communities in Vietnam; with specialized journalists whose reporting would shape the public opinion in the United States; and with U.S. Congress and the executive branch of the U.S. government. From 1975 to 1995, the U.S. government cut off all relations with the Socialist Republic of Vietnam, and the country was left to its own devices in terms of postwar reconciliation and establishing normal trade and diplomatic relations with the rest of the world.

The end of the war had been different for Vietnamese in the South than in the North. There were no more U.S. bombing raids in the North after the Paris Peace Agreement of 1973, but three more years of combat continued in the South where only the uniforms changed. U.S. troops were no longer active, but the U.S. government provided unconditional military, economic, and political support for the government in Saigon. The Thieu regime was enabled to try to undermine the process of political accommodation in the South required by the peace agreement. Thieu's contempt for the Peace Agreement, repression of "third force" opponents, and military efforts to take back territory held by the other side brought about its own calamitous collapse and the panicky evacuations that were subsequently dramatized on television.

Victory by southern revolutionaries and the North meant liberation for some and occupation for others, as I discovered during my first trip to South Vietnam for AFSC in 1978. Hundreds of thousands of southern Vietnamese fled the country as boat people. Large numbers of ARVN military and government officials were confined to re-education camps. The business and professional class that had collaborated with the U.S. military and the Saigon government left the country or were dispossessed and discriminated against.

Although one could find similarities in the mistreatment of the British loyalists after the American Revolution, and worse in Europe after World War II, and in Indonesia after the U.S.-backed military coup, postwar U.S. public opinion shifted dramatically away from majority support for normalization and humanitarian aid for Vietnam. Earlier knowledge and concern for destruction caused by U.S. bombing and out-of-control military assaults faded away, replaced by moving personal stories of refugees distributed throughout the United States. Their resettlement was often sponsored by local churches that previously hosted peace activities. There was little counter or supplementary messaging regarding the Vietnamese rebuilding of their country from an antiwar perspective.

In that context, my initial focus on normalization of relations with Vietnam and fulfillment of the U.S. promise of reconstruction aid was challenging. AFSC and other NGOs received broad backing for an Appeal for Reconciliation, but we could not stem the erosion of sympathy for the suffering caused by the war.

At the beginning of the Carter administration, normalization could have happened, but it did not. The AFSC helped brief a delegation led by former UAW President Leonard Woodcock that went to Hanoi prepared to establish relations. In my opinion, the Vietnamese made a historic misjudgment by refusing normalization unless the U.S. government followed through on its treaty agreement to help heal the wounds of war. By the time the Vietnamese could separate normalization from other issues, the United States was no longer willing to engage in normal trade and diplomatic relations with Vietnam because the priority had shifted toward building an alliance with China against the Soviet Union.

In 1979, Vietnam responded to cross-border Khmer Rouge (KR) attacks and threats from China by occupying Cambodia. The KR lost control of most of the country, countless Cambodian lives were saved and a devastated country began to rebuild with Vietnamese and Soviet bloc assistance. At the end of the Carter administration and through most of the George H.W. Bush administration years, the United States became involved politically and with covert military aid in a third Indochina war, joining with China and several Southeast Asian countries to support remnants of the Khmer Rouge, Sihanoukists, and Lon Nol republicans. Vietnam successfully defeated an invasion by China on its northern border but was isolated in the region and by policymakers in the United States.

Our AFSC efforts did, however, have enough allies in Carter's State Department (1976–80) that the Vietnamese received permission for an

annual three-day visit to Philadelphia, including a picnic with peace movement and non-governmental aid agency friends. At first, the interactions
were very formal. We would visit a factory or a pharmaceutical company or
a farm. There would be structured "dialogues." Initially, the gatherings were
men-only because of the make-up of the Vietnamese Mission to the United
Nations. The picnics continued through the hostile years of the Reagan and
Bush Sr. administrations, treasured by successive generations of diplomats
and eventually by their families as a unique opportunity to escape travel
limits confining them to New York City and to enjoy a holiday with "unofficial" representatives of the United States.

I remained involved with these outreach projects with the diminishing constituency of Americans who cared about the effect of the war and
with policy people in Washington. I was able to connect AFSC's international aid division and Operation California, a refugee aid organization.
Around Thanksgiving of 1979 we arranged with representatives of the new
Vietnamese-allied government in Phnom Penh the first air shipment of
medical supplies from the United States, despite Washington's political goal
of total isolation.

In 1981 I made my first visit to Cambodia for AFSC. I had witnessed
the evidence of KR attacks in the Mekong delta area of southern Vietnam
in 1978, but confronting the physical and psychological devastation within
Cambodia posed huge moral and political questions that to this day are still
unresolved for me. I believe that the United States created the problem by
supporting and probably sponsoring the overthrow of Norodom Sihanouk
because he allowed North Vietnamese military supply lines and safe areas
for the NLF in eastern Cambodia. "Secret" bombing of Cambodian villages, incursion by U.S. forces and military support of Lon Nol fostered the
growth of an ultra-radical Khmer Rouge.

When the KR took power on April 17th and expelled the population
of Phnom Penh, few outsiders, including myself and other peace activists,
recognized or spoke out against the horror that was being inflicted on the
population in an extreme application of communist ideology and ethnic
nationalism. While the U.S. government made a few public criticisms of
human rights violations, it did not do anything that would disturb its relations with China, the KR's only ally and source of military aid. Even worse,
after the Vietnamese overthrew the KR, Washington provided political support and weapons to an anti-Vietnamese Cambodian coalition that it knew
was dominated by the KR.

While the peace movement correctly celebrated its success in ending the
U.S. war in Indochina, few recognized the difference in how that affected

Cambodia. I still wonder whether there was anything we could have done differently that would have helped spare the country from the genocidal trauma of the Khmer Rouge.

Moving from the Quakers

In 1982, the AFSC decided that a peace education program on Indochina seven years after the war was over was no longer a priority. I moved on. I worked in Philadelphia politics as a staff person with the Americans for Democratic Action (ADA), a liberal organization that I had come to know as an elected Democratic Party official at precinct level. I was also the associate editor of the local monthly Irish paper. But I maintained connections with diplomats from Indochina and U.S. officials that I had developed at AFSC, and the picnics continued.

By chance, Bill and Cathy Rieser, whom I knew in connection with AFSC, had a small family foundation. They asked if I would I like to resume what I had been doing. I said yes and in 1985 created the U.S.– Indochina Reconciliation Project (USIRP) of the Fund for Reconciliation and Development (FfRD). Partly I was motivated by my Irish stubbornness about wanting to address the ongoing consequences of the war. My relationship with the Vietnamese, Laotians, and Cambodians was emotionally and intellectually compelling, as were the issues associated with them and with U.S. policy.

By choice and by necessity, I became a self-appointed Peace Movement Diplomat. I was doing what I wanted to do going all the way back to high school. That's the choice part. The necessity part is that there was no way that I was going to get through the State Department screening after being arrested three times during the antiwar movement. Furthermore, I was pretty alienated from anything associated with official U.S. foreign policy.

Nevertheless, I found myself engaged in fairly complex Quaker-influenced peer-to-peer dialogue with people on the National Security Council and State Department outside of their formal system. Richard Childress at the National Security Council, Ann Mills Griffeths of the League of Families, and Charles Twining at the State Department were among the counterparts who became my friends.

My goal has always been to provide the space that allows changes in U.S. policy so that other nations can figure out how they might more freely work through their own historical realities and ideologies. My early experiences greatly contributed to my perspective. Having done a lot of support work for the Student Nonviolent Coordinating Committee (SNCC) when I was at Carleton helped me. Then the Mississippi Summer Project in 1964 made me more attuned to the deep injustices and imperfections of U.S. society as well as the interplay of motives and in-group assumptions in situations of conflict.

I was also impacted by barely making it into the Peace Corps because as a student at Carleton I was the treasurer of an organization that brought controversial speakers to campus. As a result, I was the object of an FBI investigation for writing the honorarium check on behalf of the student government. From that, I had a touch of how McCarthyism still plagued U.S. politics and human rights.

During the Reagan and Bush Sr. administrations the primary public stumbling blocks to improved relations with Vietnam were the presence of its military forces in Cambodia and the problem of U.S. soldiers who were Missing in Action (MIAs). By in effect supporting the Khmer Rouge, the United States inhibited the process of Vietnamese withdrawal. However, that problem was resolved through international negotiations and a UN supervised electoral process. Both the Reagan and Bush Sr. administrations trusted General John Vessey. He and Vietnamese Foreign Minister Nguyen Co Thach negotiated a process of returning the remains of U.S. soldiers and the joint exploration of crash sites. That did not, of course, stop the U.S. right-wing from insisting for years that the Vietnamese still held U.S. POWs.

Substantial progress during the Bush Sr. administration on Cambodia and MIAs did not lead to normalization of diplomatic relations or an end to the U.S. embargo. Too much of the U.S. governing class and national security bureaucracy had been engaged in the U.S. war effort. The enduring effect of anger and resentment at the Vietnamese for having brought about the first ever military defeat of the U.S. military, and their harsh treatment of former friends in the south, cannot be underestimated. George H.W. Bush was prepared to take significant steps in the closing months of his administration, but was blocked by the active public and private opposition of Henry Kissinger and others.

Therefore, my work as a people's diplomat proceeded on two levels. I spent many hours in private conversations with State Department and National Security Council staff and in a group process led by former Senator Dick Clark at the Aspen Institute. Initially the overt debate was over whether there was any benefit for the United States to establishing relations with the three war devastated nations of Indochina. Under the surface, however, the problem was helping U.S. officials find ways to move beyond hostility toward their former enemy. Could they be led to create or believe in a positive relationship of trust? It is natural when a powerful country loses a war to blame it on the perfidy of the enemy rather than on the bankruptcy of your own assumptions and practices.

The second level of my work was to endeavor to change the public atmosphere, to refresh and modernize war-time sympathy for the victims of U.S. policy. We organized more than a dozen delegations of Americans to visit Vietnam, Laos, and Cambodia—initially composed of academics, later staff from NGOs, foundations, and private businesses. Working in coalition with other groups, we organized 10 conferences that brought together U.S. non-governmental organizations, former European and Australian government representatives who worked in the region, U.S. State Department staff, and officials of the three countries. These events were the first place that the war legacies of land mines, unexploded ordnance, and Agent Orange were discussed. Through our trips and the conferences, new and long-standing organizations came to learn how to do programs in Indochina.

Working together, we also brought people from all three countries to the United States, mostly from the academic sector for exchange and training purposes, but also personalities who had ties to the United States but stayed in their countries during the difficult post-war years. The latter posed special challenges to obtain U.S. visas. Especially rewarding was sponsoring exchange visits between former OSS members (the precursor to the CIA) and former Viet Minh, whom the U.S. military trained and supplied at the headquarters of Ho Chi Minh and General Giap in alliance against the Japanese occupation. Funding for these efforts came initially from U.S. foundations such as Christopher Reynolds and Ford. At the end, even the U.S. Information Agency pitched in.

This process of multilateral postwar negotiations came to fruition when the Clinton administration moved to end U.S. embargoes of Cambodia and Vietnam. By 1995, the U.S. government had fully normalized diplomatic and educational relations with Cambodia, Laos, and Vietnam.

Understanding Vietnam

My trip to Sweden in 1970 was not just an opportunity to discover the social democrats. Meeting the Vietnamese there also reinforced my instinct that they were not a deeply Marxist–Leninist movement.

If one looked at their theoretical publications, you would see the ideological language. But the primary message was always nationalism and independence. Marxism was an overlay rather than a substantive part of the message. It is a lot like the democracy language that comes along as a cover with USAID (United States Agency for International Development) funding around the world. My view was and is that Vietnamese Marxism–Leninism was a strategically chosen frame that Ho Chi Minh discovered was necessary if he was going to get help from anybody to obtain independence from France. I believe post-war developments have borne that out.

Many U.S. antiwar activists saw Vietnam as a righteous enemy of the United States. This includes antiwar activists who traveled to Vietnam during the war. Because of their sympathy for Vietnamese suffering and admiration for their courage, it was common to overstate as heroic or iconic what Vietnam represented as an international model and the nature of the Vietnamese revolutionary process.

The obverse side of being dissatisfied with the behavior and worldview of your own country is transferring enthusiasm to somebody else's country, culture, and history. I saw this from the perspective of having lived in Peru for two years in rural communities, having worked in Mississippi, and having dealt with the imperfections of American politics and society. I liked the Vietnamese, but I didn't have any sense that they were somehow the salvation of America's problems or for my life. They were simply people that I discovered were worthwhile and interesting.

They were very creative, hard-working people with a long and deep history and culture who had also been very brave in the face of overwhelming pressure. I don't want to emphasize it too much, but it is hard not to be in awe of what they achieved against overwhelming odds and disproportionate power, first against the French, then against the United States, and always against China.

Vietnam 2013

In the late 1990s I shifted the focus of my work to Cuba, which faced similar problems with the United States of even longer duration: embargo, diplomatic isolation, mutually hostile rhetoric, and deeply embedded distrust. But I was still engaged intellectually and personally with Indochina and periodically tried to organize trips to Indochina for people who had been involved in the antiwar movement.

It was remarkable how much traveling to Vietnam was being done by military veterans, who were sorting through their own agendas and guilt, and finding closure and reconciliation. But after the end of the war, the Vietnamese were no longer priming the pump with invitations to antiwar people or covering in-country cost of trips as they had done in the past. There were very few civilians other than humanitarian aid staff from the Quakers, Mennonites, Church World Service, and other NGOs going to Viet Nam. After U.S. travel restrictions and the embargo ended, Indochina became an important tourist destination for Americans but visits had only incidental substantive content about the war and current relations.

Activists had moved on to Central America, nuclear disarmament, the nuclear freeze, and other seemingly more worthy goals. Or they moved on to restoring their personal lives. We just couldn't find enough people with the time and money even though we made a couple of efforts with advertising and targeted mailings. That was frustrating to me. And then I noticed that friends as they retired or their kids finished school were beginning to make individual trips back to Vietnam, Laos, and Cambodia. I would get calls and provide some introductions.

As I had shifted over increasingly to Cuba, I didn't really think much more about it. But then I ran into Frank Joyce and began working on what became the January 2013 trip that created the "Hanoi 9." It became for me a chance to share what 20 years of intense work brought to me.

I have seen that the emotional and intellectual putting together of things between past and present was as important for people who had been in the antiwar movement as for military veterans, even if they weren't as aware of it as the veterans were.

Vietnam Now

I joined the 2013 trip with two central questions. One was the China/Vietnam issue. Are we witnessing just a temporary stage of heightened tension within Vietnam because of the change of leadership in China? Or are we moving towards a whole new confrontational era and threat to the safety and well-being of the Vietnamese people? I still do not have an answer to that question. I brought it up in a variety of contexts. Sometimes I got answers, sometimes I didn't.

I have the sense that for both the U.S. government and for Vietnam there is a common interest in this question but also a great carefulness about how the issue is formulated. It is certainly not going to end the Vietnamese veneration of their own history and the justice of their struggle against the United States. That insistence on Vietnamese independence from China creates a certain contradictory element that is intriguing to me.

My other question was how Vietnam continues to evolve domestically and politically independent of the United States. Again, I don't have a final answer, but I think that there is more overt discussion of the future of their political system. My impression is that the Chinese have simply reinforced the power centers in the Communist party. The Vietnamese, it seems to me, are struggling with taking seriously the implications of the ultimate master of the country being the people.

That's been part of their mantra for 20 years and it is not simply rhetoric. It is apparent in the discussion of the new constitution, the more overt opposition to the way things are now organized and the way corruption is discussed. The question is not whether corruption exists. Corruption is a problem in every society. But how is it addressed? I suppose it is my prejudice, but I think the Vietnamese are working through that process successfully in their own way.

From Ambassador David Shear, with whom our group met, and most of the postwar ambassadors that I've known, there is an assumption that the United States will set out its standards for how it thinks things should be done economically and politically. But the truth is that United States is not pushing the Vietnamese to do something that the Vietnamese are not themselves concerned about.

Economically, the two countries are deeply entwined. The United States is one of the largest foreign investors in Vietnam, Vietnam's biggest export market, and the second largest source of tourists. China is number one in terms of tourism, but many are just day-trippers.

What is also important is the number of Vietnamese students coming to study in the United States. There are many, many layers of exposure that Vietnamese people are having to U.S. society and culture. The effect is not without conflict and contradictions. But I think that Vietnamese society is changing.

When I first came to Vietnam and for years afterward, you simply could not see people except in their offices without somebody being there taking notes. Now you go to people's homes, you have private meals, and there's nobody taking notes. There are too many restaurants for them to be bugged. It's the paranoid American view that in a Communist country it means that everyone is under constant surveillance. At this point Americans may be under more constant surveillance just because of the electronics that are so dominant in our lives.

In fact, by the late 1990s, I thought the Vietnamese had achieved many things they wanted, including forging a reasonable relationship with the United States. They were on their way to where they needed to go. And I certainly came out of the 2013 trip feeling even more certain that the Vietnamese were on their own path.

The role of Americans is not central to the future of Vietnam. There are ways that we can play a helpful role and there are certainly ways we must take responsibility for the consequences of our actions, such as unexploded ordnance and Agent Orange. But Vietnam is certainly not going to live or die based on American opinions or actions.

VOICES OF VETERANS:
THE ENDLESS TRAGEDY OF VIETNAM

MYRA MacPHERSON

Editors' Note: Myra MacPherson wrote the Vietnam classic, Long Time Passing: Vietnam and the Haunted Generation (Indiana University Press, 2002), the first trade book to discuss post-traumatic stress disorder (PTSD). In 2013, MacPherson toured Vietnam with five U.S. veterans, all of whom now live in Vietnam. One of them, Chuck Searcy, met with the "Hanoi 9" in January 2013. This report first appeared in Consortium News, edited by Robert Parry. Reprinted by permission.

This is Vietnam as seen through the lens of five American ex-soldiers: They returned to their former battlefield, where three saw fierce fighting, to live full-time among and to aid the people burdened by two terrible legacies of that war. These tragedies are the thousands of children and farmers who are blown up or injured by bombs dropped half a century ago that didn't explode upon impact. And the chillingly large number of children and adults who suffer from the effects of the world's most poisonous defoliant, Agent Orange; today fourth-generation children continue to be born with twisted and useless limbs.

Throughout Vietnam today, this band of brothers in peace, travels and works tirelessly to help these victims of a war long past. The group includes a poet, a psychiatric social worker, a former aide to a United States senator, a former cop, and a long-ago gang member who found peace and purpose back here, in Vietnam.

They came here as innocent young soldiers but returned to the United States shattered. They never unpacked their pain, anger, sorrow, sense of betrayal, guilt, and disillusionment about what had been done to the people of Vietnam. They returned, burdened with memories and driven by a mission. They live from Hanoi to Ho Chi Minh City and points in between—Hue, Da Nang, Hoi An, and Nha Trang.

Whitewashing a War

Not only are they fighting for the lives of modern-day Vietnamese victims of that old war, they are—like fellow members of the 3,300 Veterans for Peace (VFP) around the world and a large contingent of distinguished Vietnam scholars, historians, and peace activists—outraged at the whitewashing they see in a mammoth Department of Defense 50th anniversary commemoration of the Vietnam War that will soon saturate the media and the public.

The Pentagon material, which will be disseminated to schools and the public, even includes the ancient lie about the Gulf of Tonkin "incident," which pushed the United States into full-scale war in 1964. The Department of Defense commemorative website states that the Gulf of Tonkin incident began with "The U.S. response to the North Vietnamese attack on *USS Maddox* (DD 731) in the Gulf of Tonkin in August 1964. [This] marked the beginning of the Navy's air and surface bombardment against North Vietnam."

However, for decades it has been known that the North Vietnamese attack never happened; this false allegation incited Congress to give the green light to go to war. As one retired Captain Carl Otis Schuster, U.S. Navy wrote, "the string of intelligence mistakes, mistranslations, misinterpretations and faulty decision-making that occurred in the Tonkin Gulf in 1964 reveals how easily analysts and officials can jump to the wrong conclusions and lead a nation into war."

"We will not leave it to the government and war hawks to tell a one-sided tale of guts and glory," blasts the VFP organization in its Full Disclosure Campaign. After protests in January, commemoration officials said they were backing off disseminating educational materials or curricula containing solely the Pentagon's views and would seek outside review. However, the Gulf of Tonkin "attack" lie, as of now, remains in their website timeline.

"The DOD commemoration of our war is a farce," explodes Chuck Palazzo, one of the former combat veterans who lives in Da Nang. "A waste of money [taxpayer cost will run into the millions of dollars] and a feeble attempt to brainwash the younger generation as well as the rest of us, that what we did was right—it was, of course, so wrong!"

The complexities of this war make it difficult for many who served; VFP members respect the idea of honoring veterans who were shunned on their return but denounce a fictionalized version of the war itself.

Bombing "Back to the Stone Age"

We are in Quang Tri Province at the DMZ, the former demilitarized zone that once separated South and North Vietnam. "You are standing in the most heavily bombed area in the history of warfare," said Vietnam veteran Chuck Searcy, the American voice of Project RENEW ("Restoring the Environment and Neutralizing the Effects of the War"), a humanitarian organization he co-founded 15 years ago that helps victims of unexploded bombs the United States dropped during the War.

Today, lush foliage belies the past. One has to look at war photos to understand such pulverizing devastation when this province was destroyed— gray, bomb-blasted fields and land, village huts incinerated, civilians racing for their lives as fighter jets screamed overhead and B-52s marauded silently at 30,000 feet, dropping bomb after bomb after bomb. Some 15 million tons of bombs were dropped on Vietnam—more than during all of World War II—much of it here at the DMZ. An estimated three million civilians were killed during the decade of war.

The serenity of a sunny day makes it equally hard to imagine the lethal presence of unexploded bombs still lurking nearby.

"To me, the U.S. bombings were an ultimate mass torture delivering fear, trauma, injuries, and death," remarked Californian Sally Benson, who, along with her husband, Steve Nichols, funded the Mine Action Visitor Center here in Quang Tri to teach awareness of the 300,000-plus tons of unexploded ordnance remaining in the province. Nichols and Benson met in Vietnam as civilian teachers during the war, returned to the United States antiwar, and maintain close ties with the five veterans, visiting Vietnam often.

How could anyone possibly survive, one wonders, imagining a daily hailstorm of bombs? We find out. We crawl deep into the Vinh Moc tunnels, moving slowly on slippery stones, hunching in the engulfing walls of earth, so close that one did not need to extend arms to feel them, cold to the touch. As we inch our way through the dark, tiny lights on our foreheads dimly pick out the winding narrow strip of earth as we go further and further down.

Suddenly a small cramped space dug out of the wall is illuminated. We gasp. A body is lying there with another crouching next to her. But they are models; a woman lying down and a woman leaning over her, holding her baby. On the wall is an incongruous sign, "maternity ward."

It is hard to imagine even one baby born there, and yet 17 Vietnamese women had given birth deep in the soil during the years of "search and destroy," when millions of bombs pummeled their peasant huts and land constantly. Villagers lived underground for months on end—children, babies, mothers, elderly parents, ancient aunts and uncles—eating, sleeping, enduring. From 1966 to 1972, when the bombing stopped, 300 Vietnamese lived in their mole-like world, digging nearly 100 feet underground.

The Loss of Limbs

Back out of darkness, squinting in the sun, we walked to meet a nearby villager. His family thought him out of harm's way; he was only four years old when the war ended in 1975. The man scooted over the ground like a crab, using his strong arms, pads protecting his knees. His legs ended in stumps just below the knees. One hand was missing. He was not wearing his artificial legs, the ones he had to sell a cow to pay for. They were too cumbersome for the work he was doing, which was dragging pieces of used lumber to build a chicken coop. He was 20 in 1991, out looking for scrap metal, when an unexploded bomb, dropped 25 years before, blew up.

"He knew the risks, but he also knew he could sell the metal for cash income. It was purely economics," said Chuck Searcy.

Cluster bombs dug six-foot circle indentations that can still be seen as dips in the green land. They contained hundreds of small but very lethal bomblets that were supposed to have exploded on impact. Only thousands did not, about 10 percent, Searcy says, citing an old Pentagon estimate. All these years later, they bring the war home again, exploding in fields and villages, killing and maiming curious children, farmers tilling their fields, poor peasants searching for scrap metal to sell. Official estimates put the number of casualties from unexploded bombs in Vietnam at around 100,000, including 34,000 killed. The true numbers are probably higher, says Searcy.

Newspapers in the province attest to the horrible ordinariness of such accidents; a recent account of a 17-year-old boy riding his bike reads: "The blast cut off Hoan's left hand, ripped his head from the forehead to the nose. The boy also suffered injuries to his left shoulder and nose and lips."

Agent Orange

We travel further south, to Nha Trang. This fashionable resort mecca—with high-rise hotels, turquoise bay, and sandy beaches—is in wild contrast to another world that tourists do not see. We visit a spotless home filled with family mementos; photos everywhere, stuffed toys near a Buddhist shrine. Lying flat on a brightly colored mat are two sisters with horribly twisted limbs, spines too weak for them to sit up, ravished by Agent Orange birth defects, carried to them genetically through a Vietnamese soldier father.

Their mother, with a smiling face and pleading eyes, moves them to a wall and props them up. Their bodies are so small that they look far younger than their ages. One is 30 and her sister is 20. An awkward silence envelops the room as visitors stand, helpless.

Don Blackburn, another Vietnam veteran who works non-stop to aid Agent Orange victims, plunks himself down between the two, as casually easy as a comforting friend. The sisters smile gratefully at him. Their father has left the family and the mother is frantic with worry about who will care for her daughters when she becomes too old or ill.

It would be hard to underestimate the damage Agent Orange dioxin caused. Between 2.1 million and 4.8 million Vietnamese citizens were directly exposed to Agent Orange and other poisonous chemicals, according to the American Public Health Association. Agent Orange poisoned the soil where Vietnamese grow crops, the rivers and streams where they fish, and created cancer, illnesses, and birth defects, now into this younger generation.

A Poisonous Herbicide

From 1961 to 1972, U.S. aircraft sprayed poisonous herbicides, until this lush country looked as grey and denuded as the moon. In all, more than 19 million gallons of herbicides were sprayed over 4.5 million acres of land. However, the United States questions the Vietnamese Red Cross projections of the numbers of victims linked to Agent Orange cancers, birth defects, and other chronic diseases.

Americans who view Vietnam as an ancient war stare in shock when visitors returning from this country tell them that the dioxin affects children born today. While American veterans who suffer from Agent Orange diseases had to fight governmental denial and scorn—President Ronald Reagan's Veterans Affairs director Robert P. Nimmo dismissed Agent Orange as causing no more than a little "teenage acne"—recognition of related illness and compensation, although often inadequate, has finally happened.

But the United States still refuses to attribute Agent Orange to diseases, illness, and defects among the Vietnamese; questions Vietnamese figures; and says more study is needed. (The United States said it has provided $54 million since 1989 to help Vietnamese with disabilities, but also stressed that such assistance was "regardless of cause.")

"It is hypocritical for the U.S. to place this unnecessary burden of proof on the Vietnamese while it does not do so for its own veterans," says Palazzo, who works here with Agent Orange victims. He cites international and Vietnamese studies linking dioxin to health and birth defects here.

The United States bristles at Vietnam claims that half a million children have been born with serious birth defects, while as many as 2 million people are suffering from cancer or other illness caused by Agent Orange. There is no measure to prove they are Agent Orange victims, but some studies estimate that the rate of birth defects here in Vietnam has quadrupled since the War, and that most of them occur where Agent Orange was sprayed or stored.

Brothers in Peace

Like the other veterans who have returned to help victims, Chuck Palazzo's past has very much informed the present. He came from a rough section in the Bronx and joined the Marines as a family tradition and to escape "from a very dysfunctional family." His often absent father was abusive when around and his mother drank heavily.

"My brother was the brains and an aeronautic engineer and I chose the gangs, stealing cars and all that," Palazzo said.

He lied about his age, joining at 17, and at 18 was a squad leader. "From 1966 to 1967, I was with the 3rd Marine Recon Battalion with stints with both the 1st and 3rd Force Recon Companies."

Today, Palazzo talks easily about his passion for the Vietnamese people, but it takes him a long time to reveal a haunting moment in the war that left him with survival guilt. One dark night in early 1971 in Phu Bai, "my best friend was in the same unit as I was. We were on a reconnaissance mission between Phu Bai and Hue and were ambushed."

Palazzo's friend saw an "NLF fighter [or Vietcong] and some NVA [North Vietnamese Army] regulars, in a tree line, very close. One was taking aim at me and instead of trying to destroy him, my friend decided the quickest and safest thing—for me—was to shove me out of the way. He saved me but took a round in the back, which hit his spine. He was paralyzed and like so many, was treated with morphine for the pain. He was flown out after the fight to the naval field hospital in Da Nang then eventually back to the States and eventually discharged."

Palazzo recalls the sad disintegration of his friend. "I think the psychological damage [of being paralyzed] was more than the physical. He went through rehab for years, but at the same time he became addicted to heroin. Many overdoses later, he finally ended it all. "

He paused, "I think that probably has had a greater impact on me than all the PTSD combined."

Burning Down "Hooches"

In Vietnam, Palazzo and six others "would receive intel reports and go confirm exact ordnances, identify air to missile sites that were shooting down our planes. If there was some movement we would blow 'em up ourselves. We saw lots of movement, NVA regulars, battalions.

"I didn't have antiwar feelings when I was here," he says as we ride in a bus through beautiful mountainous country, "but morally I knew what was wrong. I was supposed to be part of a mop-up crew, hooches torched, that sort of thing. We never killed civilians, women or children, but kids would be running out screaming, and parents running out, before the hooches were burned down. We felt they were the VC; that is what we believed. I felt it was wrong but you kind of get caught up in the mob mentality."

Living with survival guilt and his PTSD nightmares, his nervousness in crowds, and experiencing a failed marriage, Palazzo filed a claim for PTSD and received help.

Today he smiles ruefully as he recalls his nonchalance of being in "an area that was heavily sprayed with Agent Orange. We were told it was harmless, to kill mosquitoes and to keep malaria down."

Later, realizing the full impact of Agent Orange, Palazzo recalls, "The best day and the worst day of my life was the day my daughter was born. Waiting for her to be born, the anxiety was killing me; I literally popped an ulcer eating so much Excedrin. Luckily, Agent Orange did not manifest itself in her or me. So it became the best day of my life."

Palazzo did not return to Vietnam for 30 years, not until 2001, "but then I was hooked. Five years later I formed a software development company, set up shop in the United States as well as Vietnam, and, in 2008, made the move. My software career has paid the bills to allow me to focus on activism—for all victims of Agent Orange as well as UXO [unexploded ordnance], and more recently, anti-GMO."

Genetically modified foods remain controversial; they are produced from organisms that have had specific changes introduced into their

DNA using the methods of genetic engineering. GMOs are developed by Monsanto, which also produced Agent Orange.

Software expert Palazzo is a one-man information bureau, blasting off emails by the second on any news about Agent Orange or UXOs and also attacking Monsanto, the makers of Agent Orange, along with Dow.

"The same company that even today, denies they or the Agent Orange they produced was and is responsible for so much death and destruction. The same company who REFUSES to pay any compensation to the victims of Agent Orange in Vietnam and throughout the world. And now, they are brainwashing the youth of Vietnam in the form of scholarships to convince them and the rest of the people in Vietnam that GMOs are safe. This is outrageous! There is something very, very wrong with this picture."[1]

Divided Nation

Today there are still two Vietnams, but not north and south. They are the prosperous and the impoverished; the beautifully healthy young people riding motor bikes, break dancing in a bustling city, talking on cell phones—and those who have blown off limbs or lie immobile on mats or are grotesquely misshapen, such as a woman whose hands have several fingers and legs that end at the knees with flipper-like feet attached. Only the thalidomide babies of the early 1960s mirror these flipper-like defects—those subjected to the chemical thalidomide while in the womb, which was taken by unsuspecting pregnant mothers to alleviate anxiety—experienced underdeveloped limbs, deformed eyes and hearts, and deformed alimentary and urinary tracts.

"I have dedicated my life to raising awareness of the plight of the AO victims here," said Palazzo. "And assisting as best as I can, to put smiles on their faces—even when they are looking death in the eye, they manage, somehow, to smile."

Rebelling against the War

Unlike Palazzo, Don Blackburn's rebellion began in Vietnam.

"I thought I could serve my country without sacrificing my morality—a very naïve notion. But I fought harder to keep my morality/humanity than I fought the 'enemy.' It cost me. I was under near constant harassment—two article 15s, the threat of imprisonment, many restrictions and odious (literally, burning shit) details, guard duty, K.P. When I returned from Viet Nam, I was a private E-1, the lowest rank possible. But I never tried to get out of the service, and this, I think, pissed the army off even more."

After the war, Blackburn became a teacher in Oregon and, while battling PTSD, wrote searing poetry, now in a book called *All You Have Given: Meditations on War, Peace & Reconciliation* (2011). Like many veterans who came back troubled from a war fought in and around civilians, this aspect was the most disturbing. Two of his disorderly conduct actions were for refusing to go on "search and destroy" missions and to burn hooches.

Napalm was dropped from planes and shot from guns for no other use than to incinerate; bright orange walls of intense fire that spared no one and stuck to skin, impossible to shuck off. Victims were embodied in the 1972 Pulitzer Prize iconic picture of a nine-year-old girl running naked in terror, her body still burning, having torn off her clothes to escape the pain.

No doctors thought she would survive, but she did, and after years of surgery, Kim Phuc now lives in Canada. She was a carefree child when four napalm bombs were dropped on her village. As she and her family ran for their lives, several of them died that day. Nick Ut, the Associated Press photographer, scooped her up and rushed her to the nearest hospital. Today Kim calls him Uncle Ut, the man who saved her life and whose graphic photo became a rallying point for ending the war.

Like many Vietnamese, Kim Phuc astounds Americans by *saying* she has forgiven those who caused her excruciating pain: "It was the hardest work of my life, but I did it." In the end, "I learned that forgiveness is more powerful than any weapon of war."

Don Blackburn's desire to save civilians was shatteringly personal. "There was a lot of napalm used where I was." He recalls in poetry a still haunting incident:

> "Fire in the Village near Ben Cat, 1967"
>
> With all my strength I hold onto you.
> I will not, cannot, let you go.
> Together we tremble in fear and sorrow.
> Our eyes bitten blind by swirling smoke.
> Our faces stung by wind-blown, fried sand.
> The conical hat, ripped off your head,
> bursts into flame a few feet in front of us.
> In tortured anguish, you scream at the sky:
> Why? Why?
> With all my strength I hold you.
> Your heart pounds fierce through your chest.
> You kick, try to bite, strain against my arms,
> You try to pry and squirm loose.
> You yell at me to let you go.

But I cannot, will not.
You will run back into your fire-engulfed house.
Try to save, or be with, whatever/whoever
Is still inside.
Together, we tremble in fear and sorrow,
And cry, cry, cry until there is no sound.
At first light tomorrow, you will return,
to see what can be found.

Forty years later, Blackburn returned to this woman in a poem.

"To the Village Woman Who Lost Everything in the Fire"
(America 2010)

Now I know there will never be enough tears
To put out those flames.
Still I will not, cannot,
let you go.
Somehow, somewhere,
I am sure you know.

Honoring Parents

Blackburn talks of his conflicted feelings as a 19 year old. "I volunteered for the draft in 1966. I wanted to honor my parents by serving as they did. My dad was at Normandy and was a concentration camp liberator. My mother was a WAVE (Women Accepted for Volunteer Emergency Service). They were believers in America—big believers in Lyndon Johnson and his hopes to end poverty in America.

"When I was threatened with jail time at LBJ—Long Binh Jail—I told my superior officers that my parents would probably be pissed off to find out we considered LBJ to stand for Lyndon Baines Johnson.

"I was sent to Viet Nam in late 1967 with no specific M.O.S. [Military Operational Specialty] and no training beyond basic. I had never held an M-16."

Most of his year was on the Cam Ranh Peninsula, spent "unloading ordnance from ships, building bunkers, going on occasional patrols, etc. A group of us did a slow down. Finally we said we were not going to unload any artillery. Refused to do anything. We were getting high almost all the time. One guy was reading Malcolm X."

Blackburn left his post to visit a friend who was in the mental ward at Cam Ranh Hospital. For this and other acts, Blackburn feels he would have been court martialed "if it wasn't for a couple of real humanitarian sergeants I knew." When he was discharged, "One of them personally drove me to the airport."

Back home in Oregon Blackburn drifted, flunked courses in college, and married and divorced twice. Finally, in counseling, he realized his denial and seething anger. He "suddenly got interested in college, got really good grades, and started writing poetry." He found out he had a knack for teaching. But he still had problems.

He recalled: "I was great during the week with the kids teaching, but I would spend weekends in isolation. I never discussed the war."

When he became eligible for retirement, Blackburn stopped teaching. "They didn't tell me that when you retired it would leave a big vacancy in your brain. With nothing to fill the void, all my PTSD came back."

In 2002, Blackburn returned to Vietnam for a visit and stayed for good in 2004: "I went all over looking for a place to get involved. There were all kinds of crooked shit going on, people taking money, scams. Then I found Friendship Village, which was on the up and up.... The first time I was at Friendship Village, I broke down completely.... It was something I needed to do for myself as well as for the kids. It filled an incredible hole."

Blackburn pauses, reflecting on the war: "Children died and we were unable to help them. An orphanage got hit by artillery.... We didn't do anything to help them...."

Friendship Village

The Vietnam Friendship Village, outside of Hanoi, was begun by an American veteran in 1988 and is now supported by international groups. It provides therapy and medical care for 150 children with mental and physical conditions, as well as education and vocational training. No one can say for sure that any of their defects were caused by Agent Orange.

Some stare blankly, others greet visitors with smiles, handing them poems and giving them hugs. Some walk and talk awkwardly. Each year some North Vietnamese soldiers return for R&R and stay at Friendship Village. One day, when we left the village, a handful of them greeted our group that included visiting American veterans.

Soon the names of combat sites were flashed back and forth. "Were you in A Luoi?" "Phu Bai?" Yes and smiles. They had been in the same areas, fighting on opposite sides. Americans and Vietnamese men reached out and hugged one another. One Vietnamese took off his medal, reaching high up to pin it on the tall, lean chest of Chuck Searcy.

A Rebellious Marine

Another rebel both during the war and after was Manus Campbell, who saw fierce fighting from June 1967 to July 1968.

"I served with 1st Battalion 4th Marines in Quang Tri, Dong Ha, and Con Tien," he says. "I got drafted and joined the Marines because I didn't want to go in the Army. I felt the Marines were more challenging. When you come here you don't know how to act or how to be."

Struggling with "100-degree humidity, you go out with 50–60 pounds, ammo, food, water, hide behind some vegetation and wait for the enemy to come. We had a lieutenant, fresh to Vietnam, brainwashed to be aggressive. But one thing you don't do at night is move; you set up an ambush and wait for them to come to you. He moved us, upsetting everybody. We could see the VC, crawling along in black pajamas. The lieutenant shouted 'Let's go, charge!' and was shot in the head."

One time Campbell's squad was sent to secure an area following fierce fighting where Marines had been pinned down in a stream.

"The stream was filled with 30, 40 guys missing limbs, with gunshot wounds, screaming 'I want my mother,' 'I'm too young to die.' It was hell. We chopped down the trees and helicoptered them out. We dropped off the body bags and sat around them. All night we were shooting illumination flares and the next morning got out."

Campbell speaks of the survival guilt and numb inaction back then: "I had all kinds of feelings about failing, not holding these guys when they were dying or doing first aid. I felt frozen. I made the decision that if ever I was in charge, I would not do something I felt was crazy and stupid that would jeopardize others."

His horror and final disillusionment was the body count, as it was with so many combat veterans. Counting dead bodies became a perverted measurement for "winning" in a war of attrition with no fixed goals.

Squads were even given ice cream and beer for the most kills counted. A priest who worked with PTSD patients in Vet Centers once remarked, "You send Boy Scouts into war and you tell them the more people you kill, the more you'll be rewarded. Including civilians. What do you think that does to their minds?"

Campbell said, "You knew you were being used; a couple hundred would get killed taking a hill and in a few days we'd leave. They didn't really care about you. But the body count number! That's what was important."

He reflects in his low voice, "If some colonel or general found it more important to send men into harm's way just to kill some people, they would do it. After B-52 strikes, we were told to dig up graves of the NVA who had been killed and buried. A lot of times it was like mass graves."

With two months left in Vietnam, Campbell refused to send men to meaningless possible death. His commanding officer backed him and told Campbell to ignore a colonel's repeated requests to go out and "find bodies."

"Peace Time"

Returning to Bayonne, New Jersey, "was just total shock. I had no preparation either for war or for going back. I felt so crazy, mixed up, and afraid. I was downing half a bottle of gin."

He decided to become a cop "because it was exciting. As veterans, we seek stimulation. Chasing a criminal 100 miles an hour seemed pretty stimulating. I became successful at what I did. It's about learning about people; how to read people, how to react to a situation."

During rehabilitation after a severe car accident Campbell started reading about meditation. Back on the police force, he thought, "My God, I don't want to be here. This sucks. Having to deal with the dark side of life every day—murderers, children being wounded. They tell you in the Police Academy that you deal with stress two ways—alcohol and women. I did both."

Two marriages came and went following the tension of nightmares and flashbacks. He stopped drinking "for good" in 1986 and retired after 19 years as a New Jersey trooper. He then taught at-risk children, as well as alcohol and drug prevention and recovery. He said he did that "part time, and full time I struggled with PTSD."

In 2007, Campbell returned to Vietnam for the first time and visited a Pagoda in Hue where the Buddhist nun had founded a school for disabled children and an orphanage. (Poor families still have to give up their babies to adoption.) "I started to support the school financially; every month I would wire money and receive photos from the nun about her work," he said.

Campbell started his own NGO—Helping Invisible Victims of War—lived in Hue and now in Hoi An, continuing to help buy food and blankets for two very poor minority tribes who live near Khe Sanh and A Luoi. He also buys artificial legs for bomb victims, supports several children at the Khanh school for the disabled.

Palazzo and Blackburn work with VAVA (Vietnam Association of Victims of Agent Orange). A new project for Blackburn is building a house for a Rag Lai ethnic minority family in the mountains. "Three generations of this very poor family have been affected by Agent Orange dioxin poisoning."

Recollections of Saigon

Chuck Searcy, a lanky Georgian with a Southern drawl, dwarfs the Vietnamese with whom he spends his days. One night, sitting in the roof-top bar of Saigon's storied Caravelle Hotel, he remembers the night in 1967, dancing his last dance with his former fiancée, who had just arrived in Vietnam as a Red Cross volunteer.

"We could see rocket flares and hear distant artillery fire. The band was playing old Glenn Miller tunes. It was surreal."

The Caravelle, now in the renamed Ho Chi Minh City, was famously home for war correspondents; some trying to be the new Hemingway, downing drinks, watching air strikes across the Saigon River from the roof, so close but so safely removed.

Because of his role as an enlisted intelligence specialist in Saigon, except for the 1968 Tet Offensive that reached the southern capital, Searcy felt he had been untouched by PTSD in comparison to Blackburn, Campbell, and Palazzo.

However, when he returned to Georgia, this patriotic son of a World War II POW faced a "devastating awakening. All of my values, everything I had been taught and had come to believe seemed to be nothing. The United States government was not only lying to us, but perpetrating actions that were absolutely criminal. It was an awful personal trauma for me."

Searcy returned to the University of Georgia in Athens and helped form a contingent of Vietnam Veterans Against the War (VVAW). After the war, Searcy "got married and divorced a couple of times."

In 1986, Searcy helped Wyche Fowler win an incredible upset victory to become the U.S. Senator from Georgia. Searcy became Fowler's press secretary for two years.

"I was not happy with staff work in the Senate—it was static, institutionalized, frustratingly non-productive, everyone was too fawning toward the Senators. Although it was a remarkably eye-opening experience and I made many lasting friendships."

In 1992, Searcy visited Vietnam as a tourist for 30 days: "By the end, I knew that I wanted to come here and try to make a small contribution to the healing and the recovery that was slowly, but clearly, underway."

From left to right: Chuck Searcy, Rennie Davis, Ramsey Clark, Hanoi 2013.
Photo by Frank Joyce.

Fighting "Combat Fatigue"

The last of the five, Mike Cull, was a "social work technician" with the 8th Field Hospital in Nha Trang.

"I joined a bizarre Mental Health Team" whose job was to prevent what was then called combat fatigue as experienced in the Korean War, he said. Cull's cushy quarters were "near a beautiful beach and too many bars and brothels. It was the HQ for Special Forces, MACV (Military Assistance Command, Vietnam), and USAID with a very busy Air Force base."

It was jarringly different when he went weekly by chopper to other hospitals to evaluate patients near the battlefields: "The worst were suicide cases, violent criminal types, and many psychotic patients (including one psychiatrist)."

Cull's job was to help with what would later be known as PTSD patients. "We failed miserably," Cull said.

An angry Cull returned as an "unofficial Vietnam Vet Against the War in class, in bars, on the streets, and in jail for a few overnight stays." Following an ashram sojourn in India and a spiritual commune in Oregon, Cull taught urban studies and sociology at five universities for years. He quit to work in VA Vet Centers, "once again working with combat PTSD vets in Alaska."

Cull returned to Vietnam in 1998 to work for seven years for Vietnam Friendship Village, with Suel Jones (who was not in Vietnam during this interview). After retirement, Cull became a volunteer teacher at Nha Trang University and recently celebrated his marriage to a Vietnamese woman, assisted by the other American veterans in a joyous ceremony. Cull and his wife, Lan, operate the Vietnam Advanced Language Center for 150 students.

Vietnam Kaleidoscope

So many visitors to Vietnam remain startled at the friendliness of a people who were bombed and burned out of their homes and who lost family. "They love to say 'the past is the past,'" says Campbell.

Tourism is the coin of the realm in a country that swirls with constant action. Google "Vietnam" and tourist sites clog the screen—offering lush beach hideaways, silk clothes made overnight, restaurants galore, combined with trips to battlefields and museums that show graphic pictures of war crimes. Motorbikes piled with parents, children, food, and live ducks surf through Hanoi at a pace that makes crossing the street feel like running with the bulls in Pamplona. It is nigh impossible to find a bad meal in the restaurants throughout Vietnam (although one sees signs for Texas-style burgers). An upscale restaurant in Hue, a city bombarded during the 1968 Tet Offensive, has risen out of wreckage to splendor, complete with an award-winning concert pianist playing background music.

There is a tolerance for different lifestyles as well as religion; gay clubs outside Ho Chi Minh City are ignored by authorities, Miss Universe contestants are celebrated, Vietnamese who have become rich crowd a beach resort near Hoi An that charges close to $2,000 a night for two bedrooms and a private pool. Rumors abound that the Russian and Ukrainian mafia have been involved in Vietnam's tourism; until recently, there were daily nonstop flights from Moscow.

Vietnam remains Communist, but Buddhism is powerful, recognized almost as a national religion, with colorful ceremonies seen in temples everywhere with Vietnamese visiting at all hours of the day, just as they do Ho Chi Minh's tomb. Smoking barrels are ever ready at the North Vietnamese equivalent of Arlington Cemetery, where Vietnamese light incense sticks and place them on graves. We found the grave of a boy of 19, like so many of those on the side of the United States, and placed an incense stick.

Trying Tourism

Successful younger Vietnamese, heavily into tourism, have only distant memories, if at all, of the Hunger Years following the war, when the Communist regime passed a moribund Five Year Plan of Recovery, forced those who fought for the South into "re-education camps," and the United States imposed a trade embargo.

President Bill Clinton lifted the embargo in 1994 and the normalization of relations began in 1995 with Douglas "Pete" Peterson as the first U.S. Ambassador to Vietnam. As a former POW in Vietnam, Peterson brought great symbolism to this reconciliation.

Capitalism has come to Vietnam just as it had in China and some, like Searcy, an influential voice in U.S.-Vietnam relations, bemoan that it has gone too far: "It's almost impossible to explain what's going on. The economy is probably a mess, in reality, though superficial indicators look good. The Vietnamese leadership has really embraced crony capitalism, greed based on corruption and inside deals" that spawn "overnight millionaires."

Searcy says the authorities neglect environmental hazards as they fill beachfronts with fantastic hotels and ignore earlier promises to keep access to these beaches for Vietnamese families.

"Brilliant people here have explored alternative economic systems, including a healthy mix of socialism and market competition, but they are either dismissed or become threats to the ruling oligarchy," Searcy says, adding a bit sardonically, "There was a significant change when the leaders announced publicly that it was *okay to be rich.*"

Searcy is the unofficial good-will ambassador for visiting Americans and gets American press for his Project RENEW. Its "goal is to make Vietnam safe—not to 'clean up every bomb and mine' which is a misleading and distracting, and unrealistic, aim," says Searcy, the only American advisor.

He touts his team of young, educated and highly committed Vietnamese who live in Quang Tri Province: "Their families experienced the suffering of war and now live with the threat of explosives. They understand Vietnamese culture and traditions, local laws and regulations, how to get things done."

These 30-somethings, like Ngo Xuan Hien and Luong Tuan Hung, whip-smart on computers, bilingual, at home in blue jeans like their American counterparts, tell the Internet world of projects to aid poor families, like growing mushrooms and buying cows.

The Vietnamese teams are also the ones who take on the dangerous job of locating and detonating bombs, responding to daily call-ins from local residents of cluster bombs and other munitions found in their gardens and along roadways. Within hours, the teams destroy or safely remove the lethal threats.

Finding Support

These five American veterans in Vietnam have become adept beggars, in the noblest sense, in their sometimes futile pleas to raise awareness and money to aid this hidden side of Vietnam. Searcy returns to Congress, pressing for humanitarian aid, and though the U.S. government has provided significant funding, most of Project RENEW'S recent support has come from other governments—Norway, Japan, Taiwan, and Ireland, as well as assistance from Australian veterans. Modest funding has come from private American donors.

Easily found online at *http://landmines.org.vn/*, Project RENEW notes that for the price of an upscale dinner for two or three, one can buy an artificial limb (about $200–$300) for children and adults on a waiting list; however, making this happen is not easy in a complacent America.

Incensed after a trip to Vietnam in 2014, Sen. Patrick Leahy, D-Vermont, made a successful plea to Congress by asking the representatives to imagine how they would feel if their grandchildren risked death or maiming by merely playing in a field. Congress nearly tripled the small amount of funding for UXO (unexploded ordnance) removal projects throughout Southeast Asia, including Vietnam.

But humanitarian funding remains an uphill battle. A full year's education for a child affected by Agent Orange could be possible for what would amount to pennies per day for Americans. Activist Michael Moore honored his late father by recently giving money to the VFP Agent Orange effort.

Burying Lethal Dirt

Da Nang: In intense heat we climbed a ladder to the top of cement blocks, piled 20 feet high, which would become part of a giant mausoleum to bury deadly Agent Orange–contaminated soil. From the top, we could see the houses of Vietnamese close by.

Estimates of the amount of dioxin in the soil at Da Nang are staggering. A general standard is that dioxin levels must not exceed 1,000 ppt (parts per trillion) in soil. Dioxin levels of up to 365,000 ppt were found at Da Nang. Dioxin at this level calls for "immediate" remediation, experts say.

Forty years later, the U.S. government has finally begun to try to clean up this contaminated soil in Da Nang, near the airport, one of three most heavily sprayed hotspots. (The others are Bein Hoa and Phu Cat.)

The structure we visited earlier is now covered and, inside this large space, deadly dirt is being treated. The project is jointly implemented by USAID and the Vietnamese Ministry of National Defense. The initial cost was estimated at $41 million, but has reached $84 million, and may grow as the project is now expected to last until 2016.

Poisoned soil and sediment is placed in this enclosed above-ground structure. Heating rods, operating at approximately 1400 to 1500 degrees Fahrenheit, raise the temperature of the entire dirt pile to at least 635 degrees. At that temperature, the dioxin compound is supposed to decompose into harmless substances.

Chuck Palazzo is hopeful but is not certain it will work: "It's hard to convey this, but the looks in the contractors' eyes when I asked the question about this being a success, are ones of, let's say, fear. Let's hope it works, but I think Bien Hoa will go full bore *only* if Da Nang is a success."

Meanwhile, the five Vietnam Americans living here concentrate on giving their all to help victims of the Vietnam War's lasting legacies—and fighting any whitewashing by the Pentagon of that war.

10

UNWANTED MEMORIES ERASED IN ELECTROCONVULSIVE THERAPY EXPERIMENT[1]

FRANK JOYCE

Get Your FREE VIETNAM War 50th Anniversary Coin.

It's the headline of an ad at the back of the Sunday paper coupon inserts. It sits forlornly below "THE HOTTEST CONCEPT IN HAIR REMOVAL—NO! NO! HAIR." It is soliciting money for a group claiming to support the "missing" POW-MIAs from the Vietnam War.

I feel sorry for the vets trying to keep the POW-MIA issue alive. As with so many chapters in the ugly U.S. past, the electroconvulsive therapy machine is hard at work trying to erase our memory of the Vietnam War.

It won't work. Not in my case, for sure. Viet Nam as a nation and an experience is an integral part of my personal history. I have no desire to forget it. To the contrary, I think revisiting our history with the country and the war is an opportunity to learn a great deal about how we can become more powerful in waging peace.

A good place to start is by understanding how the United States came to make war on Viet Nam in the first place. More than 45 years ago I wrote a piece called, "Racism in the United States, An Introduction." In that article I said:

> The settling of the West did not stop at the Pacific Ocean, but continued on to Hawaii, the Philippines, Samoa (still called American Samoa), Japan, China, and ultimately Viet Nam. Many of the same generals who fought to the Pacific also fought in the Pacific

campaigns. And although the reasons for expansion changed as the nation became industrialized, the process of expansion is so inexorable that the United States has never had any "foreign policy" whatsoever, at least regarding the Pacific. United States Pacific and Asian involvement is, perhaps more obviously than is usually the case, simply an extension of domestic policy. *In this sense, the United States is in Viet Nam because it is in California.*[2]

As I write today, I stand by that analysis. It is even clearer now than it was then that we are a warrior nation. For as long as I have been alive, the United States has been making war somewhere. I was born during WWII. Since then, the U.S. military has attacked Korea, Viet Nam, Cambodia, Laos, Kuwait, Bosnia, Kosovo, Iraq repeatedly, Panama, Grenada, Afghanistan, and Libya. That's not counting innumerable other military interventions by clandestine forces, surrogate armies, air power, drones, and subversion. Nor does it count the 800-plus military bases the United States has outside its own borders.

Our culture is saturated with the worship of war and violence. It's so common that we mostly don't notice it. It is at the core of much of our entertainment. Likewise, the invention, manufacture, and distribution of every kind of weapon plays a key role in our economy. From handguns to grenade launchers to airplanes and missiles, we supply killing power to individuals, governments, and freelance "freedom fighters" such as Osama Bin Laden, as long as we believe they are aligned with U.S. geopolitical objectives.

Reverence for war is insinuated into every nook and cranny of our daily lives. One of my favorite examples is the TV visual of service men and women who stand by the greens in the final holes of big golf tournaments. The players and the announcers are required to gush about our "heroes" and glorify their "service."

Also illuminating was the reaction in 2014 to the disclosure of a conversation between two State Department diplomats about U.S. efforts to engineer regime change in the Ukraine (as we now know, they were ultimately successful). In the weird way of the hyper-news cycle we live in, the exchange made headlines because neo-con state department operative Victoria Nyland used the f-word in dismissing the negative reaction of the European Union to U.S. goals.[3] What caught my attention was what did *not* make news. To the best of my knowledge, not one mainstream media pundit or reporter remarked on the notion that the United States gets to decide who should be leading the government of Ukraine in the first place. It's just accepted as normal that the U.S. powers-that-be can determine the destiny of any nation they choose.

The Enduring Power of White Supremacy

Somehow this hiding-in-plain-sight reality is invisible to a majority of U.S. Americans. Every military intervention is treated as a discrete event unconnected to anything that came before. Buried most deeply is the link to the ideology of white supremacy baked into the very origin of the nation. There are two overlapping elements of the experience that shapes U.S. white supremacist culture to this day. Demonizing blacks was an essential component of the justification for slavery and then Jim Crow segregation. In a modified form it rationalizes the matrix of advantages delivered to whites today. Validating genocide against Indigenous people is also part of the DNA of the United States.

For an account of how the multiple campaigns against Indigenous nations shaped the identity, culture, organization, and strategy of the U.S. military in particular, *An Indigenous Peoples' History of the United States* by Roxanne Dunbar-Ortiz is essential reading. Understanding the arc of that history puts the U.S. war against Viet Nam in context. In one of many telling details illustrating this continuity, Dunbar-Ortiz points out that the team that assassinated Osama Bin Laden assigned him the code name Geronimo. She also points out that military use of the term "in country" is a direct descendant of "in Indian country."

Another example of the core policies and practices of the U.S. military was the use of Agent Orange to "defoliate" Viet Nam, Laos, and Cambodia. This was not a mere "echo" of the extermination of the buffalo in "settling" the U.S. American West. It is a direct descendant of the total war policies devised early in U.S. military history to decimate Indigenous people by eliminating the source of their livelihood—likewise, Operation Phoenix, the targeted assassination program in Viet Nam, and the multiple massacres of women, children, and the elderly, of which My Lai is only the most well-known example.

Total war violence was also the brutal methodology intrinsic to the U.S. brand of slavery. From ships that carried the slaves, through the slave patrols that enforced the rules of slavery, to the highly militarized twenty-first century police departments from small towns such as Ferguson, Missouri, to big cities such as Los Angeles and Chicago, violence toward civilians was routine. The works of Gerald Horne, including *The Counter-Revolution of 1776: Slave Resistance and the Origins of the United States of America*, are essential reading for understanding the military intersection of the suppression of slaves and Indigenous people in the creation of the first-ever apartheid state.

As the theory and practice of white supremacy has evolved over 500 years, it has infected and affected how most U.S. Americans, especially white Americans, see *everything*. The combination of genocidal behavior toward First Nations and the machinery of slavery required a belief system that justified the behavior. That belief system is that whites are intellectually, morally, and otherwise superior to Native Americans and African Americans. (The attitude of superiority extends to Asians and other people of color, but on a somewhat different trajectory.)

Perhaps nothing better illustrates the synergy of attitudes toward Native Americans and blacks than the viewpoint of one L. Brooks Patterson. Patterson first came to public prominence as an attorney who defended KKK members charged with burning school buses in Pontiac, Michigan, in 1971. The Klan targeted the buses because they were going to be used to racially integrate schools under a federal court order. Since 1976, Patterson has served continuously as an elected official of Oakland County, Michigan, a collection of predominantly white suburbs just north of Detroit. In 2012, he was elected to his sixth consecutive term as the county's chief executive.

Patterson once expressed his attitude toward African Americans in Detroit like this: "What we're going to do is turn Detroit into an Indian reservation, where we herd all the Indians into the city, build a fence around it, and then throw in the blankets and corn." In an interview with a writer from the *New Yorker* in 2014, he reaffirmed that perspective.

How I Got This Way

For me, the remarkable thing is that the better I understand this history, the more extraordinary the movement against the Vietnam War becomes. Why? Of all the U.S. wars, only the Vietnam War engendered such widespread resistance from the Anglo population. I am convinced that the movement helped make the war shorter. Given the enormous viciousness visited upon the citizens of Viet Nam, Laos, and Cambodia, this may seem hard to believe—but it could have been even worse were it not for the restraining force of the antiwar movement.

What made Vietnam the most opposed U.S. war before or since? The seeds were sown by the Civil Rights Movement. Without the modern struggle against Jim Crow, which I date first from the Montgomery movement in 1955 and then the Greensboro sit-ins in 1960, the U.S. assault on Viet Nam would have unfolded like Korea or other wars that drew little protest. This is true in ways big and small.

Looking at the big picture, the courage and creativity of the Civil Rights Movement proved that effective opposition to a long-established status quo was possible. It engaged blacks and whites too. It helped to stimulate the white student movement, most dramatically expressed by Students for a Democratic Society (SDS). Civil rights activists also led the way in challenging the war as an expression of colonialism and racism.

The arc of the cut-short life of the Rev. Dr. Martin Luther King traced his path from opposition to Jim Crow to his later words condemning the triple evils of racism, militarism, and materialism. My own personal evolution, starting from civil rights activism, followed a similar path. My first overt act of political resistance was to join a picket line against a segregated swimming pool in Oak Park, Michigan, in 1960.

I did not come from a liberal or progressive family. My father especially was a right-wing and racist Republican. Like others who became '60s activists of one kind or another, as a student leader, I had already participated in some challenges to the authorities at Royal Oak Dondero High School. I think many of us "rebels without causes" later found them. The causes, that is.

It was not a long trip. If there is a cauldron in which the theory and practice of post–WWII Northern urban racism was formed, Detroit, Michigan burned the hottest. My parents were white flight pioneers, leaving Detroit for a brand new suburb in the 1940s. In that context, challenging the whole apparatus and ideology of racial segregation was for sure the most rebellious thing I could do.

I guess it worked. The immediate consequence of joining the swimming pool picket line was to get me thrown out of the house when my father saw me protesting segregation on TV news coverage. Fortunately, I had a full-time factory job at the time so I was economically self-sufficient. I was able to work and attend classes at Wayne State University in Detroit. At first, I commuted from a suburban apartment but later moved into the city to be close to campus.

At Wayne State I continued to participate in student government, as I had in high school. But I also connected to the emerging Civil Rights Movement, becoming first involved in the Northern Student Movement (NSM). That later led to my helping to create People Against Racism (PAR) in 1966.

Shortly after PAR was formed, we had our first internal conflict. It was about the Vietnam War. Ultimately, we reached a consensus and issued a statement of opposition to the war. We based our case on the racism inherent in invading Viet Nam, a non-white country and on the disproportionate casualties being suffered by African-American soldiers.

Somewhere in that time frame I became a draft resister. That led to my becoming punitively inducted into the Army (a practice later ruled unconstitutional by the U.S. Supreme Court). I did report for duty as ordered, but thanks to some creative activity on my part, the military at the induction center decided then and there that I was "unfit for service." Had my plan not worked, I was prepared to refuse induction, face arrest, and then deal with those consequences.

As a result of becoming a draft resister and seeing antiwar work as an extension of anti-racism, my engagement in the antiwar movement brought me into contact with the Vietnamese. I went to meetings in Canada, Paris, and ultimately to Viet Nam in the spring of 1970. Going to Viet Nam was an especially life-changing experience. It provided an extraordinary prism through which to look at my own country.

Looking up at the sky from a village south of Hanoi at risk of being bombed at any time by B-52s, my country seemed as grotesque to me as did that segregated swimming pool in the Detroit suburb of Oak Park, Michigan. What was it about U.S. American culture that required such a permanent state of fear that a small nation 9,000 miles away represented such a big threat?

As it happened, I was in that village on a significant day: May 4, 1970. When our group of four antiwar activists was awake and gathered for breakfast, we could tell our hosts were troubled. They said they had some important news. Four students protesting the invasion of Cambodia had been killed at Kent State University.

My recollection is that the Vietnamese seemed more upset by this than we were. I was deeply moved by their distress. It may sound hokey or naïve, but I remember thinking at the time that their concern was completely genuine and authentic. It reinforced as strongly as anything that they meant it when they said they differentiated between the people of the United States and the U.S. government.

My own feeling was that I was not surprised. It was only a matter of time, I thought. The mere fact that we were in Viet Nam was proof to me that the rift at home over the war was intensifying.

I was well aware of how many Civil Rights workers had been killed. Part of my work as a staff member for the Chicago 8/7 trial had been to compile a list of those who had died in the struggle. (I use 8/7 here because the government originally charged eight activists for organizing protests at the 1968 Democratic Party convention. Early in the trial Black Panther Bobby Seale was separated as a result of his defiant courtroom behavior. The trial then continued without him.) Most U.S. Americans were aware of high-profile deaths such as Andrew Goodman, Michael Schwerner, and James Chaney in Philadelphia, Mississippi, in the summer of 1964. But my research surprised even me. As of late 1969, the list ran to well over 100

Antiwar protest in Detroit, Michigan, 1970.
Courtesy of Fifth Estate.

names and included several whites in addition to Goodman and Schwerner. Even if you are white, I realized, if you push the government too hard, it will respond with violence.

In the days following May 4, both in Viet Nam and when we got back to the United States, it became apparent that a line had been crossed. TThe national consensus of support essential to sustaining the war was over once and for all. Many friends and acquaintances, especially older people, who had been indifferent or "on the fence" about the war were now openly opposed.

The antiwar movement had changed the public mind. It was poised as never before to challenge government policy.

Even before then, and more so after my Viet Nam visit, I wondered about bigger questions. Just why are nation-states so important? What is the source of their enormous power to demand our loyalty? Why are so many U.S. Americans so obsequious toward our military? Is a nation such as Viet Nam, evolved from more than a thousand years of history, albeit fraught with its own conflicts, different than our own, descended as we are from colonialism and slavery?

I wrestle with these issues to this day. Should a "peace" movement try to end war one nation at a time, or is a transnational appeal more effective? At a time when human aggression threatens the eco-system of the planet, shouldn't our first loyalty be to *all* life-forms? Certainly, the late peace activist Lillian Genser thought so when she composed a pledge that has become a touchstone for me: "*I pledge allegiance to the world, to care for earth and sea and air, to cherish every living thing with peace and justice everywhere.*" Vincent Harding, sadly now also deceased, used to say, "*I am a citizen of a country which does not yet exist.*"

Got a Hold on Me

Throughout my lifetime of political activism, Viet Nam kept a hold on me. I returned in 2006 and again in 2013. These trips affirmed my respect and affection for the people, the culture, and the beauty of the country. I remember a powerful moment on a small boat on the Mekong River in 2006 when I marveled all over again about what could possibly have led the U.S. military to think they could even dominate the physical terrain, let alone the spirit of the people. Did it go all the way back to the frontier experience of decimating the Native Americans, also on unfamiliar terrain? Was it the legacy of thinking that U.S. prowess in weaponry, up to and including nuclear bombs, would always win the day?

Many who go to Viet Nam today, whether as returning war veterans, returning peace veterans, or tourists, are struck by the openness of the people and the lack of bitterness and resentment toward U.S. Americans. Almost everyone has a story about being told by one or more Vietnamese that the U.S. invasion was but the blink of an eye compared to the centuries of long struggles with previous invaders, especially China.

Visitors to Viet Nam are invariably impressed with the sheer energy that rises up from the streets of Hanoi, Ho Chi Minh City, smaller cities, or even rural areas. Nevermind the nauseating pettiness and mendacity of U.S. politics and the media that enables it—compared to Viet Nam, the United States seems just all around tired. Exactly what noble purpose or vision is the U.S. government fulfilling these days?

To be clear, I do not think that Viet Nam is utopia. Neither do the Vietnamese. On both of my trips back I was struck by the quality of the discussion about the direction of the country. Problems from corruption to labor unrest to income inequality to democratic participation were freely acknowledged and openly discussed.

Frank Joyce receives a gift from Vietnamese friends in Quang Tri, 2013.
Courtesy of Frank Joyce.

The New Case for Pacifism, or
Is It the Case for a New Pacifism?

I credit my engagement with Viet Nam for helping me form a realistic picture of what is wrong with the United States. But it has also been a powerful source of hope for change as well. The "David vs. Goliath" ability of Viet Nam to repel the U.S. invasion is itself inspiring. But so is the movement that arose around the world to support Viet Nam in its struggle.

I am proud to have been a part of that movement. And I believe that it proves that U.S. Americans can transcend the passivity and confusion that allows the worst aspects of our national history of racism, settler colonialism and imperial conquest to repeat themselves. Beyond that, people's diplomacy can play a part in containing war-loving policy makers.

One of the things I realized while participating in the observances of the 40th Anniversary of the Paris Peace Accords in 2013 was the continuity of the Vietnamese practice of people-to-people diplomacy, first with the French and then with U.S. Americans after the U.S. military took over the front-line job of suppressing the Vietnamese. In part, that was a legacy of the ties between Ho Chi Minh and the French Communist Party, of which he was a founder.

I am well aware that the U.S. antiwar movement and the French Communist Party were very different. At the risk of stating the obvious, the French CP was well established, disciplined, and held political power in government from municipalities to parliament. None of those things was true of the amorphous components of what came to be the antiwar movement in the United States. It was far less structured. And it took considerable time before the war became a significant issue in the electoral arena.

The "Hanoi 9" peace veterans who traveled to Viet Nam for the 40th Anniversary of the signing of the Paris Peace Accords provide a good snapshot of the makeup of a large section of the antiwar movement. As represented in this book, we were Yippies, pacifists, and new leftists. Alex Hing represents a connection both to Asian-American and African-American activism.

The dominant narrative about the Vietnam War is that it differs from virtually all other U.S. wars because the U.S. "lost." Often the "loss" is blamed on the antiwar movement. American exceptionalism requires the belief that all U.S. wars are good wars. Throughout my lifetime, World War II has been portrayed as the finest hour of the greatest generation. As a lifelong Michigander and therefore a "Yankee," I was also raised to believe in the nobility of the enormous bloodshed required to end slavery.

To be sure, emancipating slaves and defeating fascism were worthy causes, but that does not change the fact that slavery was followed by Jim Crow segregation and a century of economic exploitation of African Americans described so effectively in the book by Douglas Blackmon, *Slavery by Another Name*. Nor does it justify the pervasive institutional racism that oppresses African Americans today. Neither does it vindicate the abuse visited upon the planet by the global hegemony the U.S. government sought and obtained by using nuclear weapons to crush Hiroshima and Nagasaki.

If anything, the Civil War and World War II stand out as the exception to the rule of virtually constant U.S. war against Indigenous people in North America as well as other nations all over the planet—an endless war that has been underway since the first white colonial settlement in Jamestown, Virginia.

The purpose of the "all U.S. wars are good wars" narrative is to create a culture in which opposing war is always unpatriotic and successfully mitigating the military's ability to fight and "win" any war is thus characterized as intrinsically treasonous. Blaming the antiwar movement for the "loss" of Viet Nam serves more than one purpose. It diverts attention from the military successes of the Vietnamese. There is no denying that from a conventional wisdom perspective the failure of the enormous firepower of the U.S. military to subdue the Vietnamese is humiliating to the military establishment. Blaming war opponents for the loss also seeks to prevent opposition to present and future wars.

There is conflict between those who want to "forget everything," and those who want to use the history in support of one agenda or another. Some of the tension is individual, some institutional. Many soldiers who fought in the Viet Nam, Laos, and/or Cambodia war repress those memories as best they can. Whether they have a "clinical" version of PTSD or not, they don't talk about the war and don't like it when others bring it up. Young civilians don't have any direct experience with the war and are rarely inclined to pay attention unless required to do so in an academic setting. Older U.S. Americans, especially whites, are part of a culture that systematically operates to obliterate anything about the nation's past that is ugly. That requires a lot of obliteration.

The military has a different set of interests. It's hard for them to write Viet Nam out of their history books altogether. And so it weaves together a story to fit the war into the triumphal narrative of U.S. empire. It is from this necessity that we get the ongoing 50th anniversary commemoration of the Vietnam War. The Pentagon's Vietnam War Commission tells a story of sacrifice and heroism that ignores the opposition to the war altogether.[4] That effort is being challenged by an ad hoc coalition of veterans of the antiwar movement. Ironically, the Pentagon and the antiwar veterans share the need to combat the tendency to just forget the whole thing.

The New Case for Pacifism

Back in the day, I opposed the war against Viet Nam, Laos, and Cambodia. I would have had no problem being described as an antiwar activist, meaning that my focus was a particular war. These days, I describe myself as a pacifist. That does not mean that I have undergone training in Gandhian philosophy or the theory and practice of deep non-violence as advocated by the Rev. James Lawson and others. I have great admiration for those who do.

Nevertheless, I have reached the pacifist conclusion that there is no problem for which violence is a solution. I agree completely with the position recently taken by Steven Hawking that the supreme threat to the planet is human aggression. I concur with his observation that whatever value it once served in our evolutionary history as a species is now counterproductive.

Human violence of all kinds dominates the daily news. That is discouraging because it reinforces an apparently self-fulfilling prophecy; that such behavior is an immutable trait of our species. Admittedly, violence does beget more violence. That truth, however, also supports the possibility that peace can beget more peace.

And for those willing to look, there are many developments that seem to be leading a way to a less violent future. Perhaps most surprising are recent steps toward curtailing the mistreatment of animals. I include the decision by the Ringling Brothers circus to phase out the use of elephants in their circus performances as an example. The push-back against the exploitation of whales by Sea World is another. For many reasons, including the arguments advanced by Jeffrey Moussaieff Masson in his book *Beasts*, I am persuaded that our abuse of animals is directly related to the propensity of humans to mistreat other humans.

Also heartening is the attention now being paid to the devastating impact of bullying. Concern over the injuries intrinsic to contact sports also growing. There is probably nothing that would bring our species to a more peaceful future than the elimination of all forms of child abuse. Here, too, there is mounting awareness of the issue, if not yet that much progress in curtailing it.

The destruction of the earth by fracking, filling the oceans with trash and pollutants, damaging coral reefs by various human actions, and the manipulation of plants by genetic modification are other examples of human supremacy that threaten not just the existence of humans but the viability of all life-forms on Earth.

Finally, it is a mystery to me that anyone can deny the connection between the violence we inflict on the people of other nations and the violence that we inflict on each other within the borders of the U.S. of A. They are woven into the same cloth.

Is it not obvious that the glorification of violence places the United States—as a culture and a government—squarely on the wrong side of history? A letter written to the *New York Times* captured succinctly how we are perceived by others: "Dear America: Not that I expect to persuade you, but just so you know, most of the rest of the world regards your obsession with guns and executions as barbaric. Don't say you weren't told." Vince Calderhead, Nairobi, Kenya, April 30, 2014.[5]

The Case for a New Pacifism

It's easy to talk about "paradigm shifts." Trying to deliberately bring them about is difficult. Nevertheless, conditions are ideal for a new kind of pacifism born of the reality of our time.

Here is the contradiction we face. The urgency of onrushing eco-catastrophe compels humans to cooperate as never before. Drought and flood, water and air pollution, declining precious resources, hunger and pandemics will undoubtedly create tensions across the globe. The prospects for murderous conflict are obviously great. So is the human instinct for survival. As the crisis deepens, will it bring out the worst in humans or something better? I support something better. I don't assume it happens automatically, but that we can make it so.

A deliberate campaign by supporters of slavery, especially in the United States, elevated "whiteness" as a key component of identity in order to win support for race-based chattel slavery and capitalism. In doing so, whiteness replaced apex identities more tied to religion, ethnic heritage, or cultural interests. The point is that identity concepts are not static. Clearly, therefore, it is possible to reorder our identity priorities now to favor the unity and integrity of all life-forms.

Conversely, the power of the old identity hierarchies of patriarchy, white racism, and wealth are obstacles to achieving the cooperation necessary to save the planet. There are promising signs here, too. Most dramatic is the unprecedented speed with which the West is coming to accept a new paradigm (there's that word) of acceptable sexual identities. If that can be reordered, so can race and other categories.

As for materialism, that too must pass. Why? Global capitalism as it is currently organized is leading to extinction for humans and other life-forms. The system of producing for the sake of production and consuming for the sake of consumption is not sustainable. The only question is, how does that system end? Does it end in catastrophe or by achieving a different way of defining the purpose of an economy and a better way of organizing it? I vote for something different. Idealism and survival pragmatism can combine as never before to shape our future.

The People Make the Peace

We face a great opportunity. Appearances to the contrary, U.S. Americans are weary of war abroad and violence at home. And whether we like it or not, the temperature of the ever-simmering debate about Viet Nam is going to be turned up in the years ahead. No less a force than the Pentagon itself with the full support of Congress and the Presidency are going to see to that.

When I first became aware of this, my knee-jerk response was something like, *Oh good, we get to have arguments about Viet Nam all over again. Only now, with benefit of hindsight, we can convince even more people that we were right about Viet Nam.* I said as much in articles and speeches. But now, I think I was wrong.

Many signs from disparate places are pointing in the same direction. The point is not to engender more conflict. The point is to find the places where healing and learning can take place. In order to address the global crisis of ecocide and econocide we need to overcome divisions of all kinds—race, gender, excessive nation-state loyalty—the whole dang thing. On the other hand, working to overcome such divisions is itself a valuable contribution toward generating the unity of purpose that will allow us to transition out of destructive behaviors that threaten human and other life on earth.

This is not the place to lay out specific strategies and tactics. But some perspective, guidelines, and goals are appropriate:

- Many people who once supported the war in Viet Nam, Laos, and Cambodia, no longer do. The well-publicized doubts expressed by former Defense Secretary Robert McNamara are but one example. Whatever U.S. Americans may think or even know about the arc of U.S. genocide, racism, and imperialism, an overwhelming majority think that the Vietnam War was at best a mistake. There is virtually no one who opposed the war at the time who regrets their opposition. Furthermore, the fiascos of Iraq and Afghanistan have vindicated the opponents of those wars. In other words, conceding that a minority controls the levers of war making power, the majority of the people support peace.

- The Vietnamese helped us before; they can help us again. As former U.S. Attorney General Ramsey Clark pointed out during the 40th anniversary celebration, Viet Nam is arguably the most respected nation on Earth. Understandably, it is preoccupied with its own issues of economic development. The Vietnamese face continuing war legacy problems of Agent Orange and unexploded ordnance. Not to mention territorial threats from China. At the same time, the moral authority and real-world experience they could bring to a global peace movement is enormous.

- Just as the cost of mass incarceration in the United States is creating pressure to rethink imprisonment policies, the cost of the U.S. military machine is an obstacle to devoting resources to counteract the rush to ecocide.

- Much is made of the impact of globalization on the future of the nation-state. Often this is presented as a charge leveled at corporations not sufficiently loyal to the United States or other nation-states created in the post-feudal era, but there is more to it than that. To be sure, there is ample evidence of the enduring power of nationalism for better and for worse. At the same time, thanks in part to the Internet and social media, young people especially have access to global information as never before. It is far easier to go beyond the boundaries of one's own nation in seeking information and, for that matter, forging an identity.
- New thinking about conflict and its resolution also can contribute to new thinking about war and peace. There is a lot of this going on from the fields of neuroscience, sociology, law, and medicine. And counterintuitive as it may seem, according to Steven Pinker and other scholars, there are many metrics by which human-on-human violence is already in dramatic decline.

The people can make the peace. As a peace veteran, I look forward to working with my children, grandchildren, and others to make it happen.

CONNECTING THE DOTS

NANCY KURSHAN

Editors' Note: This essay first appeared on November 1, 2013 in Counterpunch under the title "From Tiger Cages to Control Units." Reprinted with permission.

My 1970 Trip to Vietnam

As a 26-year-old co-founder of the Yippies (the Youth International Party), I traveled to North Vietnam in 1970 as part of an all-women's peace delegation. I believed that the Vietnamese people should have been able to determine their own destiny, and that the United States had no business over there. When Ho Chi Minh said, "Nothing is more precious than independence and freedom," I understood what he meant. Despite a ban by the U.S. government on travel to North Vietnam, I took the risk of an illegal trip to see for myself what was happening there so that I could report what I saw with my own eyes and be a more effective antiwar organizer back home. I also went to express solidarity with the Vietnamese resistance and to acknowledge our common humanity. I had no idea in advance that I would also have an opportunity to address the American GIs (in between rock songs) on Vietnamese radio and encourage them to lay down their arms.

Before the trip, I already profoundly appreciated the Vietnamese. Like many others, I saw them through the lens of the David and Goliath story. Most Vietnamese are literally small in stature, and there were iconic photos in the media of a small Vietnamese woman juxtaposed with a huge, burly

American GI who she was guarding as a prisoner. But more importantly, the U.S. military was the most powerful in the world with massive weaponry and unlimited resources. On the other hand, the Vietnamese had the collective strength of their people and the love of people throughout the world.

I was a socialist (still am), and I saw in the Vietnamese struggle an attempt both to wrest control of their country's destiny and to build a society where people cared more about each other than about amassing personal wealth. Much of the population was willing to sacrifice greatly for these goals. They were led by people such as Ho Chi Minh, General Vo Nguyen Giap, and Madame Nguyen Thi Binh. I saw in those leaders individuals who were intelligent and caring, whose love for their people was their primary motivation. I was struck by the fact that Ho Chi Minh was a poet, Gen. Giap was a school teacher prior to leading the military effort, as was Madame Binh before her role in the Provisional Revolutionary Government of Vietnam and later as a negotiator of the Paris Peace Accords.

In 1970, however, it was not the leaders of the struggle who we encountered in Vietnam. Rather, we met with the "ordinary" people of Vietnam who were carrying out extraordinary tasks, some of them part of the "long-haired army," the civilian movement composed largely of women who engaged in much of the legal political work in the movement for national liberation.

As a woman, I was also impressed that the leaders of their struggle thought that women actually mattered. Ho said, "Women make up half of society. If women are not liberated, then society is not free." My visit confirmed what I had heard, that women were involved in all levels of the struggle.

Some say my view of the Vietnamese struggle was a romantic one. I continue to believe it was basically accurate. That generation of Vietnamese inspired people and movements around the world to struggle for liberation. They asserted there was a commonality among the human family and fostered a worldwide camaraderie among those who struggled. They proved that victory was possible, victory over the world's most powerful military machine ever assembled. It was a mythic battle, one that continues to reverberate today.

I left Vietnam in 1970 armed spiritually and informationally to fight harder to end the war. But I also left with lessons that would energize my political activity for the next 43 years. I left believing that ordinary people could overcome extraordinary challenges, particularly if they worked together. I left believing that people united could change reality for the better. I left believing that the pursuit of justice was a worthy life activity.

Back in the United States, I continued to participate in the movement to end the war, and later joined other social justice activities, opposing racism at home and U.S. wars in Central America. Beginning in 1985 I fought for 15 years to end long-term solitary confinement in U.S. prisons and I have the Vietnamese to thank for that. Well, not the long-term solitary confinement, of course, but the will to struggle for 15 years against the torture that exists within U.S. prisons. When we began that work in 1985, people thought I was crazy if I mentioned "torture." It was a difficult, uphill battle. I am sometimes asked why we kept on battling all those 15 years as we watched state after state build control unit or solitary confinement prisons. What inspired us to keep going with such an uphill battle? One part of the answer is the people of Vietnam during the 1960s and 1970s.

My 2013 Return to Vietnam

I had always wanted to revisit Vietnam but felt that returning as a tourist would be uncomfortable. When the Vietnamese invited American antiwar activists to return for the celebration of the 40th anniversary of the Paris Peace Accords, I jumped at the opportunity. It turned out to be an extraordinary two weeks. Very briefly, I found the land to be exquisitely beautiful, the people vibrant and welcoming. Visiting the schools attended by children who are victims of Agent Orange was a heart-wrenching, indelible experience. Crossing over the Demilitarized Zone (DMZ) into a united Vietnam was a dream come true, and climbing down into the Cu Chi tunnels, feeling the history of the guerrilla insurgency, was amazing. The most striking moment, however, was having the opportunity to exchange a few words with, and to be embraced by, Madame Binh. The experience that led me to think about my own work was the encounter with Vietnamese women and men who had been imprisoned and tortured in the Tiger Cages.

The Tiger Cages of Vietnam

At prisons such as the one on Con Son Island, 200 miles off the south coast of Vietnam, there were the Tiger Cages, five feet by nine feet cages so named because of their similarity to those that housed such animals—they were the same size and one could not even stand up in them. Many Vietnamese were tortured directly by Americans before being turned over to the Saigon authorities. The torture at the Tiger Cages was carried out by Saigon police and military, with U.S. complicity. The U.S. government paid their salaries, instructed them, delivered people to them, and was completely knowledgeable about the torture.

Nancy Kurshan greets Madame Binh, January 2013.
Photo courtesy of Nancy Kurshan.

All this was kept secret from the American people, however, until then-U.S. President Richard Nixon sent a Congressional delegation to Viet Nam in 1970. In order to visit a prison in North Vietnam that held U.S. POWs, the delegation was required by the North Vietnamese government to also visit the Tiger Cages in South Vietnam. Thanks to people such as Don Luce, who would today be considered a "whistle blower," the American public became informed about these cages. Armed with maps drawn up by a former prisoner, part of the delegation bravely took it upon themselves to deviate from the official tour in order to see what was really going on. Don Luce describes seeing a man with three fingers cut off, another whose skull was split open, and many with open sores on ankles as a result of shackling. Much of this was justified by the U.S.-backed South Vietnamese government, which claimed the prisoners were criminals, not prisoners-of-war, and therefore they were not protected by the Geneva Conventions of 1949–50.

When we returned in 2013 to Vietnam for the celebration of the 40th anniversary of the signing of the Paris Peace Accords, we spent much of a day with Vietnamese survivors of the Tiger Cages. They told us that at the time of the Accords, there were about 6,000 political prisoners, all of whom were opposed to the Saigon regime. The torture employed by the U.S.-backed Saigon regime, with the full support of the U.S. government and military, was extreme. Bamboo splinters were shoved under prisoners' fingernails. Soapy water was poured in their ears and their ears pounded. Many of the women were raped as well as tortured. Many prisoners were blinded in the course of the torture.

The people we met with had been imprisoned for 13 years, 10 years, and 7 years. They explained that the cages were down below ground level and the guards would walk overhead on the roof of the cage, which was made up of iron bars. Sometimes prisoners would be thrown in there for no reason, for 50 days at a time. The prisoner would eat, sleep, and defecate there. At times, the guards would just leave the excrement in the cell. At other times, they would throw lime powder down into the cell in order to blind the prisoner. One night in 1961, 17 people were tortured. Five of them died and were thrown in a mass grave.

Understandably, they were more excited to explain how they kept their spirits high and worked together to outsmart their torturers. Madame Hoang Thi Khanh informed us that the more active the antiwar movement, the better their life was in prison. What wonderful news that was to hear. Not one eye in our delegation was dry as Mme. Khanh sang one of the songs they sang to maintain their sanity and keep strong—in the face of U.S.-sponsored torture.

The Tiger Cages of the United States

In 1963, the United States shut down the infamous Alcatraz Prison located on an island in the San Francisco Bay. It had become too expensive to run and too infamous for its brutality. In its place, Marion Penitentiary in downstate Illinois was opened. Marion became the prison where the U.S. government would send those prisoners it most hated. Among these would be well-known political prisoners and prison organizers who had caused the U.S. government "trouble" in other prisons. In 1983, prisoners led a peaceful work stoppage when guards brutally beat a Mexican prisoner. Among those leading this strike was Rafael Cancel Miranda, a sort of Nelson Mandela of Puerto Rico, which the U.S. government held as a colony (and still does).

In response, for the first time ever, the U.S. "locked down" the entire prison (the Marion Lockdown) in retribution for the strike. This came to be called a "Control Unit" because its purpose was to totally control prisoners 24/7, frequently never even allowing them out of their cells. Two years later, some of us living in Chicago came to believe that if there was no opposition to this horror that the Lockdown would never be ended. Thus was born the Committee to End the Marion Lockdown (CEML). I was one of the founding members of CEML, as was my life partner Steve Whitman and radical attorney Jan Susler.

We stated from the beginning that such a brutal institution could not exist in a genuine democracy. The U.S. government said their intention was to put all of the "bad apples" there and thus be able to free up the rest of the prison system. We said that it was just the opposite: if we (society) gave them Marion, they would build more and more Marions, more and more Control Unit prisons. Sadly, we were correct and over the next 15 years, Control Unit prisons were built in virtually every state, each one more brutal than the next, each one condemned by human rights activists as inhumane and essentially torture chambers. Many people joined CEML over our 15 years of existence. We varied in many ways, but had as our core beliefs:

a. That U.S. prisons were mechanisms of control to stop insurgency efforts, particularly by black people and that prisons had very little to do with crime, despite the claims of the ruling elites.

b. That just as prisons were instruments of control for U.S. society, Control Units were instruments of control for the prison system.

c. That the obscene fact that black people were eight times more likely to be sent to prison than white people indicated the truth of assertions (a) and (b), and made it imperative to combat that system.

d. That unless we all did something about this injustice, this monstrous process would continue unimpeded. Consistent with all of this Steve, a statistician, analyzed "criminal" "justice" data and wrote a series of articles called the "Crime of Black Imprisonment" and the "Continuing Crime of Black Imprisonment" that became widely read throughout the movement in the United States and even beyond.[1]

I eventually wrote a history of CEML, *Out of Control: A Fifteen Year Battle Against Control Unit Prisons,* that is available in book form and online at *http://www.freedomarchives.org/CEML.html.* The African-American scholar Michelle Alexander has produced a wonderful book called *The New Jim Crow: Mass Incarceration in the Age of Colorblindness* that addresses mass incarceration. I hope that you will be able to read and study these sources.

Control Unit prisons (frequently referred to as isolation prisons) spread everywhere, most notoriously in California, which holds more prisoners than any other state. As the brutality has continued and even intensified, prisoners have said that they can no longer stand it and would rather die than live in such conditions. In July 2013, 30,000 prisoners in California's penitentiaries began a hunger strike with the abolition of long-term solitary confinement at the center of their demands. As I write, it is now Day 45. Reading the reports of their extreme sacrifice, I remind myself how important it was that we tried for years to shut down the first such Control Unit prison in downstate Illinois. Yes, for 15 years, citizens of Illinois tried to shut down Marion federal penitentiary and prevent the proliferation of these institutions. And more relevantly, how important that fight remains today.

Connecting the Dots

We can view political and social reality as a matrix of dots, as problems unconnected to one another, but doing so will leave us with a superficial understanding of reality. Or we can try to connect the dots and try to understand what patterns emerge. When we connect the dots, we can see there is an intimate connection between the Tiger Cages of Vietnam, the U.S. Penitentiary at Marion, California's Pelican Bay Prison, Abu Ghraib, Guantanamo, and all the rest.

Torture

The torture employed by the U.S.-backed Saigon regime, with the full support of the U.S. government and military, was extreme. Although there are definite instances of physical torture in U.S. prisons, more characteristically the torture is of a psychological nature. In California, 500 prisoners have been in solitary for over 10 years, 200 for over 15 years, and 78 for over 20 years! A *New York Times* editorial published on February 8, 2011, entitled "Cruel Isolation" lamented that "For many decades, the civilized world has recognized prolonged isolation of prisoners in cruel conditions to be inhumane, even torture. The Geneva Convention forbids it. Even at Abu Ghraib in Iraq, where prisoners were sexually humiliated and physically abused systematically and with official sanction, the jailers had to get permission of their commanding general to keep someone in isolation for more than 30 days."

Political Prisoners

Most of the prisoners in the Tiger Cages were political prisoners opposed to the Saigon regime. In U.S. prisons, most of the 80,000 people in long-term solitary confinement were not initially incarcerated as a result of political activity. However, the political contours of U.S. society are of course responsible for delivering hugely disparate numbers of people of color to the prison doors. Albert Hunt's article in the *New York Times* on November 20, 2011, entitled "A Country of Inmates" reported that "more than 60 percent of the United States' prisoners are black or Hispanic, though these groups comprise less than 30 percent of the population." One in nine black children has a parent in jail! As noted previously, a black person in the United States is eight times more likely to go prison than is a white person.

In addition, although the U.S. denies it, there are without a doubt, scores (perhaps hundreds) of political prisoners in the U.S. When we started our work, people such as Black Panthers Sundiata Acoli and Sekou Odinga, Native American Leonard Peltier, revolutionary Bill Dunne, Puerto Rican *independentista* Oscar Lopez-Rivera, just to name a few, were all at Marion. All of those people I just mentioned are still in prison in 2013, as are many other political prisoners. Of course the Vietnamese political prisoners have been free for many years now. None of them were imprisoned as long as Leonard Peltier, Sundiata Acoli, or Oscar Lopez-Rivera, who have all been incarcerated for more than 30 years! Just for comparison, Nelson Mandela was imprisoned for 27 years. (I wonder, will it take a liberation movement to free these political prisoners?) U.S. political prisoners are probably the longest-held political prisoners in the world. In a 2008 court hearing for the Angola 3, the prison warden Burl Cain said he would never transfer Albert Woodfox out of solitary where he's been for over 40 years because "I still know that he is still trying to practice Black Pantherism, and I still would not want him walking around my prison because he would organize the young new inmates. I would have me all kinds of problems, more than I could stand. And I would have the [whites] chasing after them."

Secrecy

It wasn't until 1970 that the American people found out about the Tiger Cages. It was because of the bravery of Don Luce and others who were willing to believe what they heard from the Vietnamese and to deviate from the official tour of the prison on Con Son Island, that the horrendous conditions were revealed. Today, American prisons are shrouded in a similar secrecy. The media are almost completely barred from entering and when they are able to enter, they are presented with a sanitized tour, allowed to speak only with handpicked prisoners.

Demonizing

The Geneva Conventions, signed after World War II, forbid the kinds of torture carried out 20 years later in the Tiger Cages. The U.S. government rationalized the torture by insisting that the prisoners were not political and therefore not protected as POWs; they were merely criminals. Madame Dang Hong Nhut explained to us during our visit that there was a major campaign to "criminalize" the prisoners so that they would not have to be released as was agreed to in the Paris Accords. This involved taking photos and fingerprints from the prisoners. There were 500 women prisoners, and they were aware the Accords had been signed thanks to a radio smuggled in by French supporters. When the prisoners found out about the scheme to "criminalize" them, they decided to resist by refusing to allow fingerprints or a normal photo to be taken. When the guards demanded photos, the prisoners closed their eyes, opened their mouths, and contorted their faces. When fingerprints were demanded, some scraped their fingers on cement to deform their prints.

Today in the California prisons, the prisoners are not even thought of as ordinary criminals. If they were, long-term solitary confinement would be difficult to defend. So the authorities justify these extreme conditions by insisting they are all gang members or affiliates, and many Americans accept this explanation as a rationale for torture.

Hunger Strike as a Tool

As one of the few options available to protest unacceptable conditions, the Hunger Strike has been a tool used by prisoners around the world from Vietnam to Ireland to Palestine to Guantanamo. The Tiger Cage survivors explained to us that in 1971 there was a 47-day hunger strike in one of the prison camps, and the following year it moved to the other camps. Even when they were on hunger strike, they tried to remain optimistic because "if we weren't happy, we couldn't survive."

The Devil's Bargain

Madame Hoang Thi Khanh told us that the Saigon regime gave them a choice: you can be killed or you can be released by renouncing the cause. "Give up your ideology, the call of Ho Chi Minh, and you will be free." In the California prisons, people have been offered better conditions in exchange for naming other people as troublemakers or gang members.

Outside Support

When we asked the survivors of the Tiger Cages how they kept their spirits up, they told us that they sang all of the time. They composed songs about prisoners' defiance, and songs about the feeling of separation and the romantic reunion that would come. But their spirits were also lifted by the knowledge of support by peace activists around the world. Similarly, the support of activists on the outside helps prisoners in the U.S. continue to struggle and to maintain the Hunger Strike.

Ho Chi Minh was a poet who himself endured harsh imprisonment. In one of his poems, he writes, "When the prison gates are open, the real dragon will fly out." Not long after I returned to the United States in 1970, I moved to Kent, Ohio, where the four students had been killed protesting the war. I returned to help rekindle the movement there, to help people overcome the fear that remained from the murders of Allison Krause, Jeffrey Miller, Sandra Scheuer, and William Schroeder. We started an underground newspaper that we named "The Real Dragon." Many of our stories were about black political prisoners in the United States and liberation struggles around the world in addition to the movement at home.

When the United States attacked Laos, we organized a protest demonstration at Kent State. I was later arrested on felony charges for spray-painting "U.S. OUT OF LAOS" on a brick wall. I was offered a deal: leave Kent and the charges would be reduced to a misdemeanor with no jail time. Kent is a small town and we had already received bomb threats at our home. I was anxious to move on and took the deal.

The following year there was a huge uprising at Attica, a prison in upstate New York that was brought to a brutal end by a murderous assault by the New York State Police that killed 43 guards and prisoners. I began to be concerned about the mass incarceration of people of color, as well as the imprisonment of political activists. I believed that the rebellion at Attica was motivated by the same spirit that proclaims, "Nothing is more precious than independence and freedom," as the Vietnamese had expressed. At Attica they said, "We are men, we are not beasts, and we will not be treated as such." This was said by L.D. Barkley, shortly before the Rockefeller-led NY State police moved in to massacre 43 men, the 24-year-old Barkley among them.

Skip now to 2013, and it is this same spirit that motivates prisoners in California to use one of the only tools available to them, the Hunger Strike, to attempt to transform their conditions. Long-term solitary confinement has been acknowledged as a form of torture by all the significant human rights organizations in the world. And yet on any given day, 80,000 people in the United States live in these conditions.

I worry about the prisoners who are risking their lives in this California Hunger Strike. I wonder if people on the outside will respond in sufficient numbers and strength. Will Americans recognize our common humanity, or will we just go about business as usual, as if these people were of another species? The State of California would have us believe that all these people are gang members or affiliates and therefore have no credibility or humanity. It reminds me of the argument the U.S. government made to justify the torture of the Vietnamese in the Tiger Cages. They said they were "criminals," not POWs, and therefore the protections of the Geneva Conventions did not apply. Across time and space, from Vietnam to Abu Ghraib to Pelican Bay, the U.S. government engages in torture. When will we demand of our "leaders" that in times of peace or times of war, at home or abroad, torture is not acceptable?

As I was finishing this chapter, Michelle Alexander placed this magnificent post on her Facebook page. She wrote:

> For the past several years, I have spent virtually all my working hours writing about or speaking about the immorality, cruelty, racism, and insanity of our nation's latest caste system: mass incarceration. On this Facebook page I have written and posted about little else. But as I pause today to reflect on the meaning and significance of the 50th anniversary of the March on Washington, I realize that my focus has been too narrow. Five years after the March, Dr. King was speaking out against the Vietnam War, condemning America's militarism and imperialism—famously stating that our nation was the "greatest purveyor of violence in the world." He saw the connections between the wars we wage abroad, and the utter indifference we have for poor people, and people of color at home. He saw the necessity of openly critiquing an economic system that will fund war and will reward greed, hand over fist, but will not pay workers a living wage. Five years after the March on Washington, Dr. King was ignoring all those who told him to just stay in his lane, just stick to talking about civil rights. Yet here I am decades later, staying in my lane. I have not been speaking publicly about the relationship between drones abroad and the War on Drugs at home. I have not been talking about the connections between the corrupt capitalism that bails out Wall Street bankers, moves jobs overseas, and forecloses on homes with zeal, all while private prisons yield high returns and expand operations into a new market: caging immigrants. I have not been connecting the dots between the NSA spying on millions of Americans, the labeling of mosques as "terrorist organizations," and the spy programs of the 1960s and 70s—specifically the FBI and COINTELPRO programs that placed civil rights advocates under constant surveillance, infiltrated civil rights organizations, and assassinated racial

justice leaders. I have been staying in my lane. But no more. In my view, the most important lesson we can learn from Dr. King is not what he said at the March on Washington, but what he said and did after. In the years that followed, he did not play politics to see what crumbs a fundamentally corrupt system might toss to the beggars of justice. Instead he connected the dots and committed himself to building a movement that would shake the foundations of our economic and social order, so that the dream he preached in 1963 might one day be a reality for all. He said that nothing less than "a radical restructuring of society" could possibly ensure justice and dignity for all. He was right. I am still committed to building a movement to end mass incarceration, but I will not do it with blinders on. If all we do is end mass incarceration, this movement will not have gone nearly far enough. A new system of racial and social control will be born again, all because we did not do what King demanded we do: connect the dots between poverty, racism, militarism and materialism. I'm getting out of my lane. I hope you're already out of yours.

And this brings us full cycle. We will either connect the dots and understand what is happening to us, or we will face barbarism. I hope we choose the former!

AFTERWORD:
A VIETNAMESE PERSPECTIVE

MADAME NGUYEN THI BINH

Editors' note: As the only woman on any side of the negotiations in Paris (1968-1972), Madame Nguyen Thi Binh quickly became an international symbol not only of Viet Nam's struggle against the U.S. military aggression, but of national liberation movements all over the world. She still actively participates in reflections about Viet Nam's past, present, and future. Because of her historic role and unique perspective, Madame Binh remains an inspirational figure for many U.S. antiwar activists today. In January 2013, several of the authors in this book met with her over dinner. At that gathering, as in the passage below, Madame Binh emphasized her appreciation for the antiwar movement. More importantly, she rejects the idea of a "victory" and speaks instead of a "useless and destructive war" that "provided no benefit for the American people."

This following passage has been excerpted and condensed with permission from Family, Friends, and Country: A Memoir by Nguyen Thi Binh (translation by Lady Borton, Tri Thuc Publishing House & Phuong Nam Book Co., Ltd., 2015). We are grateful to Judy Gumbo and Randy Ross for preparing an earlier selection of excerpts that they read at the VIETNAM: POWER OF PROTEST conference held in Washington, D.C. in May 2015.

For fourteen years, between 1962-1976, I was active in foreign relations for the National Liberation Front and the Provisional Revolutionary Government of South Việt Nam. In addition to taking part in the Paris

Peace Conference, my other primary work was mobilizing international support for our resistance.

One of our key objectives was to gather the support of antiwar and peace groups in the United States. The first time I met representatives of the American antiwar movement was at a two-day conference held in Bratislava in 1967. I was not impressed with these Americans at first sight. They were not dressed tidily, and their way of speaking seemed overly casual.

Yet when I described the situation in Việt Nam, the American participants listened attentively and asked many questions. I spoke especially about the war in the South, including the American military's crimes, and I expressed our people's aspirations for peace and independence. By the end, we were holding hands, promising to alert the public, especially in the U.S. [to] the reality of what was happening in Việt Nam. We asserted that, together, we would strengthen our solidarity to end the war, a war the American public had never wanted.

Up until now U.S. officials, particularly in the military believe that, had the Americans "plunged headlong" by using their full military strength, the United States probably would have "achieved victory." These are the shallow and blind views of those who saw apparent facts but not the essence of the issue. They saw the temporal unfold before their eyes, but they did not see the whole. Therefore, they could neither perceive nor foresee the underlying, inevitable, and ultimate conclusion.

Suppose Việt Nam had not enjoyed an international solidarity movement, particularly in the United States. If so, we could not have shaken Washington's aggressive will. The U.S. administrations had to address the widespread public opinion opposing the meaningless war they had created in Việt Nam. The U.S. antiwar movement...drew from many forces—communists, leftists, progressive people, those who simply love peace and justice, and others. This political and material strength shook the most stubborn, conservative, and warlike minds in the U.S. political leadership.

The Vietnamese people have great appreciation for the peace and antiwar movements in the United States and view those movements' contributions as important in shortening the war and re-establishing peace in Việt Nam. Not long ago, an American film team visiting Việt Nam asked me, "Is it true that Việt Nam profited from the divisions within the United States?"

"No," I answered. "We don't think that way. The work that we did took advantage of the American people's spirit, which prizes peace and justice, to oppose again and again the useless and destructive war in Việt Nam, which provided no benefit for the American people."

It is fortunate that many Americans, particularly the women, understood this point and stood on the side of common sense and peace. That made possible the base leading to later reconciliation between the people of our two nations.

NOTES

Introduction

1. For many readers, this sentence will bring to mind white students. But it is important to note that white students were not the only ones who gave up their lives in protesting the War. In addition to the four white students at Kent State University in Ohio, black students at Jackson State University in Mississippi were also killed. In addition, four people were killed during the Chicano moratorium.

2. We understand that language often carries the baggage of war, imperialism and racism. We want to acknowledge that "Vietnam" is much bigger than a U.S. war; it is also a people, a culture, a land, and an era. We refer to the U.S. war in Viet Nam as "the Vietnam War." We call the country "Viet Nam." Acknowledging that "America" is a large continent made up of many nations and cultures, we use the term U.S. Americans to refer to citizens and residents of the United States. However, rather than require everyone to follow our unusual and admittedly awkward rules, individual authors use whatever spellings and terms they prefer in their chapters.

3. Michael H. Hunt and Steven I. Levine, *Arc of Empire: America's Wars in Asia from the Philippines to Vietnam* (Chapel Hill, NC: University of North Carolina Press, 2012).

4. Roxanne Dunbar-Ortiz, *An Indigenous People's History of the United States* (Boston: Beacon Press, 2014).

5. Jeffrey Kimball, *Nixon's Vietnam War*, (Lawrence, KS: University Press of Kansas, 1998).

6. Fredrik Logevall, *Embers of War: The Fall of an Empire and the Making of America's Vietnam* (New York: Random House, 2012), p. xiv.

7. David L. Anderson, *The Columbia Guide to the Vietnam War* (New York: Columbia University Press, 2002), p.173.

8. Ibid. p. 171.

9. The speech is accessible at *whitehouse.gov.*

10. Susan Sontag, *Regarding the Pain of Others* (New York: Farrar Strauss and Giroux, 2003).

11. David Anderson, p. 113.

12. Elizabeth Sutherland Martinez, *Letters from Mississippi* (New York: McGraw-Hill, 1965).

13. Clark Dougan and Samuel Lipsman, *The Vietnam Experience: A Nation Divided* (Boston: Boston Publishing Company, 1984), p. 63.

14. For information on Chicano and Native/American Indian resistance to the Vietnam War, see: Lorena Oropeza, *Raza Sí!, Guerra No!: Chicano protest and patriotism during the Viet Nam war era* (Berkeley: University of California Press, 2005), also Paul Chaat Smith and Robert Allen Warrior, *Like a Hurricane: The Indian Movement from Alcatraz to Wounded Knee* (New York: New Press, 1996).

15. Kimberley L. Phillips, *War! What Is It Good For?: Black Freedom Struggles & the U.S. Military from World War II to Iraq*, John Hope Franklin Series in African American History and Culture, (Chapel Hill, NC: University of North Carolina Press, 2012), p. 242.

16. Tavis Smiley and David Ritz, *Death of a King: The Real Story of Dr. Martin Luther King Jr.'s Final Year* (New York: Little, Brown and Company, 2014).

17. "Which Way Home?" radio interview with Asian American veterans by Gina Hotta, 1991, available on soundprint.org.

18. Steve Louie and Glenn Omatsu, eds., *Asian Americans: The Movement and the Moment*, (Los Angeles, CA: UCLA Asian American Studies Center Press, 2001).

19. Tram Quang Nguyen, "Caring for the Soul of Our Community: Vietnamese Youth Activism in the 1960s and Today," in *Asian Americans: The Movement and the Moment*, eds. Steve Louie and Glenn Omatsu (UCLA, 2001), p. 288.

20. Philipps, p. 254.

21. Tom Wells, *The War Within: America's Battle over Vietnam* (Berkeley, CA: University of California Press, 1994). See also: Nancy Zaroulis and Gerald Sullivan, *Who Spoke Up?: American Protest Against the War in Vietnam, 1963-1975* (Garden City, New York: Doubleday & Company, 1984), p. 361.

22. David Cortright, *Soldiers in Revolt: The American Military Today* (New York: Anchor Press, 1975).

23. Melvin Small, "Bring the Boys Home Now! Antiwar Activism and Withdrawal from Vietnam—and Iraq," *Diplomatic History* 34, no. 3 (June 2010), p. 551.

24. According to Mary Hershberger, the idea to form a committee to carry the mail first emerged out of discussions between North American and Vietnamese women at an international meeting in Canada; see *Traveling to Vietnam: American Peace Activists and the War* (Syracuse, NY: Syracuse Univ. Press, 2003). The proposal to set up a clearinghouse for prisoner mail delivery occurred after several years of cultivating trustworthy relationships with the Women's Union and other officials in Vietnam. For information about the Committee of Liaison with Servicemen Detained in North Vietnam based on interviews with Cora Weiss, see Judy Tzu-chun Wu, *Radicals on the Road: Internationalism, Orientalism, and Feminism during the Vietnam Era* (Ithaca, NY: Cornell University Press, 2013).

25. Hershberger, 2003. Hershberger says that pressure from the State Department prevented black civil rights activists including the Rev. Dr. Martin Luther King from going to Viet Nam during the War.

26. In 1969 and 1971, meetings held in Vancouver and Montreal between one thousand North American women and a small group of Vietnamese, Cambodian, and Laotian women enabled the antiwar movement to express itself in terms of

sisterhood, motherhood, and families. In tandem to these meetings, the PRG's iconic representative, Madame Binh, was able to build international support for the Vietnamese struggle for liberation on the basis of the shared experience of women around the world. For a discussion of the impact of the antiwar movement on U.S. feminism, see Wu, *Radicals on the Road.*

27. The only woman involved in the Paris Peace Accords, Madame Binh represented the Provisional Revolutionary Government (PRG). Soft spoken and petite, she became an international icon and a symbol of Viet Nam's struggle for independence.

28. According to Ngô Vĩnh Long, four decades since the signing of the Paris Peace Treaty, "the problems of reconciliation and accommodation are still extremely pronounced. He argues that Viet Nam's "military victors" need to turn their attention to the growth of civil society and the rule of law. See: Ngô Vĩnh Long, "Military Victory and the Difficult Tasks of Reconciliation in Vietnam: A Cautionary Tale." *Peace & Change* 38, no. 4 (October 2013): pp. 474–86.

29. Michael S. Foley, *Confronting the War Machine: Draft Resistance During the Vietnam War* (Chapel Hill, NC: University of North Carolina Press, 2003).

30. https://en.wikiquote.org/wiki/John_Kerry. Testimony before the subcommittees of the U.S. Senate (April, 1971).

31. David Steigerwald, "Teaching the Antiwar Movement: Confronting Popular Myths, Teaching Complexity," in *Understanding and Teaching the Vietnam War*, eds. John Day Tully et al. (University of Wisconsin Press, 2013), pp. 202–222.

32. Bao Phi, *Song I Sing: Poems.* (Minneapolis, MN: Coffee House Press, 2011). See also, Yen Le Espiritu, *Body Counts: The Vietnam War and Militarized Refuge(es)* (Berkeley, CA: University of California Press, 2014).

33. James Max Fendrich, "The Forgotten Movement: The Vietnam Antiwar Movement," *Sociological Inquiry* 73, no. 3 (August 2003): pp. 338–358. Fendrich points out the scant attention given by social scientists to the antiwar movement. This is not to diminish the many excellent analyses provided by other researchers, many of which we list in the Resources section.

1. Seeing Vietnam With My Own Eyes

1. Nguyen Thi Binh, *Family, Friends, and Country: A Memoir by Nguyen Thi Binh*, trans. Lady Borton (Tri Thuc Publishing House & Phuong Nam Book Co., Ltd., 2015).

2. Viet Nam Time Travel, 1970–2013

1. Susan Sontag, *Trip to Hanoi* (New York: Noonday Press, 1968).
2. John McCrea, "In Flanders Fields."

4. The People's Peace Treaty

1. The authors of this chapter were members of the 1970 National Student Association (NSA) Peace Treaty delegation to Vietnam.
2. Tom Wells, *The War Within, America's Battle Over Vietnam* (Oakland, CA: University of California Press, 1994), 397.
3. Ifshin later became general counsel for Bill Clinton's 1992 presidential campaign committee, and an attorney and lobbyist for the American Israel Public Affairs Committee and other pro-Israel causes. He died in 1996.
4. Greer went on to play a crucial press role for the Bill Clinton presidential campaigns. He also worked on campaigns by Barack Obama, South African President Nelson Mandela, Czechoslovakian President Vaclav Havel, Guatemalan President Alvaro Colom and President Horacio Cartes in Paraguay.
5. Ngô Vĩnh Long, "Legacies Foretold: Excavating the Roots of Postwar Vietnam," in *Four Decades On: Vietnam, the United States, and the Legacies of the Second Indochina War*, eds. Scott Laderman and Edwin A. Martini (Durham and London: Duke University Press, 2013), 16–43.
6. Mam was later charged with "treason" for his part in the Saigon student protests of 1970, and was imprisoned for two years. He was released soon after the Paris Peace Accords were signed.
7. In 1967, an expose in *Ramparts* magazine revealed that the CIA had been funding and manipulating the NSA for at least

15 years. It's extremely ironic that only three years later, the same CIA was *spying* on the NSA. A 2009 PhD dissertation by CUNY historian J. Angus Johnson on the history of the NSA reveals that the CIA's infamous MHCHAOS program investigated our 1970 People's Peace Treaty trip to Vietnam, and that the FBI spied on at least two members of our delegation, Mark Wefers and David Ifshin. See https://studentactivism.files. wordpress.com/2012/07/johnston-diss-5-81f.pdf. In addition, delegate Becca Wilson learned that the FBI tailed her for at least several months during 1971, after her return from Vietnam. See her accompanying essay in this volume. According to researcher James Kirkpatrick Davis, the FBI not only spied on, but conducted dirty tricks to discredit another member of our delegation, Keith Parker. See *Assault on the Left: The FBI and the Sixties Antiwar Movement,* by James Kirkpatrick Davis, Praeger, 1997, pages 189-191.

8. This passage is from a transcript of the Nixon White House tapes. The transcript is available at the Nixon Library's online database, www.nixonlibrary.gov/forresearchers/find/tapes/watergate/wspf/491-014.pdf.

9. Charles DeBenedetti and Charles Chatfield, *An American ordeal: the antiwar movement of the Vietnam era* (Syracuse, NY: Syracuse University Press, 1990), 316.

10. James A. Henretta, Rebecca Edwards, and Robert O. Self, *America: a Concise History, Combined Volume* (New York, NY: Macmillan), 842.

11. www.commondreams.org/views/2014/08/12/george-will-confirms-nixons-vietnam-treason.

12. Nick Turse, *Kill Anything That Moves: The Real American War in Vietnam* (New York: Macmillan, 2013).

5. A Pacifist in the War Zone

1. Quảng Nam Province was split in two, creating Quảng Tín province in the southern part of Quảng Nam so it would be easier to pacify. After 1975, Quảng Tín was absorbed back into Quảng Nam Province, as it was before 1965.

2. When Quảng Tín became absorbed back into Quảng Nam, Tam Kỳ was no longer the provincial capital.

6. Journeys to Remember

1. Dana Sachs, "Small Tragedies and Distant Stars: Le Minh Khue's Language of Lost Ideals," in *Crossroads–An Interdisciplinary Journal of Southeast Asian Studies* 13, no.1 (1999): 1–10.
2. Le Minh Khue, "The Stars," in *The Stars, The Earth, The River* (Willimantic, CT: Curbstone Press), 20.
3. Ibid., 186.
4. *The Catonsville Nine: Investigation of a Flame*. Lynne Sachs, Director. With Tom Lewis, Daniel Berrigan, Marjorie Melville, John Hogan, Mary Murphy, and Tom Melville. 2001. www.investigationofaflame.com/.
5. www.history.com/topics/vietnam-war/agent-orange.

7. From Hanoi to Santa Barbara

1. Before she joined the National Liberation Front, Nguyen Thi Chau had been a deeply engaged student antiwar activist in Saigon. As a result she had suffered a long sentence in the Tiger Cages, the Thieu regime's notorious torture chambers. When we met her, she had become an NLF hero, legendary among fellow prisoners because of her ability to sing even while being tortured.

9. Voices of Veterans: The Endless Tragedy of Vietnam

1. Chuck Palazzo cites the website "Monsanto and Vietnam University of Agriculture Collaborate to Develop Talents in Agricultural Biotechnology." http://monsantoblog com/2014/10/13/monsanto-and-vietnam-university-of-agriculture-collaborate-to-develop-talents-in-agricultural-biotechnology/.

10. Unwanted Memories Erased in Electroconvulsive Therapy Experiment

1. Newspaper headline about new techniques of manipulating human memory from the *Wall Street Journal*, December 22, 2013.
2. My essay appeared in a book titled *The New Left: A Collection of Essays*, edited by Priscilla Long, 1969, Porter Sargent Handbooks, p. 130.

3. www.nbcnews.com/storyline/ukraine-crisis/f-bomb-flap-did-rU.S.sia-snoop-senior-u-s-diplomat-n24316 (accessed April 4, 2015).

4. www.vietnamwar50th.com (accessed April 4, 2015).

5. *New York Times*, May 1, 2014.

11. Connecting the Dots

1. Find this important document at www.freedomarchives.org/Documents/Finder/DOC3_scans/REDOOO3.continuing.crime.black.imprisonment.pdf.

RESOURCES:
LEARN MORE AND GET INVOLVED

Some of the biggest lessons of the Vietnam antiwar movement include the importance of access to information and of working with others to teach ourselves. We offer this list of resources as a way to encourage the spirit of inquiry that is so necessary to a democratic society. We hope this book and these resources we list here will help to spur meaningful discussions and debates that span communities, cultures, and generations across the globe.

Resources on the War and the antiwar movement are far too many to name. We list some of the most important ones here. For information on the topic of Agent Orange and unexploded ordnance, we direct you to the organizations that are directly involved.

The Vietnam War and U.S. Wars
Books

Anderson, David L. *The Columbia Guide to the Vietnam War*. New York: Columbia University Press, 2002.

Appy, Christian G. *Patriots: The Vietnam War Remembered From All Sides*. New York: Penguin Books, 2003.

———. *American Reckoning: The Vietnam War and Our National Identity*. New York: Penguin Publishing Group, 2015.

Dunbar-Ortiz, Roxanne. *An Indigenous Peoples' History of the United States.* Boston: Beacon Press, 2014.

Ernst, John. *The War That Never Ends: New Perspectives on the Vietnam War.* Edited by David L. Anderson. Lexington, KY: University Press of Kentucky, 2007.

Espiritu, Yen Le. *Body Counts: The Vietnam War and Militarized Refuge(es).* Berkeley, CA: University of California Press, 2014.

Herring, George C. *America's Longest War: The United States and Vietnam, 1950-1975.* 2nd ed. New York: Alfred A. Knopf, 1986.

Hunt, Michael H., and Steven I. Levine. *Arc of Empire: America's Wars in Asia from the Philippines to Vietnam.* Chapel Hill, NC: University of North Carolina Press, 2012.

Karnow, Stanley. *Vietnam, a History.* New York: Viking Press, 1983.

Logevall, Fredrik. *Embers of War: The Fall of an Empire and the Making of America's Vietnam.* New York: Random House, 2012.

MacPherson, Myra. *Long Time Passing: Vietnam and the Haunted Generation.* New York: Doubleday, 1984.

Turse, Nick. *Kill Anything That Moves.* London: Picador, 2013.

Tully, John Day, Matthew Masur, and Brad Austin, eds. *Understanding and Teaching the Vietnam War.* Madison, WI: University of Wisconsin, 2013.

Viñh Long, Ngô. *Coming to Terms: Indochina, the United States, and the War.* Edited by Douglas Allen. Boulder, CO: Westview, 1991.

———. "Military Victory and the Difficult Tasks of Reconciliation in Vietnam: A Cautionary Tale." *Peace & Change* 38, no. 4 (October 2013): 474–86.

Young, Marilyn Blatt. *The Vietnam Wars, 1945-1990.* New York: HarperCollins, 1991.

Multimedia

Pentagon commemorative website: www.vietnamwar50th.com
National Archives: www.archives.gov/research/military/vietnam-war/
Veterans for Peace: www.vietnamfulldisclosure.org
About Laos: Legacies of War.org

The Vietnam Antiwar Movement

Books

Anderson, Terry H. "Vietnam Is Here: The Antiwar Movement." In *The War That Never Ends: New Perspectives on the Vietnam War.* Lexington, KY: University Press of Kentucky, 2007.

Buzzanco, Robert. *Vietnam and the Transformation of American Life.* Malden, MA: Blackwell Publishers, 1999.

Cushing, Lincoln. *All of Us or None: Social Justice Posters of the San Francisco Bay Area.* Berkeley, CA: Heyday, 2012.

Dougan, Clark, and Samuel Lipsman. *The Vietnam Experience: A Nation Divided.* Boston: Boston Publishing Company, 1984.

Flacks, Richard. *Making History: The American Left and the American Mind.* New York: Columbia University Press, 1988.

Hayden, Thomas, and Staughton Lynd. *The Other Side.* New York: New American Library, 1965.

Heineman, Kenneth J. *Campus Wars: The Peace Movement at American State Universities in the Vietnam Era.* New York: New York University Press, 1993.

Hershberger, Mary. *Traveling to Vietnam: American Peace Activists and the War.* Syracuse, NY: Syracuse University Press, 2003.

Lewis, Penny. *Hardhats, Hippies, and Hawks: The Vietnam Antiwar Movement as Myth and Memory.* Ithaca, NY: ILR Press, 2013.

Onishi, Yuichiro. *Transpacific Antiracism: Afro-Asian Solidarity in Twentieth-Century Black America, Japan, and Okinawa.* New York: New York University Press, 2013.

Phillips, Kimberley L. *War! What Is It Good For?: Black Freedom Struggles & the U.S. Military from World War II to Iraq.* John Hope Franklin Series in African American History and Culture. Chapel Hill, NC: University of North Carolina Press, 2012.

Randall, Margaret. *Spirit of the People.* Vancouver, BC: New Star Books, 1975.

Small, Melvin. *Antiwarriors: The Vietnam War and the Battle for America's Hearts and Minds.* Vietnam: America in the War Years. Wilmington, DE: Scholarly Resources, Inc, 2002.

———. "Bring the Boys Home Now! Antiwar Activism and Withdrawal from Vietnam—and Iraq." *Diplomatic History* 34, no. 3 (June 2010): 543–53.

———. *Covering Dissent: The Media and the Anti-Vietnam War Movement.* New Brunswick, NJ: Rutgers University Press, 1994.

Sontag, Susan. *Trip to Hanoi.* New York: Noonday Press, 1968.

Steigerwald, David. "Teaching the Antiwar Movement: Confronting Popular Myths, Teaching Complexity." In *Understanding and Teaching the Vietnam War,* edited by John Day Tully, Matthew Masur, and Brad Austin. Madison, WI: University of Wisconsin Press, 2013.

Vickers, George R. "The Vietnam Antiwar Movement." In *Coming to Terms: Indochina, the United States, and the War.* Boulder, CO: Westview Press, 1991.

Wells, Tom. *The War Within: America's Battle over Vietnam.* Berkeley, CA: University of California Press, 1994.

Westheider, James E. *Fighting on Two Fronts: African Americans and the Vietnam War.* New York: New York University Press, 1997.

Wu, Judy Tzu-Chun. *Radicals on the Road: Internationalism, Orientalism, and Feminism during the Vietnam Era.* Ithaca, NY: Cornell University Press, 2013.

Zaroulis, Nancy, and Gerald Sullivan. *Who Spoke Up?: American Protest Against the War in Vietnam, 1963–1975.* Garden City, New York: Doubleday & Company, 1984.

Multimedia

Alper, Loretta, Jeremy Earp, Sean Penn, and Norman Solomon. *War Made Easy: How Presidents & Pundits Keep Spinning Us to Death.* New York: Disinformation Co, 2008.

Jean-Luc Godard, Agnès Varda et al. *"Far from Vietnam = Loin du Vietnam."* Brooklyn NY: Icarus, 2013.

Pearson, Andrew, and Martin Smith. *"Vietnam, a Television History."* Bethlehem, PA: Lehigh University, 2015.

U.S. War Veterans

Books

Cortright, David. *Soldiers in Revolt: The American Military Today.* New York: Anchor Press, 1975.

Ehrhart, W.D. *Passing Time: Memoir of a Vietnam Veteran Against the War.* Amherst, MA: University of Massachusetts Press, 1986.

O'Brien, Tim. *The Things They Carried.* Boston: Houghton Mifflin, 1990.

Multimedia

David Zeiger. *"Sir! No Sir! : The Supressed Story of the GI Movement to End the War in Vietnam."* Displaced Films, 2006.

Winterfilm, Vietnam Veterans Against the War, and Milliarium Zero. *"Winter Soldier."* Harrington Park, NJ: Milliarium Zero, 2006.

Organizations

Vietnam Veterans Against the War: www.vvaw.org

Veterans for Peace: www.veteransforpeace.org

Veterans Vietnam Restoration Project (although this project has closed down, this link has valuable information): www.vvrp.org

Iraq Veterans Against the War: www.ivaw.org

Committee Opposed to Militarism and the Draft: www.comdsd.org/aboutus.htm

William Joiner Center for the Study of War and Social Consequences: www.umb.edu/joinerinstitute

Agent Orange and Unexploded Ordnance

Organizations

Susan Hammond, War Legacies Project: www.warlegacies.org

Veterans for Peace, Agent Orange Campaign: www.veteransforpeace.org/our-work/vfp-national-projects/agent-orange/

Project Renew: http://landmines.org.vn/

Viet Nam, Laos, and Cambodia: Past And Present

Books

Branfman, Fred. *Voices from the Plain of Jars: Life under an Air War.* New York: Harper & Row, 1972.

Caswell, Michelle. *Archiving the unspeakable: silence, memory, and the Photographic Record in Cambodia.* Madison, WI: University of Wisconsin Press, 2014.

Chandler, David P. *A History of Cambodia.* Boulder, CO: Westview Press, 2000.

Hinton, Alexander Laban. *Why Did They Kill?: Cambodia in the Shadow of Genocide.* Berkeley, CA: University of California Press, 2005.

Power, Samantha. *A Problem from Hell: America and the Age of Genocide*. New York: Basic Books, 2002.

Shawcross, William. *Sideshow: Kissinger, Nixon and the Destruction of Cambodia*. New York: Simon and Schuster, 1979.

Tyner, James A. *The Killing of Cambodia: Geography, Genocide and the Unmaking of Space*. Aldershot, Hampshire, England: Ashgate, 2008.

Vickery, Michael. *Cambodia, 1975-1982*. Boston, MA: South End Press, 1984.

Warner, Roger, and Roger Warner. *Shooting at the Moon: The Story of America's Clandestine War in Laos*. South Royalton, VT: Steerforth Press, 1996.

Contemporary Culture and Experiences of Vietnamese Americans, Hmong, and Other Southeast Asian Americans

Books

Chan, Sucheng. *Survivors: Cambodian Refugees in the United States*. Urbana: University of Illinois Press, 2004.

Faderman, Lillian, and Ghia Xiong. *I Begin My Life All Over: The Hmong and the American Immigrant Experience*. Boston: Beacon Press, 1998.

Fadiman, Anne. *The Spirit Catches You and You Fall Down: A Hmong Child, Her American Doctors, and the Collision of Two Cultures*. New York: Farrar, Straus and Giroux, 1998.

Hillmer, Paul. *A People's History of the Hmong*. St. Paul, MN: Minnesota Historical Society Press, 2010.

Lieu, Nhi T. *The American Dream in Vietnamese*. Minneapolis: University of Minnesota Press, 2011.

Moua, Mai Neng. *Bamboo Among the Oaks: Contemporary Writing by Hmong Americans*. St. Paul, MN: Minnesota Historical Society Press, 2002.

Pelaud, Isabelle Thuy. *This Is All I Choose to Tell: History and Hybridity in Vietnamese American Literature*. Philadelphia, PA: Temple University Press, 2011.

Phi, Bao. *Song I Sing: Poems*. Minneapolis, MN: Coffee House Press, 2011.

Quincy, Keith. *Hmong, History of a People*. Cheney: Eastern Washington University, 1995.

Truong, Monique T.D., and Luu Truong Khoi. *Watermark: Vietnamese American Poetry and Prose.* Edited by Barbara Tran. New York: Asian American Writer's Workshop, 1998.

Yang, Kao Kalia. *The Latehomecomer: A Hmong Family Memoir.* Minneapolis: Coffee House Press, 2008.

Multimedia

Vietnamese diasporic arts, culture, and politics: diacritics.org

Hmong Women's Oral History Project: collections.mnhs.org/ioh/index.php/10000825

Hmong History Paintings by Cy Thao: www.chgs.umn.edu/museum/responses/hmongMigration/

ABOUT THE CONTRIBUTORS

RENNIE DAVIS coordinated the largest coalition of antiwar and civil rights organizations during some of America's most impactful demonstrations. With Tom Hayden, he led the antiwar activities at the Democratic National Convention in 1968, watched on television by more people than the first man landing on the moon. He was one of the Chicago 8, the most significant political trial in U.S. history, according to the *New York Times*. He organized the largest civil disobedience arrest in American history. In 1967, he traveled to Hanoi to witness the U.S. bombing of North Vietnam from the ground. In 1969, he returned to Vietnam to bring U.S. pilots shot down and captured as prisoners of war back to the United States. In the fall of 1971, when John Lennon joined the American antiwar movement, Rennie worked with Lennon to bring a million people to the Republican Convention. Lennon was subsequently pulled out of that campaign by the Justice Department that initiated deportation proceedings against him. In January 1973, Rennie was a guest of Madame Binh at the ceremonies that signed the Paris Peace Accord. He returned to Hanoi in January 2013 and again in 2015 to begin a new campaign for healing the wounds of war. Today he is chairman of the Foundation for Humanity and president of the environmental technology company iPower Living LLC. He is currently preparing a book called *Generation Arise* about a new generation that needs to change the world again. Find him at *www.renniedavis.com.*

JUDY GUMBO is an original member of the Yippies, who used ridicule as a weapon to help end the Vietnam War. In the late 1960s the Yippies "levitated" the Pentagon, brought the New York Stock Exchange to a halt to satirize greed, and ran a pig as the most appropriate candidate for president of the United States during the 1968 Democratic Convention. Judy went on to help start one of Berkeley's original women's groups and wrote for two underground newspapers, the *Berkeley Barb* and the *Berkeley Tribe*. In 1970, Judy visited the former North Viet Nam, returning to help organize the women's April 10th march on the Pentagon and May Day demonstrations; she then traveled around the country agitating against the war and for the liberation of women. In 1975, Judy discovered a tracking device on her car and became part of a lawsuit that successfully challenged warrantless wiretapping.

Judy spent the majority of her professional career as an award-winning fundraiser for Planned Parenthood. She also has a Ph.D. in sociology and has taught at the State University of New York at New Paltz and at Mills College. Judy is co-author of *The Sixties Papers: Documents of a Rebellious Decade* (1984) and is currently completing her memoir, *Yippie Girl*. She recently published "Bugged" in *The Times They Were A-Changing: Women Remember the '60s and '70s* (She Writes Press, 2013). Portions of "Viet Nam Time Travel, 1970-2013" have appeared in *CounterPunch* (www.counterpunch.org/2014/01/13/back-to-vietnam). Her slideshow about the 2013 trip can be found at http://yippiegirl.com/vietnam.

Judy is the widow of Yippie founder Stew Albert and of David Dobkin, a founder of Berkeley Cohousing. Find Judy Gumbo at www.yippiegirl.com or on Facebook.

ALEX HING is a sous chef at a hotel in the United Nations complex in New York City, where he has been working for over 30 years. He began his career as a dishwasher and night porter in San Francisco in 1965. Hing has presented the cuisines of many countries around the world at the hotel's restaurant and has been featured on television and at the James Beard Foundation. As a trustee of Local 6 UNITE HERE, of the New York Hotel Trades Council, he is proud to be an activist in one of the most progressive unions in the country. In San Francisco's UNITE HERE Local 2, he was in the leadership of the 1980 six-week citywide strike. Hing is a founding member of the Asian Pacific American Labor Alliance, the only national organization of Asian and Pacific Islander union members. In 1969, he was minister of education of the Red Guard Party, a revolutionary organization based in San Francisco's Chinatown, closely allied with the Black Panther Party, that fought to break the power of the Kuomintang (KMT) over the community, and end police harassment and brutality of youth. The Red Guard fought for relevant education, affordable housing, jobs and community wellness. He was and continues to be active in the peace, justice, and environmental movements.

Hing is also a martial artist, having trained in Okinawan karate for nearly 15 years as a student of the late sensei Dr. Richard Kim in San Francisco. He is presently a tai chi master in New York with more than 20 years of training with Grandmaster William CC Chen. He has won numerous national and international awards in martial arts competition and teaches tai chi in several Manhattan venues.

Hing presently lives in Harlem with his wife, Heike Jarick. He was elected to the board of his condominium and is organizing against the corrupt condominium real estate developer in the interest of affordable housing for the building residents. He has two adult sons, Van Troi and Michael, who live and work on the East Coast.

 **DOUG HOSTETTER** is the Director of the Mennonite Central Committee United Nations Office. Doug was a conscientious objector during the Vietnam War, and chose to do his alternative service working for Mennonite Central Committee in Tam Ky, Quang Tin Province, from 1966 to 1969. In 1970, Doug participated in the U.S. National Student Association delegation to Vietnam, which negotiated the People's Peace Treaty. He was active on the staff of the People's Peace Treaty, which brought the treaty to be ratified by hundreds of U.S. colleges and universities. Doug was the treasurer of Medical Aid for Indochina (MAI), which provided medical assistance to a Quaker rehabilitation center in Quang Ngai and to hospitals and clinics in the Democratic Republic of Vietnam and areas controlled by the Provisional Revolutionary Government. When the U.S. military bombed the Bach Mai Hospital in December of 1972, MAI changed its name to the Bach Mai Hospital Fund and contributed significantly to the reconstruction of the Ear Nose Throat wing of the Bach Mai Hospital. Doug returned to Vietnam with a Bach Mai Hospital Fund delegation in 1974 to visit the newly reconstructed Ear Nose Throat wing of Bach Mai and visit a variety of medical clinics in the DRVN and Quang Tri, which was then under PRG control. After the end of the Vietnam War, the Bach Mai Hospital Fund changed its name to Friendshipment and continued the same medical assistance to hospitals and clinics throughout Vietnam. In 1979, Doug returned to Vietnam with a Friendshipment delegation, which visited Bach Mai Hospital and a small medical clinic that Friendshipment had helped to build at My Lai, Quang Ngai Province.

When the war ended, Doug was one of the organizers of "The War Is Over" celebration at Sheep's Meadow in Central Park, which brought together U.S. antiwar political and cultural activists to celebrate the end of the Vietnam War. He was part of a small group of New York antiwar activists in welcoming the first post-war Vietnamese delegation to the United Nations, and helping them get settled in New York. Doug was also active professionally in faith-based organizations in antiwar efforts during the war and friendship and reconciliation efforts after the war ended. He worked as resource specialist for peace at United Methodist Office for the UN. Later he directed the New England Regional Office of the American Friends Service Committee in Cambridge, Massachusetts. He was the director and later international/interfaith director for the U.S. Fellowship of Reconciliation. As a visiting scholar at Northwestern University in Evanston, Illinois, Doug taught a course called "War and Nongovernmental Organizations," which examined the Vietnam War and several other recent U.S. wars, and the civil society and nongovernmental organizations that opposed those wars. Doug has published widely on the subjects of war, peace, and the nonviolent movement. Doug has a webpage of some of his pictures from Vietnam at *www.pictureofpeace.org* and has contributed pictures, journal entries, and stories from Vietnam to the Civilian Public Service webpage (www.civilian-publicservice.org/storycontinues/vietnam/hostetter).

Photo by Matt Kiedaisch

JAY CRAVEN is an award-winning producer, independent film writer/director, impresario, and community arts activist. He directs the film studies program at Marlboro College and the college's biennial "Movies from Marlboro" program where 20 professionals mentor and collaborate with 30 students from multiple colleges, to produce a feature film for national release.

Craven's feature films include *Where the Rivers Flow North* (with Rip Torn and Tantoo Cardinal); *A Stranger in the Kingdom* (with Ernie Hudson, David Lansbury, Martin Sheen); *Disappearances* (with Kris Kristofferson); *Northern Borders* (with Bruce Dern and Genevieve Bujold), and *Peter and John* (with Jacqueline Bisset and Christian Coulson).

Craven has also made several films that grow specifically from his political activist experience. They include "Dawn of the People" (with Doreen Kraft), about the 1980 Nicaraguan National Literacy Crusade; the documentary "After the Fog: Interviews with Combat Veterans" and the narrative film, "The Year That Trembled" (with Marin Hinkle, Jonathan Brandis, Fred Willard), set in the shadow of the 1970 events at Kent State. Writing about "The Year That Trembled," *Chicago Reader* lead film critic Jonathan Rosenbaum wrote, "This is more believable than most depictions of the period because the politics are informed by historical reflection."

In 1970, Craven traveled to Vietnam as part of the People's Peace Treaty delegation of college newspaper editors and student body presidents organized by the U.S. National Student Association. Their purpose: to forge a "people's peace treaty" with elected Vietnamese student leaders from Saigon, North Vietnam, and the liberated areas in South Vietnam. After returning from Vietnam to the United States, Craven helped lead the 1971

May Day demonstrations in Washington that resulted in the largest mass arrest for non-violent civil disobedience in U.S. history.

BECCA WILSON The People's Peace Treaty trip Becca made in 1970 led her to vow that activism for peace and justice would be a lifelong calling of the heart, not merely a phase of her youth. After her return, she became one of the leaders of Santa Barbara's antiwar movement, helping to organize a statewide People's Peace Treaty conference at UCSB, as well as weeklong demonstrations in conjunction with the May Day 1971 protests in Washington, D.C. While serving time in jail for her part in one of the local May Day protests, Becca and a visiting friend hatched a plan to establish an alternative weekly newspaper to challenge the hegemony of the stodgy, conservative *Santa Barbara News Press*. She and a small group of friends formed a collective, and with just $5,000 in capital, launched the first issue of the *Santa Barbara News-Review* in late 1971.

Beginning in 1972, Becca became active in the Indochina Peace Campaign (IPC) and helped organize and coordinate two more statewide conferences of antiwar groups. She remained active in the IPC through the fall of Saigon in 1975. At the *News & Review*, she wrote about the war, especially the air war and the Vietnamization program, and after the peace agreements were signed in 1973, about the political situation in South Vietnam.

In 1976, Becca moved to Los Angeles and worked for several years in documentary film production. In 1984, the staff-owned and -operated *News & Review* was facing imminent bankruptcy. To save the paper, shareholders sold it for one dollar to a group of investors, who arranged a merger with a competing, more yuppie-ish newspaper. The publication survives today in a new incarnation called the *Santa Barbara Independent*.

For the last 25 years, Becca has been an editor and writer working primarily for unions and progressive nonprofits.

JOHN McAULIFF After working in the civil rights movement in Mississippi, McAuliff served with the Peace Corps in Peru. Upon return to the United States in 1966, he obtained conscientious objector status but later turned in his draft card and refused assignment for several years. He served as the first national president of the Committee of Returned Volunteers, participating in many national demonstrations and in the leadership of antiwar coalitions. He met representatives of Vietnam at the Stockholm Peace Conferences. He headed the Indochina Program of the Peace Education Division of the American Friends Service Committee from 1972 to 1982, which led to his arrival in Ha Noi on the day the war ended. In 1985, he founded the Fund for Reconciliation and Development to work for the normalization of relations between Viet Nam and the United States. The Fund sponsored many trips of academics and professionals to Vietnam, brought delegations of Vietnamese political figures and university staff to the United States, and organized 10 international conferences of NGOs working with Vietnam, Laos, and Cambodia. Their annual picnics allowed Vietnamese diplomats to go beyond New York and visit the Philadelphia area. After President Clinton ended the embargo and normalized relations, the Fund supported the trade agreement and WTO membership, then refocused on similar work with Cuba.

MYRA MacPHERSON An award-winning author, former *Washington Post* journalist Myra MacPherson has written five books. Her landmark *Long Time Passing: Vietnam and the Haunted Generation* (Doubleday, 1984), considered a "Vietnam classic," was the first trade book to discuss post-traumatic stress disorder (PTSD). Updated versions remain in print (accessible on Amazon and Barnes and Noble). A member of Veterans for Peace (VFP), she has continued to lecture and write about the aftermath of Vietnam. Her contribution to this book grew out of a trip to Vietnam in 2013 when MacPherson met five amazing Vietnam Veterans—three of whom experienced heavy combat—who now dedicate their lives to helping the thousands of Vietnam Agent Orange and landmine victims forgotten as casualties of the Vietnam War.

NANCY KURSHAN As a college student, Nancy participated in the early antiwar movement in Madison, Wisconsin, and traveled to Washington, D.C., for the first national antiwar demonstration organized by Students for a Democratic Society (SDS). As a graduate student in Berkeley, California, she went door to door with SDS talking to people about the war, and participated in teach-ins and demonstrations. In 1967, she moved to New York and worked as a paid staff member of the National Mobilization Against the War in order to prepare for the 1967 March on the Pentagon. She was arrested, along with more than 800 others, at the Pentagon in a mass civil disobedience action. Nancy was a founding member of the Yippies, one of the groups that helped organize for the demonstrations at the 1968 Democratic Convention. When the Chicago 8 were indicted, she moved to Chicago to help with the work and attend the trial. During and after the trial, she spoke at a number of places about the trial and the importance of continuing to fight to end the war. In 1970, Nancy attended a Stockholm Peace Conference where she met with the Vietnamese delegation. In May of that same year she traveled to Vietnam, spending two weeks in Hanoi and Thanh Hoa province. On her way back through Moscow, Nancy and two companions staged a three-person antiwar demonstration outside the U.S. Consulate that was covered in much of the Western press.

Upon her return to the United States she moved to Kent, Ohio, and spent the following year producing, with others, an underground newspaper and preparing for a demonstration against the war on the first anniversary of the murder of the four students the previous year. During that time she organized women from Kent to travel to Washington, D.C., to participate in a women's demonstration against the war and was active in carrying out a protest against the February 1971 U.S. invasion of Laos. She was later arrested on a felony for spray-painting political slogans at the time of that demonstration (reduced to a misdemeanor on condition that she leave Kent). Happy to leave, she worked in New Hampshire during the primary of 1971, not on the campaign per se, but organizing antiwar demonstrations and trying to raise consciousness about the war. After the primary she moved back to California and engaged in work around prisons. She participated in the joyous street demonstrations when the Peace Treaty was signed. She reprinted the Weather Underground's statement entitled "Common Victories" and joined that organization.

More recently, Nancy was a social worker in the Chicago public schools for 20 years and active in the Chicago movement around the wars in Central America as part of the Pledge of Resistance. Her primary focus, however, has been work around prison conditions in the United States as part of the Committee to End the Marion Lockdown. For 15 years she attempted to draw attention to the racist nature of incarceration in the U.S., the discriminatory internment of political prisoners, and the proliferation of long-term solitary confinement. She recently completed a book *Out of Control: A 15-Year Battle Against Control Unit Prisons* published by the California-based Freedom Archives. She previously wrote a historical piece on women in prison that has been widely distributed, including in a major women's studies textbook. In the intervening years she raised two children, both of whom participated in Occupy Oakland's General Strike. Her daughter is a fourth-grade teacher, and the entire staff of her school participated in the strike. She is on the board of directors of a high school in Chicago's Puerto Rican community. Nancy has written a memoir that has thus far not seen the light of day.

 **NGUYEN THI BÌNH**, also known as "Madame Binh," was born in Sài Gòn in 1927. She came from an educated and elite family. Her grandfather, Phan Chu Trinh, was a Nationalist. Madame Binh led a series of student protests in Sài Gòn against the French and the United States, and was imprisoned for her political activism for three years. After her release, she helped to found the National Liberation Front (NLF) and the Women's Union for the Liberation of South Vietnam. When the Provisional Revolutionary Government of the Republic of South Vietnam (PRG) was formed in June 1969, Madame Binh was appointed as Minister of Foreign Affairs and head of the PRG delegation to the Paris Peace Talks. She was one of the signers of the Paris Peace Treaty in 1973. Madame Binh served two terms as vice president of the Socialist Republic of Vietnam from 1992 to 2002.

ACKNOWLEDGMENTS

The Vietnam antiwar movement was a collective endeavor and so was this book. As editors, we express our gratitude to all of the contributors. The authenticity of the ideas and reflections in each chapter extend the positive legacies of the antiwar movement and make this a truly unique project.

Our 2013 visit to Viet Nam could not have happened without the support of Mr. Vu Xuan Hong, president of the Vietnam Union of Friendship Organizations (VUFO). We are grateful to this champion of world peace and understanding and to the entire staff of the Viet Nam USA society.

Prof. Judy Tzu-Chun Wu, author of *Radicals on the Road*, joined the 2013 trip and supported this project in many ways still to unfold. Amanda Wilder filmed the trip and conducted interviews with the "Hanoi 9" that were very helpful in putting this book together.

Our publisher, Just World Books, saw the value in this project when it was just four pages long. We are especially grateful to Helena Cobban, Diana Ghazzawi, and the other editorial and production staff who patiently waited for our ideas to come to fruition, and then polished us up so that we could meet the public.

Frank's Acknowledgments

My wife, Mary Anne Barnett, was, is, and always will be essential to anything worthwhile I do. Or write. Her feedback is invaluable. I personally owe all of our contributors a lot for what they brought to the trip and to the book. More than that, though, for the part they each played in building the Viet Nam antiwar movement in the first place. It is not easy to live a moral life in the belly of the empire that is the United States. The antiwar movement made that possible for millions and I am proud to have been a part of it. I cherish the lifelong relationships that came from it.

If I have ever used the English language to write anything helpful to others there are four people who made it possible. My mother who instilled in me a love of reading and language. And on a good day getting the spelling and grammar right too. (Props to public school teachers as well.) Then there are three guys who push me, cajole me, and edit me to be better at writing and other things: Dave Marsh, Peter Laarman, and Don Hazen.

And finally, Karin. What a treat it's been to do this together. What's our next project?

Karin's Acknowledgments

Right on, Frank! It has been such an honor and joy to struggle over words, ideas, and politics with you.

This project fulfills many dreams. I could not have befriended Frank Joyce or Mary Anne had we all not participated in the 2006 trip to Viet Nam led by the late Prof. Erwin Marquit. Erwin and his wife, Doris, were rare examples of wit and hope in a complex world.

My journey through Vietnamese America has a spiritual component, and for that I am grateful for my friendship with Prof. Gina Masequesmay. She and Mr. Nguyen Van Muoi helped us with incorporating Vietnamese language into this book.

Where would activism be without research? For expert help in locating original sources, I turned to Julie Herrada (Labadie Radical Political History Archives, University of Michigan) and Dave Collins (Instruction and Research Librarian, Macalester College). In the last hours, three undergraduates also pitched in: Kathryn Anastasi, Kong Vang, and Samuel Faulkner.

People need love to make the peace. For daily life support, I owe Sharon Haire.

For giving me life, and instilling in me a sense of commitment to a world in struggle, I owe my parents, Delia Aguilar and E. San Juan Jr. (aka Sonny).

ABOUT THE EDITORS

 **KARIN AGUILAR-SAN JUAN** is a second-generation Filipino American and a second-generation writer/activist. She is a former member of the South End Press book publishing collective, and a former editor/production manager of *dollars & Sense* magazine. Karín received her M.A. and Ph.D. in sociology from Brown University and her B.A. in economics from Swarthmore College. She is an associate professor of American Studies at Macalester College, where she teaches "The School-to-Prison Pipeline," "Hunger Games: Map and Mirror for the 21st Century," and "U.S. Imperialism from the Philippines to Viet Nam." Her book, *Little Saigons: Staying Vietnamese in America* (2009) examines the relationship between community and place for Vietnamese Americans in Boston, Massachusetts, and Orange County, California. Her edited volume, *The State of Asian America: Activism and Resistance in the 1990s* (1993) gave visibility to Asian-American activism for an earlier generation. She serves on the boards of Clouds in Water Zen Center in St. Paul and Volunteers of America–Minnesota. Karín has practiced Asian martial arts since 1986. She and her spouse, Sharon T. Haire, live with two urban and unemployed border collies, Bosco and Bella.

FRANK JOYCE The lifelong political activism of Frank Joyce began with the Civil Rights Movement. He joined the Northern Student Movement (NSM) in the early 1960s and later helped found People Against Racism (PAR). He has been involved in many labor, anti-racist, human rights, and antiwar campaigns since. He has won journalism awards in print, radio, and television. He was a member of the UAW International Union staff for 18 years, including 12 years as director of the public relations and publications department.

Currently he is a communications consultant to labor and community organizations. He is active in building the emerging New Work/New Culture movement in Detroit and elsewhere. Joyce is president of the board of The Working Group (TWG), a nonprofit media production company that supports the anti-hate movement Not In Our Town (NIOT) and Not In Our Schools (NIOS). He has served for many years on the board of the Michigan Coalition for Human Rights (MCHR). He is a member of the Coordinating Committee of the National Council of Elders (NCOE).

His writing is frequently published at AlterNet (*www.alternet.org*) and elsewhere. His essay on race and the new left appears in *A New Insurgency: The Port Huron Statement and Its Times* (Michigan Publishing, 2015).

He and his wife, Mary Anne Barnett, have three adult sons and three grandchildren. They live in Grosse Pointe Park, Michigan, and Paso Robles, California.

CPSIA information can be obtained at www.ICGtesting.com
Printed in the USA
LVOW06s2206080915

453385LV00013B/374/P

9 781935 982593